Hamish McDonald was born in 1948 and graduated from the University of Sydney in 1968.

He has worked as a journalist for the *Sydney Morning Herald* from 1969 to 1974. From 1975 to 1978 Hamish McDonald was a freelance correspondent in Jakarta, Indonesia, for the *National Times*, the *Australian Financial Review*, the *Sydney Morning Herald*, the *Age*, the *Washington Post* and the *Financial Times* (London).

He is currently Tokyo correspondent for the *Sydney Morning Herald* and the *Age*.

SUHARTO'S INDONESIA

Hamish McDonald

Fontana/Collins

© HAMISH McDONALD 1980
First published in Fontana Books 1980
Printed and bound in Australia by
The Dominion Press, Blackburn, Victoria 3130

National Library of Australia
Cataloguing-in-Publication data
McDonald, Hamish, 1948-
  Suharto's Indonesia.
  Index
  Bibliography
  ISBN 0 00 635721 0
  1. Indonesia – Politics and government – 1966-.
  I. Title.
959,8'037

CONDITIONS OF SALE: This book is sold subject to the condition that it shall not, by way of trade or otherwise, be lent, re-sold, hired out or otherwise circulated without the publisher's prior consent in any form of binding or cover other than that in which it is published and without a similar condition including this condition being imposed on the subsequent purchaser.

Contents

Acknowledgements

1 Java — 1
2 The Suharto Group — 24
3 Suharto to Power — 49
4 The Technocrats — 68
5 The Politics of Order — 87
6 The Feudal State — 112
7 The Rise and Fall of Ibnu Sutowo — 143
8 Village and Kampung — 166
9 War and Diplomacy: The Timor Case — 189
10 The Prisoners — 216
11 'Regeneration' — 232

Glossary — 260

Index — 269

Acknowledgements

I wish to offer my thanks to Professor Peter Worsley, head of the Department of Indonesia and Malayan Studies, the University of Sydney, for his assistance in providing a place for me to write this book at the university in 1978–9. His staff and students also provided welcome advice and encouragement, as did Dr David Reeve, of the Sydney Technical College. I am also very grateful to Dr Peter McCawley and Mr Chris Manning of the Australian National University, Dr Michael van Langenberg, of the University of Sydney, Mr Max Suich and Mr Andrew Clark for reading drafts and making many helpful suggestions. Many Indonesians contribute consciously or unconsciously to the preparation of this book. I thank them for their patience in explaining the workings of their country's political system. To my friends in the Jakarta press corps, in particular, I wish to state my thanks and my admiration for their insight, determination and professionalism.

Hamish McDonald

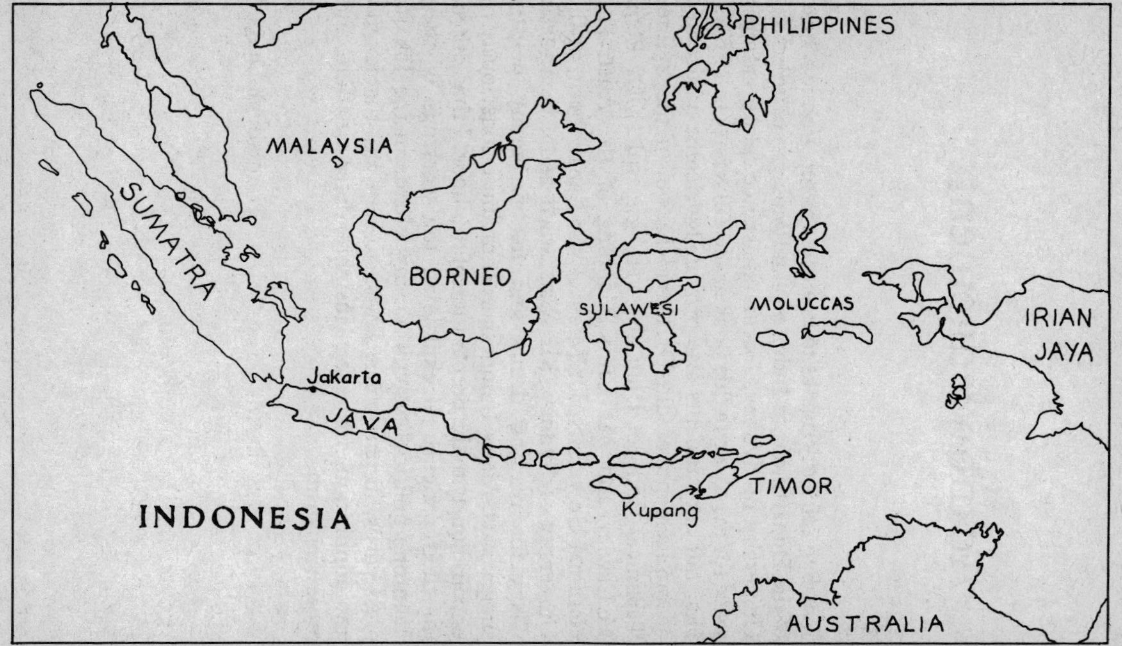
PHILIPPINES
MALAYSIA
SUMATRA
BORNEO
SULAWESI
MOLUCCAS
IRIAN
JAYA
Jakarta
JAVA
TIMOR
Kupang
INDONESIA
AUSTRALIA

1. Java

In September 1974 one of the more extraordinary encounters of contemporary international politics took place in a cave in Central Java. It occurred during informal talks between President Suharto of Indonesia and the Australian Prime Minister, Gough Whitlam, in the small town of Wonosobo. These talks greatly deepened relations between their two countries and are alleged to have sealed a tacit bargain for the Indonesian takeover of the small neighbouring territory of Portuguese Timor.

During a break from the discussions Suharto took Whitlam on a tour of the nearby Dieng Plateau, a misty upland plain surrounded by volcanoes and dotted with ancient Hindu temples. Suharto led Whitlam to a cave called Gua Semar. They entered alone, Suharto shutting the iron gate in front of his Cabinet Secretary, Lieutenant-General Sudharmono, who was trying to follow. It was a rare sign of favour from Suharto. The cave is one of several places in Java popularly believed to be dwellings of the clown-god Semar, who in the *wayang* (traditional theatre) is the founding father of the Javanese and guardian of their island. Suharto, who is deeply influenced by Javanese mystic beliefs, is said to identify strongly with the character of Semar and to travel occasionally to the cave on the Dieng Plateau and similar sacred places to meditate. While Suharto and Whitlam concurred in their discussions on Timor, the unspoken dimensions of their meeting were also important. Suharto felt he had reached an intuitive understanding with Whitlam. Taking Whitlam into the cave was perhaps the most intimate gesture Suharto has made to any foreign leader. It explains much of the surprise and hurt later, in 1975, when Australia found Indonesia's interpretation of the Timor accord irreconcilable.[1]

The clown-god Semar entered Indonesian politics on another occasion. When the late President Sukarno was talked into handing over executive powers to the then General Suharto on 11 March 1966, the title of the transferral decree was ingeniously reduced to the acronym 'Supersemar' (from the Indonesian for '11 March Order'). Suharto's masterly stroke of political salesmanship made good the invidious comparison being drawn between Sukarno's dazzling personality and his own lack-lustre sobriety: in the shadow-play the bumbling Semar is often the one who rescues the situation when more refined characters have failed.

Instances like these exemplify the Javanese way of politics and it is impossible to understand the currents of Indonesian events without some reference to mythology. Indeed, one political counsellor at a large Western embassy in Jakarta during the 1970s told visitors that in weighing up a situation he listed normal political considerations, and then threw in what he called 'Factor X', the possible influence of mystic or intuitive thinking among certain key figures in the Javanese-dominated Indonesian Government. The passage of time draws out the similarities between Sukarno and Suharto. Behind their vastly different respective calls for 'revolution' and 'development' lies an essentially conservative ideology derived from Javanese tradition.[2]

The Javanese stamp on Indonesia does not result simply from the force of numbers, although the island holds 85 million of Indonesia's 131 million people (of whom some 55 million live in the central and eastern provinces dominated by ethnic Javanese). Although the peoples of the 'Outer Islands' made great contributions during the formation of Indonesia, it was Java that carried the heaviest burdens of colonialism and war-time occupation, and it was in Java that the decisive steps were taken in the four-year war of independence. For many years afterwards the weight of Java crushed separatist rebellions and drew power towards the capital city, Jakarta.

The openness of Java's people to outside influences disguises resilience. Waves of foreign ideas dissipate their force in its tolerance. The Javanese claim Java to contain the 'navel' of the universe on a mountain near Jogjakarta, and the world outside this magically endowed island is *Sabrang*, literally meaning 'overseas' but implying that its amorphous peoples, even those now within the present boundaries of Indonesia, are not graced with higher civilization.

On Java there are hundreds of holy places where spiritual force is believed to be concentrated like magnetic poles. Sendang Semanggi, a spring near Jogjakarta, or Gua Sirandil, a sea-cave near Cilacap, or the misty uplands of the Dieng Plateau are such places where, with patient meditation and self-denial, the force may be absorbed. Like Suharto's Cave of Semar many of these holy places are associated with characters in the shadow-plays based on the great Indian narratives: the *Ramayana* (recounting the exile of Prince Rama and the rescue of his wife, Sita, from an evil abductor, and the *Mahabharata* (the complex epic of dynastic war between the five Pandawa brothers and their cousins, the Kurawa). According to Javanese mythology 'before there were people' these characters lived and fought on Java. Like the *wayang* heroes, famous men are believed to leave behind some of their power at the sites of decisive events in their life, their dwellings, and their graves. Their weapons and trappings are imbued with mystic force and, as *pusaka* (sacred heirlooms) add their unseen radiance to the powers of their inheritors.

At its higher levels Javanism shades into the science of *kebatinan* (mysticism) whose followers can progressively attune themselves to the inner harmony and clarity of the universe and the Almighty. They achieve this by fasting, meditation, and contact with more enlightened people who may be *gurus* in informal teacher–pupil arrangements. At a more popular level the teacher's wisdom is sought on how to cope with illness, love affairs and other everyday problems. In these cases the mystical practitioner is more a healer who dispenses folk medicines and spells than a philosopher.

On auspicious occasions (say, every thirty-fifth day on the eve of the day when the fifth day of the (five-day) Javanese week coincides with the fifth day of the Western week) holy places are still crowded with devotees. The royal cemetery of the Mataram dynasty at Imogiri near Jogjakarta is one. Javanese climb the 345 steps to the summit of a rocky outcrop, change into ceremonial court dress, and enter the tomb of the great Sultan Agung (1613–46) to sprinkle flower-petals on the sarcophagus.

Perhaps the strongest recent proof of the power of superstition was the widespread belief in the famous Joyoboyo prophecy during the Second World War. Joyoboyo, king of an East Java principality in the fourteenth century, forecast that the 'white buffalo' would rule in Java until expelled by the 'yellow chicken' who would govern for the life of the maize plant (three years) before a *ratu adil* ('just prince') took power to usher in a golden age. When Japan occupied the Dutch East Indies in 1942 the prophecy appeared on the way to being fulfilled and cheered Indonesian hopes during the hard years that followed.

The Cornell-based scholar, Benedict Anderson, has argued in a very influential essay[3] that the Javanese have quite distinctive concepts of political power. For the Westerner power is an abstract quality, derived from many sources, with no limits (depending on the, say, military or economic resources available), and capable of being employed for good or bad. For the Javanese power is a concrete discernible substance that concentrates in the ruler, radiating like light from a bulb. Power has the same quality from ruler to ruler. It is limited: a powerful ruler takes power from other concentrations. Power is essentially amoral, neither legitimate nor illegitimate.

As expounded in the *wayang* and the histories of the pre-colonial Javanese kingdoms, power was gained by a process of accumulation. Both *wayang* heroes and successful usurpers often prepared for campaigns by long periods of withdrawal and self-discipline to focus power within themselves. A ruler would reinforce his power by having around him powerful things, *pusaka*, or people who included 'extraordinary human beings such as albinos, clowns, dwarves and fortune tellers'. He would also draw power from invocatory words and ceremonies, and Anderson here makes a comparison with the rallies, anniversaries and jargon of modern Indonesian public life. The powerful man displayed his power by being able to weld opposing forces into unity, by vigorous sexual activity, and by a feeling of well-being in the community.

Anderson sees this idea of power as concentration and weakness as diffusion as basic to the great emphasis among the Javanese on unity. It helps explain the appeal of nationalism, and the quick disappearance of a federal state after the transfer of sovereignty from the Dutch in 1949, as well as the unease Javanese feel at such Western concepts as separation of powers, government and opposition.

In the old kingdoms the government was an extension of the ruler's household and all wealth belonged to him. Officials were appointed by the ruler, and their wealth was a portion of revenues flowing upwards from royal domains and monopolies. Those in power therefore owed loyalty upwards. To ensure this flow of loyalty they were deliberately moved around to avoid their forming any local attachments. With the crushing of regionalism in the 1950s and coinciding economic decline, Anderson sees the Indonesian bureaucracy as having shifted away from the 'rational–legal' mechanism established by the Dutch in the last fifty years of their rule, towards this traditional 'patrimonial' model, with all the implications of a pyramid of patron–client relationships developing as well as, from the legal standpoint at least, corruption. Power means refinement. The Javanese official, as a powerful and therefore *halus* (refined) person, disguises his commands in polite, indirect language.

> The man of power should have to exert himself as little as possible in any action. The slightest lifting of his finger should be able to set a chain of actions in motion. The man of real Power does not have to raise his voice and does not have to give overt orders. The *halus*ness of his command is the external expression of his authority. The whole Javanese style of administration is therefore marked by the attempt, wherever possible, to give an impression of minimum effort.[4]

But while traditionally power was absolute, it was also inherently unstable. The ruler governed under divine revelation of authority known as the *wahyu kedaton*, which made opposition to him an attack on God. However, according to the Indonesian historian, Ong Hok-ham, this *wahyu* could shift at any time to anyone else. Power was not inherited but reincarnated. A new just prince would seize power by virtue of his *wahyu* and launch a golden age. But gradually civil wars, palace struggles, taxation and inflation would increase. The rich would hoard money, Java's wealth would escape abroad, and heirlooms would disappear. The *wahyu* would move and a new cycle would start.[5] Anderson points out that the tendency was for power to dissipate through the indulgence and lack of discipline of the sovereign, giving rise to an underlying pessimism in Javanese thought but also a susceptibility to messianic movements.[6]

These may appear anachronistic concepts to be considered in the running of a modern-day state. But in September 1976 the Suharto Government caused a sensation in Jakarta by announcing the foiling of a plot against the president by a would-be just prince. The candidate was Sawito Kartowibowo, a 45-year-old Agriculture Department functionary on half-pay. With a group that included a former ambassador to Sweden and a well-known army major-general, Sawito was involved in mystical practices. In 1972 some of the group had made a tour of the mystical power-points of Java. After a night's meditation on Mount Saptorenggo, near Kudus, they claimed to have found a stone which had been revealed by a beam of light penetrating the ground. This stone was engraved on one side with the features of Jesus Christ and on the other with those of Sawito. Later they journeyed to the Ketonggo Forest, near Madiun, and were welcomed by the gate-keeper. He had been told in a dream that 'a leader from Jakarta' would arrive. After many such experiences Sawito was convinced he possessed the *wahyu*. The activities came to government attention four years later in July 1976 when Sawito began circulating pamphlets, one calling for the resignation of Suharto. He planned to send this by mail to the presidential palace.

More dangerously, Sawito drew up a document attacking the moral decline he saw in the nation. He brought it to the attention of five respected national figures including the former Vice-President, Mohammad Hatta, and leaders of the major religious groupings. They all signed. Sawito and seven others were immediately arrested, and delegations of ministers were despatched by Suharto to persuade the five signatories to disavow the document. It was an absurd plot, but a sensitive nerve had been touched. The then deputy head of the State Intelligence Co-ordinating Body, Lieutenant-General Ali Murtopo, remarked: 'From the rational viewpoint the Sawito case is just a comedy. However, from the irrational point of view.' Sawito was later put on trial for subversion and, after some months of spectacular court proceedings, sentenced to eight years in prison.[7]

Events of this kind emphasize the traditional substrata of the Indonesian political landscape. It should be noted that the cultures of the many non-Javanese peoples, of whom there are over a dozen major groups, are in many respects radically different. The American sociologist, Clifford Geertz, has defined three main cultural 'streams' in Java, with some correlating division of social and economic activity.[8] The *abangan* stream tend to be the people of the village: shrewd, earthy, absorbing Hindu and Muslim elements into a basic animism and folk tradition. The second stream is the *santri*, the devout Muslim, strongly influenced by the Arab world, the more vigorous trader and landowner, and part of an egalitarian religious community. The third type is the *priyayi*, the traditional bureaucratic elite. Deeply ingrained with the hierarchic ideas of Hindu–Javanese tradition, the *priyayi* moved easily from the position of court official to that of colonial civil servant, and then to administrator of the republic.

Since Geertz published his study in 1959 most political studies of Indonesia have employed his classifications to some degree. The *santri* community was the base for a series of vigorous nationalist movements, and mounts the most direct and potent political opposition to the present army rule. The *abangan* people tend to follow the prevailing political wind. They responded to the nationalism of Sukarno, and now dutifully record their votes for Golkar (Functional Groups), the army's political organization. Yet the poorer *abangan* areas became strongholds of the Indonesian Communist Party which, paradoxically, was often able to convey its revolutionary ideas through traditional *wayang* concepts and forms. The cultural variants in Java have contributed to the bloodiest civil conflicts in recent Indonesian history and still cause the most bitter competition.

Suharto was born on 8 June 1921 in a small house with plaited bamboo-slat walls and a sagging tiled roof in the hamlet of Kemusu, part of Godean village, about 12 kilometres west of Jogjakarta. This area was and is decisively under the cultural sway of the Jogjakarta royal court. Narrow roads run out to it from the city through level green rice lands. Even today the infrequent motorized traffic must slow for pedestrians, bicycles, pony traps and bullock drays ambling between the small market centres of tiny wooden-shuttered stalls and shops. On a clear day the volcano Merapi, trailing steam, towers to the north, and to the west are a range of bare, low hills running towards the 1000-year-old Buddhist monument, the Borobudur. Tall trees and clumps of bamboo every few hundred metres mark small settlements: the region conceals a dense population well. Buildings are weather-beaten and in shady spots moss marks the progress of rising damp in ancient masonry.

Something of a mystery surrounded Suharto's family background until his rule was quite advanced. Perhaps the deliberate needs of Javanese statecraft made this so. It was certainly a curious instance of palace intrigue that finally forced out much of the real story from the secretive president. When Suharto gained power, despite his own avowal that he was just a peasant's son, rumours persisted that he was a lost or unacknowledged son of the father of the present sultan of Jogjakarta, Hamengkubuwono VIII. One widely accepted variation was that Suharto's grandfather had been a distinguished officer in the sultan's private army, but that after experiencing a moral awakening at the sight of a dying beggar he had removed himself to a life of meditation and study in the countryside. That such rumours gained currency without strenuous contradiction could be ascribed to the processes of power accretion employed by newly arrived Javanese rulers, not so much to establish the legal right to rule but to absorb the hovering authority left by such a noble connection.[9] But by 1974, when Suharto had become a powerful figure in his own right and the centre of a burgeoning family and palace-centred power group, it was taken as presumption when a magazine devoted to sport, film and pop music published yet another version of Suharto's alleged aristocratic links. An angry Suharto then gave his first detailed public account of his family-tree, to prove that he was what he said: a country boy.[10]

Even by Javanese standards, which accommodate a high rate of divorce and remarriage and the frequent fosterage of children by relatives, Suharto's early life was a remarkably disturbed one, full of family disruption, and to-ing and fro-ing across the boundary of peasant and official classes. Though there is practically no sign Suharto was touched by the growing Indonesian nationalism between the wars, it was a time of economic difficulty. His father appears to have been a restless, rather ambitious man whose frequent changes of name suggest a lack of satisfaction (a Javanese custom is to change a name, particularly a child's, after a run of bad luck or illness). Son of a man called Kertoirono (presumed to be of peasant background), Suharto's father was brought up under the name Wagiyo but known as Panjang (Long). On his first marriage, which bore two children, Wagiyo changed his name to Kertorejo. On his second it became Kertasudiro, and on the third it became Notokariyo. Suharto was the only child of his father's second marriage with a local woman named Sukirah. She was distantly descended from Sultan Hamengkubuwono V by his first concubine.[11] His father had four more children from his third marriage, and his mother had another seven in her second marriage (including Probosutedjo, whose accession to business success and wealth under the Suharto Government was to become a continual focus of corruption allegations). *Pak* Kerto, as the father was known, was a village irrigation official controlling the vital distribution of water to the local wet-rice cultivators. He wore both traditional Javanese dress of sarong and batik head-cloth, and an approved official air of undisturbable equanimity which disguised his unsettled personality. Sukirah, Suharto's mother, seems to have been less stable. Before Suharto was forty days old his mother went into a kind of withdrawal state. She disappeared for some days, and was found in the dark central room of an empty house near by, weak from lack of food and drink. She was unable to suckle the child any longer. Suharto was given to his paternal great-aunt, *Mbah* Kromodiryo, the midwife at his birth. At the age of three he was returned to his mother, who had remarried a local farmer, and spent a conventional rural childhood helping his stepfather in the paddy-fields. Close to the age of eight he started attending the local Javanese-language elementary school.

Then a tussle over the child began between father and mother. One day in 1929 Suharto was summoned by his great-aunt to meet his father. Kerto told him he was disappointed at the lowly way he was being raised: he had decided to take him away from Kemusu to live with his sister who was married to an agricultural supervisor, Prawirowihardjo, then serving at Wurjantoro, a small town south of Wonogiri. Eight-year-old Suharto was taken without being allowed to farewell his mother. Fitted out in new clothes, his old ones discarded, Suharto and his father travelled by train to Jogjakarta (it was the first time Suharto rode on a train), then by bus and cab through Solo and Wonogiri to his uncle Prawirowihardjo's household in Wurjantoro. A year later his stepfather arrived unannounced during the Muslim fasting-month holiday, and took Suharto back to his mother. After a further year in his old home in Kemusu, Suharto was again removed by his father to Wurjantoro.

This town has probably not changed much since then. There is a new school, an administrative building and a tarred road going the few miles north to Wonogiri. But the houses are small and shabby, and the people poor. The surrounding hills are deforested and eroded, the farming yields poor, and the dry season long and severe. During the 1970s thousands of families have been moved to make way for a giant dam that may transform this officially acknowledged 'minus' area. When Suharto moved there the Dutch Indies economy had collapsed as the Great Depression cut back commodity export markets. Labour flooded back to Java from the plantations of Sumatra. Workers left the towns to go back to their villages. Java retreated deeper into subsistence economy. Food was hard to buy on reduced cash earnings among the landless. Wonogiri was among the worst affected areas.

Poor as the district was, Suharto's surroundings were of a distinctly higher social level than in his mother's home. The Prawirowihardjo house, a low wooden-walled and windowless building with a well and bathing place behind, looks mean by present Indonesian city standards, but by the measure of the time and place it was quite substantial. Prawirowihardjo, although not an aristocrat, was a member of the official class, possessing some education and refinement. Suharto stayed in Wurjantoro for the rest of his four years of primary schooling. He also attended Koran-reading classes and joined the Muslim boy scout organization, Hisbulwathan (in preference to the more Javanized Javaanse Padvinders Organisatie), organized by the Mangkunegaran royal house of nearby Solo which governed the town. Later Suharto moved to Wonogiri to attend middle school, staying first with an elder foster-brother and then with a friend of his foster-family, Hardjowijono, a railways pensioner. The household was poor, and Suharto acted as servant while also helping the pensioner's wife sew brassieres and other clothes for sale in the market.[12]

Hardjowijono was also of the *priyayi* (official) class and strongly interested in the Javanese mystic arts of *kebatinan*. Through this connection Suharto transferred to the household of Daryatmo, a noted *guru* and *dukun* (a wise man and mystical practitioner), who also combined the functions of Muslim teacher. Daryatmo was known around Wonogiri and Solo for his science, which blended into Islam the traditional Javanese mysticism based on self-denial and meditation. In addition to this spiritual concern, he also offered advice on marital problems and other everyday affairs as well as herbal cures for physical complaints. Daryatmo also functioned as an irrigation official, like Suharto's father, and one of his unsuccessful efforts while Suharto was apprenticed to him was to persuade local peasants to adopt a new water distribution system. Daryatmo was to remain a constant source of advice for many years during Suharto's later career.

Suharto returned to his father in his old village, Kemusu, and in 1939 finished his middle-school education aged eighteen. He found work in the village bank at

Wurjantoro, but was forced to resign when a bicycle mishap tore his only set of working clothes. During this period of unemployment Suharto was finally caught up in the political turmoil that had seized the Dutch Indies. In 1940, with the Netherlands under German occupation and Japan pressing for access to its oil supplies, the Indies Government was isolated. It desperately organized defence and opened the ranks of the Royal Netherlands Indies Army (KNIL) to large intakes of Javanese and other ethnic groups previously excluded in favour of more loyal recruits from Ambon and other eastern islands. Suharto joined and quickly rose to the rank of sergeant. But three months after Pearl Harbor the Allied Forces on Java were surrendered by their Dutch commander. Suharto was soon back in Wonogiri, unemployed.

Japan's interest in the Indies was not a sudden development. Long set on a programme of industrial development and colonial expansion in Asia it had extended its economic interests in the archipelago since the 1920s, although barred by the Dutch from purchasing strategic materials. Japanese shops, staffed by smiling and polite men who contrasted favourably with the often abrupt Chinese traders, sprang up in towns throughout the Indies. Although Japanese Muslims numbered only a few hundred, a Japanese Islamic Association was created to promote contacts with South-East Asian Muslims. It sent students to study abroad, organized visits, built mosques, and in 1939 held an international Islamic conference.

The Japanese Army was given a friendly welcome in many areas, and the nationalist leadership of Sukarno and Hatta agreed to co-operate with occupation forces as a step towards independence. As already mentioned, due to belief in mythology it was commonly thought that Japanese rule would be temporary. Suharto was one of thousands of Indonesians who volunteered for security organizations set up by the Japanese to overcome manpower problems and to rally support for Japanese war aims. After some months with an auxiliary police unit in Jogjakarta he was inducted to the newly formed Volunteer Army of Defenders of the Homeland, PETA, in 1943. Again Suharto was singled out for advancement, becoming a platoon commander at Wates (a few kilometres from his home village) before attending the PETA higher military training school in Bogor, near Jakarta. On graduating as a company commander in 1944 he was subsequently attached to units in Solo and Madiun at a time of growing disillusionment with the Japanese, in both the PETA and the community. A tightening blockade by the Allies, harsh food collection, and neglect of non-strategic industries led to severe deprivation. Islamic sensibilities were offended by the occasionally demanded public demonstrations of worship of the Japanese Emperor. Up to 270 000 young men were transported overseas for forced labour, of whom only about 70 000 eventually returned. Unrest led to revolt in February 1945 when the PETA battalion of Blitar, a remote East Java town, rose against the Japanese. The uprising was quickly put down and its leaders executed. Although Suharto is now said to have shared the general resentment and nationalist aspirations of the time, he was chosen by the Japanese to reform the shattered Blitar unit. He spent the rest of the war quietly training new commanders in the countryside near by.[13]

Suharto disbanded his unit upon the orders sent out by the Japanese command in compliance with the terms of surrender on 15 August 1945. He drifted back to Jogjakarta to stay with relatives. The end of the war had put the city into ferment because of the profound social changes which had taken place in the previous few years. In part, these were due to the young sultan, Hamengkubuwono IX, who had ascended the throne late in 1939. As crown prince he had been abruptly called home by his ailing father from nine years of study in the Netherlands. The story is told that the aged sultan met his son in Jakarta (then called Batavia) and travelled home with him by train. Midway in the journey he handed the prince a sacred *kris,* one of the most valued heirlooms of the dynasty, before sinking into unconsciousness. When the prince helped his father (who died within hours) from the train a loud clap of thunder burst in the clear sky, a portent for the Jogjakarta people of great leadership.[14]

The new sultan used the Japanese occupation to reform his administration. He removed feudal barriers to his own direct involvement in administration, placed himself in contact with the commercial classes for the first time, and established consultative committees. Under the Japanese thousands of young men had been given their first military experience, and the population had seen the former colonial rulers humiliated by fellow Asians. On 9 September 1945, Sultan Hamengkubuwono and the head of the tiny Pakualaman principality enclosed by Jogjakarta issued statements declaring their territories a special region of the Indonesian Republic (proclaimed by Sukarno and Hatta in Jakarta on 17 August) with the sultan as its head. This was confirmed almost immediately by the new Indonesian Republican Government in Jakarta.

Largely self-appointed republican forces were springing up throughout the Dutch East Indies, often based on former PETA units and other less formal groups with names like 'Black Dragon' and 'Black Fan'. The latter had been organized in the last days of the war and in some cases allowed to use the Indonesian red and white national colours. A primary aim was to seize weapons from the Japanese who were under orders to stand fast and maintain order until the arrival of the Allies. Numerous attacks on Japanese installations took place, often by crowds armed only with knives, parangs and sharpened bamboo poles. Suharto joined a new unit of the republic's main army in Jogjakarta in September 1945, and by virtue of his PETA experience was elected deputy commander. Almost immediately he was involved in a mass attack on the local Japanese garrison which gained hundreds of weapons for the Indonesians, although he was obliged to recruit their new owners in many cases to gain the rifles. When the republican forces were formally organized in October

1945, Suharto became a battalion commander.

By then the Allies had arrived in Jakarta and were cautiously accepting the Japanese surrender, releasing prisoners of war, and attempting to maintain order until the Dutch could return. Bitter fighting broke out, especially in the East Java capital of Surabaya, where frenzied resistance by Indonesian youths lasted some three weeks from 10 November, a date now celebrated as the national Heroes' Day. In Jakarta the Indonesian Government existed uneasily alongside British, Japanese and Dutch elements. In January 1946 after an assassination attempt by Ambonese soldiers in the Dutch forces on Prime Minister Sultan Sjahrir, the republican government decided to move to Jogjakarta, which saw an influx of about 50 000 republican troops and administrators in the following months. Suharto took part in fighting against Allied troops around Magelang and Semarang before returning to Jogjakarta at the head of a brigade, with the rank of lieutenant-colonel and some repute as a field commander.

By November 1946 the Allied forces had been withdrawn, leaving some 55 000 Dutch and colonial troops in Java. These occupied some major towns along the north coast. Elsewhere the Netherlands was attempting to form puppet states among more amenable ethnic groups, or, as in the case of South Sulawesi (Celebes), resorting to forcible suppression. In the republican territories varying degrees of social revolution were taking place. This in some instances involved the overthrow of established administrations, particularly in eastern Sumatra where the wholesale slaughter of the feudal ruling classes occurred. The next three years saw a confusing struggle, half-diplomatic, half-military, in which the Dutch tried to establish, on the basis of the enclaves they controlled, a tractable federation, and the republicans tried to establish a unitary state extending throughout the former Indies. Internally the republicans were beset by rivalries, the most serious based on differing degrees of commitment to social change, ranging from communism to traditional feudalism.

Sharp conflicts arose over the use of diplomacy between the older, Western-educated civilians in the government and the young, Japanese-trained, locally raised fighting men.

Although Suharto scarcely rates a mention in most accounts of the Indonesian war of independence, photographs from that period show him at the side of national leaders, such as the army commander, General Sudirman, at several historic moments. His military role as garrison commander in the republican capital was to enable him to see at close quarters the machinations of the Indonesian leadership. He showed some deftness on one celebrated occasion when his immediate superior became involved in a move with other military leaders against the government of Sutan Sjahrir in June 1946. Suharto demurred at a direct order in person from Sukarno to arrest his commander, thereby earning the appellation *koppig*, Dutch for pigheaded. But he maintained a watch on his superior and kept the president informed. When the general concerned came to demand a new cabinet Sukarno was prepared and had the general arrested, thereby preventing a possible coup.

After months of deadlocked negotiations the Dutch began a major offensive against republican areas on 20 July 1947, the first of two so-called 'Police Actions'. On Java large numbers of troups fanned out from Jakarta and Bandung in the west and from Surabaya in the east. Although control remained confined to towns and main roads, with republican forces still operating in between (especially in West Java), the Dutch had swiftly increased their apparent territorial control by the time international pressure achieved a ceasefire on 4 August. An agreement fixing new lines was signed aboard the American warship, *Renville*, off Jakarta in January 1948. It was a humiliating moment for the Indonesians, although the Dutch had actually failed in their aim of forcing the republic into a federation of easily manipulable states. The shrunken territory of the republic in Java was in great turmoil, with the inward retreat exacerbating inter-unit rivalries. Early in August a new factor entered politics with the return of the Stalinist-line communist, Musso, from Moscow, where he had lived most of the time since the Communist Party (PKI) uprising. Taking leadership of the PKI and associated left-wing elements, Musso turned it towards direct action to force land redistribution and overthrow 'feudal' village hierarchies.

Because larger landholdings were often in the hands of the more devout Muslims, the conflict tended towards a confrontation of two traditional Javanese cultural streams (*santri* and *abangan*) since the PKI drew much of its support from landless peasants who were more likely to be nominal Muslims. In Solo clashes developed between unruly local troops and the West Java 'Siliwangi' Division, whose 22 000 men had retreated eastward from the Dutch. When the Siliwangi expelled these local units from Solo on 17 September, a socialist youth group seized power next day in the nearby town of Madiun and broadcast formation of a regional government based on a left-wing alliance.

At some stage close to this date the Indonesian Army attempted to head off the looming civil war. Lieutenant-Colonel Suharto was sent to Madiun and surrounding areas to try to talk rebellious units over to the government. But events were moving too fast. Musso and certain other PKI leaders had gone to Madiun, although the party did not immediately come out in support of the revolt. On 19 September Sukarno broadcast a forceful speech calling on Indonesians to rise up against Musso and the PKI. Musso was stung into condemning Sukarno and Hatta over Madiun Radio as 'Quislings' to the Japanese and 'slaves' of American imperialism. Java, from Solo and Wonogiri, east to Kediri near the Dutch lines, slid into communal slaughter. Perhaps as many as 25 000 local troops sided with the rebels, but they could not withstand the well-armed and disciplined Siliwangi Division which drove eastward. By December the rebellion was smashed, its leaders executed; unknown thousands had been killed, and some 35 000 people had been arrested by the government.

The Madiun affair left a grim heritage of hatred and suspicion – part political, part religious – that was to explode again in 1965. The reaction of Suharto and his army colleagues to the attempted coup that year cannot be explained without reference to Madiun.

On 4 December 1948 with this turmoil barely subsided, the Dutch issued an ultimatum to the republic and followed this up early in the morning of 19 December with a successful paratroop assault on Jogjakarta Airport. This seized, reinforcements flew in and fought their way into Jogjakarta the same day. Sukarno and his Cabinet stayed in the city and allowed themselves to be captured, but the army withdrew to prearranged positions in the surrounding countryside. Its commander, General Sudirman, set up secret headquarters in the rugged Gunung Kidul area south-east of Jogjakarta where he established radio contact with an emergency republican government based in West Sumatra.

Suharto's regiment regrouped outside the city on the evening of the Dutch attack, then marched west of Jogjakarta down to the area around the small hamlet of Bibis, about 30 kilometres south of the city. Suharto set up his own headquarters in the house of the village headman and lived for some months watching the situation in Jogjakarta. This same area had been occupied in the 1825–30 Java War by the anti-Dutch rebel Diponegoro. Two caves, Gua Wurung and Gua Selarong, had been used as temporary bases by Diponegoro and had become sacred places for the Javanese. Suharto used them for meditation, and spent at least one full night absorbing Diponegoro's cosmic powers in Gua Selarong. On occasions he dressed as a peasant and slipped into the city for reconnaissance. During these visits he held meetings with Sultan Hamengkubuwono whom the Dutch left untouched for fear of local reaction. Through him, Suharto was given the order to carry out one of the most daring exploits of the war, the 'General Attack' of 1 March 1949. This was a marked departure from the normal Indonesian tactic of avoiding direct clashes. Suharto's brigade infiltrated Jogjakarta, then, when the sirens marking the lifting of the night curfew sounded at 6 a.m. on 1 March, his troops attacked the unprepared Dutch garrison. Simultaneous assaults were made from all four sides outside the city, and irregular units harried Dutch patrols in the countryside. Suharto and his men remained inside the town until midday when they withdrew as a Dutch armoured column arrived.

The incident, later made into a film called *Six Hours in Jogjakarta*, embarrassed the Dutch who were claiming that the republic was finished. As intended, it changed the atmosphere for forthcoming negotiations. Although they still occupied the main towns throughout Java the Dutch were increasingly on the defensive as republican forces fanned out to wage guerilla warfare under the loose direction of the brilliant former West Java commander, thirty-year-old Colonel A. H. Nasution. Their determined resistance, combined with increasing international pressure (particularly from the USA which had cut Marshall Plan aid to the East Indies over the second 'Police Action'), destroyed Dutch confidence. By mid-1949 the republican leadership was restored to Jogjakarta and a ceasefire proclaimed as the Dutch withdrew to their earlier lines. Even so, the Indonesian Army remained suspicious of diplomacy and it required a major effort of persuasion by army men (who included Suharto) and a threatened resignation by Sukarno to induce the dying, tuberculosis-ridden General Sudirman to come in from his guerilla base. Negotiations later that year resulted in the transfer of sovereignty on 27 December 1949 to a federal Republic of the United States of Indonesia, covering all the former Indies except Western New Guinea.

By the end of the struggle for independence Suharto was not a prominent man in the Indonesian National Army, but enjoyed a reputation for sound military ability and political caution. Apart from his brief PETA training in West Java and his few months in East Java after the Blitar uprising, no mention is made in biographical data of any other trip outside Central Java. Within this province Suharto operated mostly in the area covered by the traditional principalities of Jogjakarta and Solo. Like many of his fellow army men he was therefore quite different in upbringing from the civilian leaders of the Indonesian Republic like Sukarno, Hatta and Sjahrir. His education had been to the middle levels of local Javanese and Islamic schools, and his social contacts had not at any stage included Westerners. He had matured in the Dutch and then Japanese military systems. He was untouched by the appeal of social revolution, despite his poverty-stricken background. Indeed, his fosterage had introduced Suharto to the first rung of the social ladder, and his contact with the young sultan had shown him the best side of the traditional system of rule.

This must have been reinforced by his marriage, in 1947, to Siti Hartinah, daughter of a minor noble. The union was suggested and arranged, as was and often still is the Javanese custom, by his guardians, in this case the Prawirawihardjos. Tien, as Mrs Suharto is called, is the daughter of the late *Raden Mas Ngabei* Sumoharjomo, a fifth generation descendant of the second ruler, the Mangkunegaran royal house in Solo, as was his wife by another branch of the family. As such Sumoharjomo still enjoyed aristocratic office, although, by Javanese convention, getting close to the seventh-generation cut-off point where nobility joins the wide official class. He benefited from the system of apange, then applying in the Javanese principalities, whereby local offices (and incomes) were handed out to favoured courtiers. Sumoharjomo first received the office of *mantri gunung* (supervisor of mountain land), then served as an assistant *wedana* (district administrator) in Wonogiri before becoming *wedana* in Wurjantoro, around the same time Suharto lived there.

Although the town was small and Hartinah attended the same primary school two years behind Suharto, contact at that time appears to have been slight, if any. The rather impoverished *wedana* lived in a Western-style house, probably the only one in the town. His household was a stronghold of traditional aristocratic Javanese values. Hartinah received only a primary school education, and spent her later childhood in the seclusion thought appropriate to unmarried girls. She practised *batik*, the art of painting and dyeing fabric using wax, and occasionally sold her work in the market – batik and jewellery dealings being the acceptable economic field for upper-class women. Whereas Suharto joined the Muslim boy scout movement, Hartinah belonged to the Mangkunegaran equivalent. Sumoharjomo was another one immersed in the mystic side of Javanism, often practising various kinds of self-deprivation of food, drink or sleep. Hartinah was versed in this way of thinking, as well as acquiring traditional styles of behaviour and taste (including chewing of betel) that she has never lost. A part of the Javanese upper-class tradition was that in hard times it was permissible for wives to indulge in genteel commercial transactions to help the family budget, while the husband maintained his dignity as warrior, courtier and administrator.[15]

Personally, Suharto was reserved and abstemious. He had become thoroughly versed in the Javanese process of consultation, and liked to suppress any outward sign of strong emotion or difference of opinion. A long time later he was to expound principles of leadership that were probably well on the way to being worked out by 1949. They owe little to any non-Javanese influence. Four basic objectives given were: be rich without possessions, make war without an army, win without humiliating, give without losing. The leader should be patient, tactful and pious combining the character of a king (wise, just and fair), of a *pandito* or seer (far-sighted and cautious), and of a peasant (simple, honest, straightforward and punctual). A leader should not be easily excited or shocked, or become proud of his power. He should not be cunning like the mouse-deer, proud like the elephant, nor feel himself skilful like a snake with its poison. He should look for virtue rather than friends, follow religious teachings, and be dedicated and self-correcting.[16]

NOTES

1. Lee Khoon Choy, *Indonesia between Myth and Reality*, Nile & Mackenzie, London, 1976, pp. 156–7.
2. Willard A. Hanna, 'The Magical–Mystical Syndrome in the Indonesian Mentality' part 1, *American Universities Field Staff Reports Service*, South-East Asia Series, vol. XV, no. 5, November 1967, pp. 1–3.
3. Benedict Anderson, 'The Idea of Power in Javanese Culture' in Claire Holt (ed.), *Culture and Politics in Indonesia*, Cornell University Press, 1972.
4. Ibid., p. 43.
5. Ong Hok-ham, 'Wahyu Dalam Sejarah Raja-Raja Jawa', *Tempo* (Jakarta), 30 October 1976, pp. 14–15.
6. Op. cit., p. 21.
7. See accounts in *Tempo*, 16 October 1976; 13 August 1977; 19 November 1977.
8. Clifford Geertz, *The Religion of Java*, Free Press, Glencoe, Illinois, 1960 and University of Chicago Press, 1976.
9. See Hanna, op. cit., part V, vol. XV, no. 9, December 1967, and Anderson, op. cit., pp. 25–8.
10. The so-called '*Pop* affair' will be discussed in chapter 6. See *Tempo* (Jakarta), 11 November 1974. Many new details of Suharto's background are contained in the revised edition of O. G. Roeder, *The Smiling General*, Gunung Agung, Jakarta 1969, published in Indonesian as *Anak Desa, Biografi Presiden Soeharto* (1976). Much of subsequent data is confirmed by this semi-official source.
11. *Tempo* (Jakarta), 11 November 1974.
12. See various Jakarta newspaper reports, 27 January 1978.
13. Nugroho Notosusanto, 'The Peta Army during the Japanese Occupation of Indonesia', doctoral dissertation, University of Indonesia, 1977, p. 186 footnote.
14. Selosoemardjan, *Social Changes in Jogjakarta*, Cornell University Press, 1962, p. 23.
15. Roeder, op. cit., pp. 194–200, and Suripto, *Soeharto: Sautu Sketsa Karier dan Politik*, GRIP, Surabaya, 1972, pp. 69–74.
16. Remarks made on 5 November 1973, quoted in *Indonesia Times*, 7 April 1977.

2. The Suharto Group

The constitution of Indonesia was still unsettled after the transfer of sovereignty in 1949, and popular hopes of a new 'golden age' were soon to be disappointed. An immediate challenge to Jakarta's authority came from regional administrations and colonial army elements left by the Dutch, chiefly in the 'Eastern Islands'. All over Indonesia the government faced resistance from surplus army units and a multiplicity of irregular forces which it wanted to demobilize. In certain devoutly Muslim areas, particularly West Java, a rebellion in favour of an Islamic state, whose movement was commonly known as Darul Islam (house of Islam), had government forces hard pressed.

Nationalist pressure against the Dutch-enforced federal structure toppled the weaker state governments within four months, aided by a clumsy coup attempt in Bandung and Jakarta by ex-colonial troops under the notorious Dutch 'counter-insurgency expert', Turk Westerling. In contrast the state of East Indonesia, stretching from Sulawesi to the Moluccas and Timor, was four years established and a traditional supplier of military manpower against Java and Sumatra. In April 1950 troops formerly in the Royal Netherlands Indies Army (KNIL) under Captain Andi Abdul Aziz arrested republican military officials attempting to exert authority in Makassar and prevented republican troops from landing. Aziz obeyed an order to report to Jakarta, where he was promptly arrested. Meanwhile the Indonesian National Army formed an expeditionary force under Colonel Alex Kawilarang of the (West Java) Siliwangi Division. Together with troops from

East and West Java, Lieutenant-Colonel Suharto's Garuda Mataram Brigade from Central Java sailed for Makassar. They landed on 18 April, two weeks after the Aziz rebellion, and met little resistance.[1] Most of the ex-KNIL troops surrendered the next day, and a new East Indonesia Government agreed within three weeks to join a unitary state.

Suharto's troops were later involved in at least one major clash, during which they appear to have behaved beyond the control of their officers. Suharto's troops earned a reputation for harshness among the Bugis and Makassarese people of South Sulawesi. One historian reports that Suharto's Javanese soldiers were 'widely described as behaving like an occupation army, and displayed a degree of arrogance which alienated large sections of the population'.[2] Suharto remained in Makassar while Colonel Kawilarang, now commander of the East Indonesia area, pursued the 'mastermind' behind Aziz, Dr Soumokil, Minister of Justice in the local Cabinet who had fled to his native Ambon where, on 25 April, he proclaimed the 'Republic of the South Moluccas' (RMS). Bitter fighting from July to November 1950 expelled ex-KNIL troops supporting the RMS from Ambon, the Moluccan capital. Fighting continued on nearby Ceram Island for several years, and RMS supporters who went into exile in Holland remain an unreconciled problem for Jakarta to this day.

In November 1951 Suharto was transferred to command the 'Pragola' Brigade based at Salatiga in Central Java. This unit had been formed from several battalions from the Indonesian National Army, KNIL, and Islamic-based Hisbullah (Army of Allah) during military consolidation and proved difficult to bring into line. One Hisbullah unit, Battalion 426 of Kudus, resisted incorporation and took up arms against the republic in Central Java around that time. Suharto mounted a cautious blocking operation, until the lightning strikes of a new elite force called the 'Banteng (Wild Buffalo) Raiders' under Ahmad Yani broke the back of the insurrection.

For the rest of the 1950s Suharto remained mostly in Central Java with the Diponegoro Division, whose territorial area covered both the province of Central Java and the Special District of Jogjakarta. The army units in West Java (the province in which Jakarta is situated) were increasingly involving themselves in national politics and Suharto, being in Central Java, remained an obscure figure. Army leaders were concerned about the impotence of successive short-lived civilian cabinets. In the Outer Islands the regional army commanders asserted warlord-style powers. A busy barter trade grew between Singapore and Sumatra, Manila and northern Sulawesi, openly evading the duties imposed by the central government. In Jakarta itself, the Army Chief of Staff, General Nasution, was suspended for more than two years following an unsuccessful army ultimatum to Sukarno demanding dissolution of Parliament. In November 1956 the army's Intelligence chief, Colonel Zulkifli Lubis, attempted a *coup d'état* in which the army's new elite commando regiment, the RPKAD, marched on Jakarta.

Following the 1955 general election, which had seen support flow to the PKI and the Muslim parties, Sukarno became disillusioned with parliamentary government. During 1956 and 1957 he proposed its replacement with a National Council based on the traditional concepts of *musyawarah* and *mufakat*, consultation and consensus. The cabinet should be formed of the four main parties: the Indonesian Nationalist Party (PNI), the Indonesian Communist Party (PKI), Nahdatul Ulama (the conservative Muslim Scholars' League based mainly in Java) and Musyumi (a modernist Muslim movement strongly supported in West Java and parts of the Outer Islands). This proposal was opposed by anti-communist forces, principally the Muslims. Although not fully implemented it led to some army commanders in the Outer Islands declaring martial law and cutting their ties with the central government. Sukarno declared a state of siege on 17 March 1957. This, together with increasing antagonism to

Dutch occupation of West Irian and a consequent army takeover of Dutch property throughout Indonesia, was to expand greatly the military's role in government and the economy.

Early in 1958 Sukarno's regional opponents formed the Revolutionary Government of the Republic of Indonesia (PRRI) with its capital in Padang, West Sumatra. It attracted many leaders, particularly from Masyumi and the small but influential Indonesian Socialist Party (PSI), whose hopes for modernization were being thwarted under Sukarno. The rebels occupied the enormously wealthy island of Sumatra, containing the large Caltex and Stanvac oil-fields, while an allied movement, Permesta, held the rich plantation province of North Sulawesi. Seeing the PRRI and Permesta groups as essentially anti-communist, and Sukarno moving towards the communist bloc, the USA gave the rebels covert support through the Central Intelligence Agency (CIA). Arms and advice were supplied to Sumatra, and CIA combat aircraft flew missions in support of the Sulawesi rebels from US bases in the Philippines. Yet the revolt in Sumatra where it counted most was a bluff. Central government forces struck quickly, sending paratroops to seize the Sumatran oil-fields, and finally mounting an amphibious assault on Padang. Many rebels accepted amnesty offers, while others went into exile in Malaya and other refuges. By mid-1959 resistance was confined to small pockets. The army had gained immensely in authority, and in the crisis Sukarno was able to establish his concept of 'Guided Democracy' which involved a return to the strong presidential rule that the constitution originally adopted in 1945. The consequent banning of Masyumi and the PSI saw an eclipse of alternative, more pragmatic sources of leadership. In a system that grew more akin to ancient Javanese kingship, Sukarno, the ruler, showed his mystic grace by including three contradictory elements – the army, the PKI and the now Nahdatul Ulama dominated Muslim camp – in his court life. The unity achieved under this 'Nasakom' doctrine was, of course, superficial.

Suharto, back in Central Java, was beginning to take sides, as commander of Infantry Regiment 15 in Solo from 1953-6 and then, after a brief spell with Nasution's General Staff in Jakarta, as Chief of Staff, acting commander, and commander, successively, of the Diponegoro Division. Suharto's most noteworthy contribution to national politics at the time came during attendance at a National Conference convened by Sukarno in September 1957. Suharto spoke out strongly against appeasement of the rebels in Sumatra and Sulawesi.[3] In the PRRI–Permesta revolt that soon followed, the Diponegoro, like the other two Java commands, contributed most of its available fighting troops to central government expeditionary forces. Suharto's few reported public statements typically stressed the need for unity and harmony, but warned that this did not mean a 'neutral' approach, rather firmness and the willingness to take risks. *Rame ing gawe, sepi ing padudon* (Busy at your task, free of argument) was one old Javanese maxim he urged.[4]

Suharto was not neutral in the great political struggle being waged for Central Java. Between the general elections in 1955 and regional elections in 1957 the Communist Party had dramatically increased its representation and relegated the Nationalist Party (PNI) to second place. The PKI's new portion of the vote had come almost entirely at the expense of the PNI, from the great *abangan* constituency. By 1957 the communists held majorities in the assemblies of nine out of the thirty-four regions in Central Java including Semarang, the provincial capital. Semarang became a focus of the battle, since one of the PNI's most doughty fighters, Hadisubeno Sosrowerdoyo, had managed to remain mayor despite a PKI majority in his local assembly and attempts by non-PNI ministers in Jakarta to dislodge him. Hadisubeno belonged to the *priyayi* bureaucratic elite who had tended to gravitate to the PNI and had been placed in positions of favour when that party was ascendant. It was towards

Hadisubeno's *priyayi*, anti-communist world that Suharto leaned after moving in 1956 to Diponegoro Division headquarters in Semarang. Official biographical material published since the 1965-6 change of regime stresses that during his tenure as regional commander Suharto was constantly warning government leaders (including Sukarno) about increasing communist strength.

The link with Hadisubeno extended to another area of activity in which Suharto is acknowledged to have been perhaps too conspicuously successful: fund-raising. By the mid-1950s conventional sources of revenue were so inadequate that irregular local resources became essential to keep the army going. It was not the only poorly provided institution. Civil servants and professional people were taking second jobs or running private businesses to supplement official pay which could not carry them through the month. Company registration documents of the time even show a Roman Catholic bishop in Central Java establishing a diocesan soap-making business. Seizures of Dutch assets in 1957 left army officers running factories, trading companies and plantations. They directed funds back to their units as much as to official revenue, and in areas with export produce 'administrative smuggling' flourished.

Suharto's is the epitome of the patronage style of leadership in the Indonesian Army. In a highly personalized relationship such a commander looks after his troops in both material and moral ways. Once trust is given, it is hard to break by outside criticism. Mutual loyalty and support may continue long after the immediate link is severed. The concept has seen certain trusted associates move up with Suharto through his career, in some instances at the expense of competence. The welfare of his men is a prime concern for Suharto. In 1950 he had already received one warning from his commander, Colonel Gatot Subroto, over a transport enterprise established with army vehicles in Jogjakarta to provide jobs for his veterans.[5] While commander in Central Java (known as the Fourth

Military Region as well as the Diponegoro Division) Suharto looked after his own in a curious financial structure that attempted to combine philanthropy with making money. This was to bring about Suharto's removal from the job.

Semarang is unlike the gentle royal cities of Solo and Jogjakarta near the south shore of Java. It sits on Central Java's hot northern plain, and has the only port open to large ships on that stretch of coast. Under the Dutch it became a busy trading and administrative centre. Joining the Muslim entrepreneurs of the north coast came great numbers of Chinese traders and their families. Even in the depressed 1950s great wealth flowed through the city: sugar and other agricultural produce going out, industrial raw materials and finished goods coming in.

Key figures in the Diponegoro Division's efforts to divert some of the province's wealth were the officers of its Finance and Economic Planning Staff, known as Finek, whose job was not only to keep the books but to raise cash.[6] This money came from nationalized Dutch enterprises and by the influence of officers placed on the boards of revenue-raising state bodies. For example in 1957 a Diponegoro major was placed on the board of Permigan, a small state-owned oil company, located at Cepu, east of Semarang.[7] With the divisional commander holding martial law powers from 1957, direct entrepreneuring became possible. In a pattern that was to cause the army considerable unpopularity, it was often a Chinese partner who provided the bulk of capital while the *baju hijau* ('green shirt', i.e. uniform) gave easy progress through or around bureaucracy and taxes.

A young officer, Major Sujono Humardani, who unusually combined a Solo *priyayi* upbringing with early business experience, became head of the finance section of the FINEK staff. Together with his superior, Colonel Sutomo, and acting on behalf of Suharto he set up enterprises including a shipping company and a general-purpose trading venture. Allied with the two officers were

Chinese businessmen, such as Mohammed (Bob) Hassan who had been raised as a foster-child by the division's Colonel Gatot Subroto. Later the PNI leader, Hadisubeno, joined two firms as president of their boards of commissioners, representing Suharto as the Martial Law chief of Central Java, and stood in for Suharto in the founding of another trading venture.

Another avenue of enterprise came through two foundations established in 1957 by Suharto: the Yayasan Dana Pembangunan Territorium IV (Territory IV Development Contributions Fund) and the Yayasan Territorium Empat (Territory IV Foundation). The first was intended to 'repay the debt' owed for the people's support during the revolution by way of assisting agricultural enterprises. The second was to aid soldiers' welfare and provide jobs for retired personnel. These foundations became partners in companies directed at taking over marketing and distribution of key commodities.[8] Suharto gained a reputation as an efficient money-maker. His reasoning was that where commercial opportunities existed it might as well be the authorities who benefited; this would support them in their public duties.

The army's involvement in commercial enterprise was attracting public hostility, particularly as some army units had been vigorously pursuing an anti-corruption drive against similar ventures by civilians. Late in 1958 a scandal erupted over a smuggling or 'barter' case in which the main culprit was the army's Operations chief, Colonel Ibnu Sutowo. Ibnu had ordered the clearance of goods through Tanjung Priok, the port of Jakarta, in order to effect payment in Singapore for military supplies. The army commander, General Nasution, felt obliged to temporarily suspend Ibnu from office, although he was allowed to continue running an army-controlled oil firm, Permina.[9] Nasution was then arguing for extension of the state of emergency by another year, which was opposed by the political parties who cited military corruption to justify a return to civilian rule.

Towards the end of 1958 Nasution had introduced his concept of the 'Middle Way' for the military in politics: neither completely in control nor simply a professional fighting force. As Sukarno moved the debate on Indonesia's constitutional form towards Guided Democracy, the army's concern was to gain official recognition for this Middle Way. Corruption caused Nasution continual concern. In August 1959 he announced that the army had to 'cleanse itself',[10] and followed this with an investigation of regional commands. According to informed accounts, an investigation by Nasution's budgetary controller found Suharto to be involved in the smuggling of sugar and other produce as part of a barter trade through Semarang to Singapore.[11] Another inquiry into the activities of the Diponegoro Division also drew action from headquarters. The army's Inspector-General, Brigadier-General Sungkono, told the press in Semarang on 13 October 1959 that the division's Development Contributions Fund had been financed by unauthorized levies. General Sungkono pointedly observed that the fund was the only such venture set up in any of the military regions of Indonesia.[12]

Some time between 13 October, when Suharto made his last reported appearance as Diponegoro Commander, and 16 October, when a brief announcement of a new appointment was made,[13] he was relieved of his command without fanfare. According to sources close to Nasution, Nasution and his deputy, Gatot Subroto, took a conscious decision 'because of the political climate' not to take further action. Suharto was assigned to the army's Staff and Command School (Seskoad) in Bandung.[14]

Behind the immediate political expediency of Nasution's move against Suharto and Ibnu Sutowo was a clash of values. Nasution is a Sumatran, a devout Muslim, and was one of the handful of Indonesians trained as army officers by the Dutch. His own life-style is comfortable but unacquisitive. He is more loyal to ideas than people, and ideologically able to accept a separation of powers. The two Javanese colonels had little time for theory, valued comradely understanding highest of all, and saw separation of functions as wasteful and divisive.

Bandung lies in the cool uplands of West Java, a city of dignified public buildings, comfortable Dutch villas along tree-shaded streets, and crowded *kampung*s climbing up the sides of steep valleys. It billets some of Indonesia's brightest students attending leading universities, such as the Institute of Technology (ITB) where Sukarno first emerged as a nationalist force. Bandung reflects both an outward-looking intellectual preoccupation and the directness of the Sundanese people of West Java. It also contains, in the elegant and well-maintained former headquarters of the KNIL, the command centre of the Siliwangi Division, long the Indonesian Army's best equipped and most professional force.

When 38-year-old Colonel Suharto arrived to begin a ten-month course at the Army Staff and Command School, he plunged into the Indonesian Army's most vigorous centre of political thinking. Between 1958 and 1962 the students of the staff school, under a brilliant Siliwangi Division officer, Suwarto, formulated a doctrine that greatly extended the army's political role and brought it into a position to challenge the fast-expanding Communist Party. From Nasution's 1959 statement of a Middle Way and the idea of 'territorial warfare' found in the guerilla struggle against the Dutch, it paradoxically built on the weakness of Indonesia's armed forces. Because the navy and air force could not, in the foreseeable future, become strong enought o block an enemy landing, national defence had to be built on the deterrent of an army that never surrendered but continued, in the last resort, an indefinite guerilla struggle. To be successful in such 'territorial warfare' the army had to be accepted and supported by the people. Therefore, to prepare against such an eventuality the army had to be permanently in contact with the people at local level to build up a stock of goodwill. From this Suwarto's students evolved the idea of 'Territorial Management', the establishment of a parallel administration down to village level so that resident army personnel could supervise and prod the civil authorities. Around 1962 Nasution further tuned the idea with a 'Civic Mission' programme, equipping idle units in peace time for public works. The army's allies also became involved. A group of American-trained economists, later known as the 'Berkeley Mafia', who were then based at the University of Indonesia in Jakarta, helped to refine the Territorial Management concept. Through personal contact between Nasution and General Maxwell Taylor, the US Government initiated a plan to provide equipment for civic action having, since its unfruitful covert support for the 1958 rebellion, decided to assist sympathetic elements in Jakarta.[15]

Attending Seskoad for most of 1960, Suharto was one of the students who contributed to the Territorial Management and Civic Mission doctrines, attending a key seminar organized by Suwarto in December 1960. Suharto recovered quickly from the set-back posed by the fundraising controversy in Semarang. It seems to have been quickly forgiven by his senior army colleagues, many of whom, as they themselves learnt to enjoy the good life of the Jakarta elite, were becoming rather impatient with the homilies of General Nasution. General Gatot Subroto who had chaired the army's council on officer promotions since 1956 was most likely exerting his influence to reverse the set-back, if for no other reason than the involvement of his own protégé, Bob Hassan, in Suharto's projects. Suharto became a brigadier-general soon after arriving in Bandung. At the end of 1960 he was placed in charge of Intelligence as First Deputy to the Army Chief of Staff.

New responsibilities began to be piled on Suharto. In 1961 he was given, simultaneously with his Intelligence function, command of the army's new Strategic Reserve force which was later to become known as Kostrad. This reserve fulfilled Nasution's long-held desire for a well-equipped, highly mobile fighting force directly at the disposal of the General Staff, avoiding any hell-dragging or even outright opposition from regional commanders. The best units of the three Java commands were to be upgraded to airborne status, and together with elite units like the commando regiment (RPKAD), were to be ready for immediate dispatch to any outbreak of trouble. Later in 1961 Suharto accompanied Nasution on a tour of Yugoslavia, France and Germany. In January 1962 he was promoted to major-general and given command of the 'Mandala' campaign to capture West Irian, the one part of the former Indies not relinquished by the Dutch.

Given his lack of prominence in the army General Staff and his non-participation in the 1958–9 fighting, Suharto's rapid rise is puzzling, particularly because of the implications of success or failure in West Irian for national prestige. The explanation may lie precisely in his withdrawn character and political caution, since Nasution was reluctant to take on the Dutch while the military balance remained heavily in their favour (the Netherlands moved, among other modern armaments, an aircraft carrier to Western New Guinea in 1962). It might have been thought Suharto would be competent but unadventurous: at the same time he posed little political threat to his superiors.

As head of the Strategic Reserve and of the West Irian campaign Suharto gathered a wide circle of military acquaintances into a tight military clique. Based on old Diponegoro Division links, it extended into other units of the army and even into the other services, particularly the navy. A navy colonel, Sudomo, became Suharto's deputy, beginning an association that was to last nearly two decades. A young commando officer, Benny Murdani, who was to win acclaim for leading a parachute jump into West Irian, became one of Suharto's confidants. On the island of Dobo in the Arafura Sea, Major Ali Murtopo was put in charge of testing a new 'combat intelligence' unit attached to the Strategic Reserve and which was to evolve into a body notorious for political manipulation under the Suharto Government: Special Operations, or Opsus.

The military task was a difficult one. About the time of Suharto's appointment the Dutch had underscored Indonesia's air and naval supremacy by sinking two or three torpedo boats heading towards the Irian coast, and killing the flotilla commander. Throughout 1962 Indonesian forces infiltrated West Irian in small boats across the shallow seas from nearby islands or by night-time parachute drops. The latter were made on the swampy south coast away from the main concentrations of Dutch forces. The commandos were thwarted by tall jungle trees which snared their descent and swamp that kept them permanently soaked and ill. Equipment was lost and ruined. Worst of all the Irianese population declined to welcome the Indonesians as liberators, having been prepared by the Netherlands for eventual independence. Mostly they either attacked the paratroopers or turned them over to the Dutch authorities. According to one set of official statistics, of the 1419 troops dropped on West Irian, 216 were killed or never found and 296 captured. Suharto's plan to swiftly resolve the campaign was a combined air and sea assault on Biak Island, a centre of trade and communications for the territory, which contained a big Dutch military base and the only jet airstrip. This highly risky operation was fortunately never attempted, since the Dutch abruptly capitulated to pressure by the USA in August 1962 and agreed to terms that led to an Indonesian takeover the followng year after a six-month United Nations interregnum.

Many Indonesians hoped the successful West Irian campaign would bring them a period of internal consolidation. Instead, Sukarno soon took the country into another international adventure, to 'crush' the new neighbouring state of Malaysia created from the former British territories of Malaya, Singapore and North Borneo on 16 September 1963. Indonesia, which six years previously had welcomed independence for Malaya, dubbed the new federation an imperialist plot. The 'Confrontation' of Malaysia and concurrent drain on the already prostrate economy distanced Jakarta from both Western powers and the USSR, the latter of whom had supplied large amounts of sophisticated weaponry for use in Irian. Sukarno moved closer to Peking.

At home, Sukarno had staged a successful strike at the army by promoting Nasution to the new and essentially powerless position of Armed Forces Chief of Staff, since the individual services remained directly responsible to himself as Commander-in-Chief. A gap soon developed between Nasution and the new Army Minister and Chief of Staff, Major-General Ahmad Yani, a Javanese who had settled easily into the frivolous life-style of the Jakarta elite suburb of Menteng and who 'enjoyed the same hobby' as Sukarno: womanizing. Similar splits developed in other parts of the army. As Confrontation shifted the balance of power to the PKI, the military found themselves less and less able to pursue the line of resistance worked out a few years before at the Staff and Command School in Bandung.[16] The anti-imperialist emotion created by Confrontation thwarted an attempt in 1963 to attack worsening inflation. Many moderate, technically qualified people were hounded from public life. Some, like the Socialist Party leader, Sutan Sjahrir, were jailed. Sukarno, created President for Life with such grandiose titles as 'Great Leader of the Revolution', was playing with wild and unpredictable forces.

The first armed clash of Confrontation took place in Sarawak a few days after Malaysia was formed. In Jakarta mobs stormed and burnt British property, including the British embassy. Nasution, according to some Indonesia watchers, decided to align himself with Confrontation to further the army's influence, and issued orders direct to field commanders over Yani's head. Perhaps sensing widespread reluctance among army officers corps, Sukarno appointed the air force commander, Air Vice-Marshall

Omar Dhani, to head the anti-Malaysia 'Alert Command' (Komando Siaga) in May 1964 with the intention of invading the Malayan peninsula a year later. Yani remained unconvinced that Indonesia could prevail against the British Commonwealth forces defending Malaysia, an opinion justified by disastrously incompetent air drops of ill-prepared guerilla units in August and September of 1964. In deft staff reshuffles, Yani placed officers with like opinion in the front-line positions and made sure no transport was available for offensive action. Yani then used the repulse of the early raids to argue for a 'strengthening' of the anti-Malaysia commands by the addition of seasoned fighting men. On 1 January 1965 Major-General Suharto was made Omar Dhani's deputy with new powers over all Confrontation activities in Sumatra and Kalimantan.[17]

Suharto was the man for Yani's ploy. According to one study, Suharto's intelligence advisers in Kostrad, the Strategic Reserve, had already told him six months before that active pursuit of Confrontation requiring the transfer of key units out of Java would dangerously weaken the army's political stance against the communists. Lieutenant-Colonel Ali Murtopo, head of Kostrad's Special Operations group, had opened secret contacts with Malaysian and British officials in August and September 1964,[18] particularly with the Permanent Head of the Malaysian Foreign Ministry, Ghazalie Shafie. In November that year Ali Murtopo and another Suharto confidant in Kostrad, Colonel Tjokropranolo, went to Bangkok for secret negotiations aimed at limiting Confrontation. Ali Murtopo also communicated with several of the Indonesians exiled in Malaya and Singapore since the 1958 rebellion. These included men as diverse as the noted economist, Sumitro Djojohadikusumo (later a minister in the Suharto Government), and the Arab–Indonesian businessman, Des Alwi. Suharto's sway over the rich plantation areas of Sumatra and Kalimantan combined with Ali Murtopo's links across the Malacca Straits, and help from navy friends like Colonel Sudomo soon led to a burgeoning of traditional regional smuggling, diverting huge amounts of rubber and other commodities. Some Western intelligence agencies rate Ali Murtopo as Indonesia's 'biggest smuggler' by late 1965. The commerce did not go completely unnoticed. At one cabinet meeting of the time, Trade Minister Adam Malik flourished a wad of Singapore customs clearance papers at military men, accusing the army of undermining Confrontation.[19]

But the 'Crush Malaysia' campaign provided the political excuse for the PKI to lift itself from the rut of 'domestication' where some observers saw it placed by 1963. The party had advanced steadily since 27-year-old Dipa Nusantara Aidit took over its leadership in 1950 after the rout of Madiun (which had sent Aidit himself into brief exile in China). With his four politburo members, Lukman, Njoto, Sakirman and Sudisman, Aidit had used the openness of the 1950s to rebuild the PKI according to a long-term strategy which emphasized co-operation with other political forces and the widest extension of influence through affiliated mass organizations, at the price of ideological purity. Under Guided Democracy the communists followed Sukarno's Nasakom concept, and worked with nationalist and religious forces. By 1963 PKI membership had passed 2 million. The party's criticism of other political groups sharpened as the current orthodoxy set by Sukarno took a more revolutionary turn. The PKI-associated Peoples' Cultural Institute (Lekra) harassed artists, writers and journalists deemed not sufficiently progressive. In 1964 in the countryside of East and Central Java, which formed the real base of the PKI, the party's organization of peasants (BTI) led 'unilateral action' against large landholdings, plantations and state forests to force compliance with a 1960 land reform law. Early in 1965 it began pressing for appointment of political officers in the military and creation of a new 'Fifth Force' by giving arms and training to volunteers from the masses. In this it won the support of the air force chief, Omar Dhani, and certain other air force, navy and police leaders.

The tumult created by these moves may have disguised the precarious nature of PKI influence. The party lacked real strength in the Outer Islands. In West Java the strength of Islam and the Siliwangi Division's highly developed Territorial Management programme overwhelmed the PKI in competition for village loyalties. The West Java commander, Major-General Adjie, was in the habit of telling visitors he could wipe out the PKI within twenty-four hours. Even in the ethnic Javanese provinces to the east, the army remained a strong countervailing force in alliance with Muslim and anti-communist nationalist elements who tended to be the target of 'unilateral action' in their capacities as landowners and defenders of government property. Subsequent Suharto Government studies have alleged that parallel with its 'legal' activity the PKI was attempting to build an underground organization around potential guerilla bases in remote areas.[20]

By 1965 the PKI and the army were circling each other, pre-occupied with a struggle they believed must break out when the ageing Sukarno died. Rumours circulated of army plots, fuelled by Foreign Minister Subandrio's announcement of a draft note allegedly written by the British Ambassador, Sir Andrew Gilchrist, referring to 'local army friends' of Britain and the USA. Sukarno was prompted to raise with the army chief, Yani, allegations that a 'Council of Generals' had been formed to push the army's political ambitions. Yani is said to have replied, and his successors still maintain, that the only such body was a commission on senior promotions sometimes known by that name which confined itself strictly to its personnel function. But the insinuation certainly lodged in many minds.

In the early hours of 1 October 1965 army trucks drove through the quiet, shadowy streets of the suburbs of Menteng and Kebayoran Baru in Jakarta. Squads of soldiers burst into seven substantial houses in search of Nasution, Yani and five other members of the army General Staff. Yani and two others were shot down when they put up resistance and their bodies carried off. Nasution ran to the rear of his house and scrambled over a high wall into a neighbouring garden, injuring an ankle, while a violent search took place in which his five-year-old daughter was fatally wounded and his aide abducted. Three other generals were abducted to the air force base at Halim, on the south-eastern edge of the city. At an empty part of the airfield known as Lubang Buaya (Crocodile Hole) the security force commander of the base was waiting with 2000 civilian volunteers from the PKI's women's and youth organizations who thought they were assembled for paramilitary training in preparation for an 'imperialist' attack on Indonesia. The three surviving generals and Nasution's aide were executed and all seven bodies buried in a disused well. In the city two battalions of troops in town for the scheduled Armed Forces' Day parade on 5 October took over the presidential palace, the Jakarta station of Radio Republik Indonesia and the Telecommunications Centre which all face on to the central Merdeka Square.

To Halim Air Base hurried Aidit, Omar Dhani and Sukarno, the latter who had been wakened at the house of his young Japanese wife, Dewi, and warned of strange troop movements. At 7.10 a.m. the leader of the putsch came on air. It was Lieutenant-Colonel Untung, a well-known hero of the West Irian parachute drops who, since January 1965, had commanded a battalion of the elite Cakrabirawa Regiment guarding Sukarno in Jakarta. Untung announced that a '30 September Movement' (which had thus apparently taken a final decision the previous day) had acted to foil a planned *coup d'état* by the 'Council of Generals' on Armed Forces' Day, 5 October. A Revolutionary Council would be formed in Jakarta, with corresponding moves at local level. Untung called on the military to purge their higher ranks.

> Power-mad generals who have neglected the lot of their men and who above the accumulated sufferings of their men have lived in luxury, led a gay life, insulted our women and wasted

> Government funds must be kicked out of the Army and punished accordingly. The Army is not for generals, but is the possession of all soldiers of the Army who are loyal to the ideals of the Revolution.

Untung mentioned no party connection, stressing that the movement was 'an internal army affair'. He did not mention Sukarno's presence at the coup headquarters.

The earlier shooting at the homes of the seven generals had quickly drawn a response from the city garrison. The Jakarta commander, Brigadier-General Umar Wirahadikusumah, arrived at Nasution's house and dispatched troops to look for the abductors. The Strategic Reserve (Kostrad) commander, Suharto, had also been alerted by the head of his neighbourhood association, a lawyer named Mashuri. After finding out who was missing, Suharto decided to assume temporary command of the army, a role he had customarily assumed during Yani's absences. Throughout the day Suharto methodically tested the strength of the coup forces and marshalled his own. One of the out-of-town units around Merdeka Square was from the East Java Brawijaya Division. A former chief of the Brawijaya with Suharto casually strolled up to its soldiers and successfully persuaded them to change sides. The other battalion, formerly under the command of Colonel Untung in Central Java, deserted its position and withdrew to Halim.

With Sukarno holding back from recognition of the coup and his presence at Halim not known to the public, Suharto was able to gain the psychological advantage of portraying the coup as the overthrow of the president. Ignoring a decision by Sukarno to appoint an old rival, Pranato Reksosamudro, as acting army chief, Suharto tightened his blockade around Halim. After hearing that Sukarno had left for a presidential retreat at Bogor, some 40 kilometres south, Suharto ordered the RPKAD commando regiment to move in. The base fell without much struggle early in the morning of 2 October, about an hour after Aidit and Omar Dhani had flown out to Jogjakarta aboard an air force Hercules.

The Suharto Group 43

It was in Central Java that the 30 September Movement mounted its biggest challenge. After hearing Untung's first broadcast, the Diponegoro Division Intelligence chief, Colonel Suherman, seized control of divisional headquarters in Semarang. Fellow conspirators took action in other big towns, including Jogjakarta (where the local commander was abducted and later murdered), Solo and Salatiga. But the Diponegoro commander, Brigadier-General Suryosempeno, eluded arrest and joined a tank regiment in Magelang. The next day he retook Semarang largely by show of force. By 5 October Colonel Widodo, a former company commander in Suharto's 1949 'General Attack', had taken over Jogjakarta for Suharto while in nearby Solo General Suryosempeno's forces had gained a more fragile ascendancy.

The degree of PKI complicity in the 30 September Movement is still contested and may never be satisfactorily determined. The use of the Council of Generals target did associate Untung with the communists, as did the role of communist women and youth at Halim. Yet a close analysis of the events of 5 October shows that PKI support was tentative. Aidit was at Halim, but like Sukarno seems to have been passive in his behaviour. A demonstration of support was organized in Jogjakarta by the PKI, and the PKI mayor of Solo declared his support, but these seem local initiatives. Implication came more from an editorial carried by the communist newspaper *Harian Rakyat* (*People's Daily*) in Jakarta on the morning of 2 October, expressing cautious support for the coup – curiously, since the Untung movement was visibly collapsing well before the edition would normally have gone to press. Another major question is Sukarno's involvement. Why did he rush to Halim? Why did he express such little concern over the dead generals, either on 1 October or on many appropriate occasions afterwards?

Largely through the subsequent trials of alleged plotters and through two official histories,[21] the Suharto Government has claimed that the PKI was the mastermind behind the 'Gestapu' affair, as it has been dubbed in a sinister acronym. The most recent version asserts that since 1957 the PKI had been attempting to subvert the armed forces through a special branch known first as the Biro Penghubung (Contact Bureau) and from 1964 as the Special Bureau or Biro Khusus. The leader of this force was the mysterious Syam, alias Kamaruzaman bin Mubaidah, who set up the coup by manipulating gullible left-wing officers. Syam, who was captured and tried in 1967, was said to have been a long-time informer on communist activities for military intelligence in his many-layered career. The existence of the Biro Khusus was said to have been known only to Aidit in the PKI leadership. Syam's testimony in court was the only direct evidence attesting to an Aidit–Untung link.

Statements made by certain prominent PKI figures in their own trials have conceded that Aidit was involved. Although such confessions from the dock were probably often coerced, some independent scholars have given credence to this aspect, and it has been supported in works of 'self-criticism' published by PKI figures either while still at large inside Indonesia or from exile in Albania and elsewhere. But did the initiative come from Aidit, or from the Diponegoro–Untung group? Was the motive a genuine fear of an impending military coup, resulting in a hasty pre-emptive move? Or was the 30 September Movement a more premeditated strike to make the army more amenable under a continuing Nasakom system, with Sukarno regarding the communists as the loyalists? In either case it would have been preferable to stage the strike as an internal army affair. The failure of the PKI to call out its huge membership (Aidit ordered the party to remain calm) can be cited as a sign of limited involvement or aims. But Aidit would have known the army would have certainly learnt of such a plan well in advance since its intelligence had thoroughly penetrated the party structure. An alternative scenario could see a successful Untung putsch as a preliminary to mobilizing the party masses.

The loose ends have prompted some observers to look in different directions from the version put out by Suharto's New Order that it was a PKI plot. An early foreign study came from two of Cornell University's Indonesia specialists, Benedict Anderson and Ruth McVey, who made an exhaustive search through contemporary Indonesian press accounts. Their tentative conclusion, entitled 'Preliminary Analysis', emerged early in 1966 as a private paper but was given unexpected publicity. The 'Cornell Paper', as it became known, postulated that the coup was centred in Semarang and that Untung was merely its 'Man in Jakarta'. The plotters were zealous young Sukarnoist officers seeking to clean out their corrupted generals who were selling out Indonesia to the Western powers. The PKI had been deliberately enticed into the affair to lend physical support. But the plot came unstuck because it neglected Suharto and garrison commander, Umar Wirahadikusumah, in the Jakarta kidnappings, because of Sukarno's wavering, and because of public reaction against the killings of the generals in which communist organizations were closely involved.[22]

The continued work of Anderson and McVey on the origins of the coup has taken them towards more radical conclusions. They assert that even anti-communist accounts, such as the official CIA study released in 1976,[23] fail to produce a credible explanation for the PKI to have mounted such a coup. The genuineness of Sjam is also questioned, particularly since Aidit, the only other witness even claimed to have known of the existence of the Biro Khusus, was summarily executed. (Sjam himself has not been executed like all the other alleged chief conspirators.) Why was the *Harian Rakyat* editorial of 2 October allowed to appear, after Suharto had already placed controls on the Jakarta press? Anderson and McVey say that if such evidence (as some of it does) suggests the coup might have been aimed *against* the PKI, the coup would obviously not have come from the army leadership who lost six generals and nearly lost Nasution. The finger they point is at the eventual winner, Suharto, who was on cool terms with both Nasution and Yani, and who was a puzzling omission from any attack on the General Staff, given his seniority and key role as Kostrad commander. The lack of any attempt to take over or isolate Kostrad headquarters, with its nationwide communications system (installed by US military aid) is also noted. Finally they question the interest of the CIA in having an alternative conclusion accepted by release of its own account, the only such study on Indonesian politics it has published so far.[24] However, Anderson and McVey do not yet claim to have made out a case.

Sukarno protested to his death that he was not involved in or informed about preparations for the coup attempt. Although military interrogation teams periodically produced new 'evidence' of Sukarno's involvement and support for Untung on 1 October, Suharto appears to have been unconvinced of this himself, and was certainly concerned for sound political reasons to maintain an ambivalence about Sukarno's role. On one hand it suited him to implicate Sukarno, in order to thoroughly discredit him among groups already disillusioned with Guided Democracy. On the other this raised again the question of which was really the loyalist force. After castigating Sukarno for his actions at Halim, Suharto in his 1967 opening address to the Indonesian Congress concluded that Sukarno could not be marked down as a 'direct instigator, or the mastermind, or even an important figure' in the 30 September Movement. In 1978, when it had become politic to allow a measured rehabilitation of Sukarnoism, a government report cleared Sukarno. It stated that he had gone to Halim under a pre-arranged plan to disperse the national leadership in the event of trouble. After hearing of unidentified troops in Merdeka Square, Sukarno had rushed to Halim where his personal aircraft was ready to carry him to safety in Jogjakarta. Sukarno had not known that the airbase was the plotters' Jakarta headquarters. When informed about the abduction of the generals he had warned he expected proof that the Council of Generals had planned to act.[25]

Whatever the provenance of the quickly dispersed 30 September Movement, the events of 1 October were a decisive moment in the history of the Indonesian Republic. Both Sukarno and the PKI had become tainted by the murders. Restraints maintained under Guided Democracy had been critically weakened. Pent-up political and social forces were released. Indonesia was carried towards a dramatic change of political regime, accompanied by one of the most terrible massacres of this century.

NOTES

1 Herbert Feith, *The Decline of Constitutional Democracy in Indonesia*, Cornell University Press, 1962, p. 68.
2 Ulf Sundhausen, 'The Political Orientations and Political Involvement of the Indonesian Officer Corps 1945-1966: The Siliwangi Division and the Army Headquarters', PhD thesis, Monash University, Melbourne, 1971, p. 188; and O. G. Roeder, op. cit., 213.
3 Daniel S. Lev, *The Transition to Guided Democracy: Indonesian Politics, 1957-59*, Monograph Series, Modern Indonesia Project, Cornell University Press, 1966, p. 29.
4 *Kedaulatan Rakyat* (Jogjakarta), 18 August 1959.
5 From confidential interviews by the author in Jakarta, 1978.
6 See R. A. Robinson, 'Towards a Class Analysis of the Indonesian Military Bureaucratic State', *Indonesia*, Cornell University Press, no. 25, April, 1978.
7 Anderson G. Bartlett *et al.*, *Pertamina, Indonesian National Oil*, Amerasian, Jakarta, Singapore and Tulsa, 1972, p. 206.
8 *Berita Negara Tambahan Berseroan Terbatas, Jakarta*, nos 826, 1959; 263, 1960; 270, 1960; 825, 1959; 880, 1959; 893, 1959; 897, 1959.
9 Lev, op. cit., p. 195 and, for example, *Harian Rakyat*, 7 January 1959 and 3 March 1959 among wide press coverage.
10 *Duta Masjarakat*, 8 August 1959.
11 From confidential interviews by the author in Jakarta 1978, and also referred to in Harold Crouch, *The Army and Politics in Indonesia*, Cornell University Press, 1978, p. 40.
12 *Duta Masjarakat*, 16 October 1959.
13 See *Kedaulatan Rakyat*, 14 October and 17 October 1959.

48 Suharto's Indonesia

14 Confidential interview sources. A different version put about by Suharto's supporters is that he was moved for acting against communists in his command (see Howard Palfrey Jones, *Indonesia: The Possible Dream*, Harcourt Brace Jovanovich, New York, 1971, p. 438).
15 See Sundausen, op. cit.; and Guy S. Pauker 'The Indonesian Doctrine of Territorial Warfare and Territorial Management', Rand Corporation Memorandum, November 1963. A less sympathetic account which exaggerates the US influence is given by Peter Dale Scott in Malcolm Caldwell (ed.), *Ten Years Military Terror in Indonesia*, Spokesman, London, 1975. For the shift in US policy see Jones, op. cit.
16 See Sundhausen, op. cit.; Crouch, op. cit.; and Guy S. Pauker in John J. Johnson (ed.), *The Role of the Military in Underdeveloped Countries*, Princeton University Press, 1962.
17 Sundhausen, op. cit., pp. 578-83.
18 Peter Polomka, 'The Indonesian Army and Confrontation: An Inquiry into the Functions of Foreign Policy under Guided Democracy', MA thesis, University of Melbourne, 1969, p. 176.
19 Confidential interviews by the author in Jakarta, 1978.
20 *Tempo* (Jakarta), 5 August 1978.
21 Nugroho Notosusanto and Ismael Saleh, *The Coup Attempt of the '30 September Movement' in Indonesia*, Jakarta, 1967, and Nugroho Notosusanto and other army personnel, *Buku Putih tentang Peristiwa Gestapu/PKI*, limited preliminary issue, 20 July 1978, reported in *Tempo* (Jakarta), 5 August 1978.
22 Benedict Anderson and Ruth McVey, 'A Preliminary Analysis of the 1 October 1965, Coup in Indonesia', *Interim Report Series*, Modern Indonesia Project, Cornell University, 1971.
23 CIA Directorate of Intelligence, *Indonesia 1965: The Coup That Backfired*, Washington, 1968, released in 1976.
24 Letter by Benedict Anderson and Ruth McVey in *New York Review of Books*, 1 June 1978. Ruth McVey has also investigated links between 30 September Movement officers and Suharto in the earlier West Irian campaign in 'A Preliminary Excursion Through the Small World of Lieutenant-Colonel Untung'. Unpublished paper, University of London.
25 Nugroho Notosusanto *et al.*, op. cit.; *Tempo* (Jakarta), 5 August 1978.

3. Suharto to Power

The Palace of Bogor is a cool white building in the elegant style of European classicism, a working resort for successive rulers of the archipelago who retreat from the steamy heat and clamour of the capital, a little over an hour's drive away. It backs on to the town's famed botanical gardens, and is protected from Bogor townlife by an iron picket-fence, sentry boxes and acres of grass and shady trees where scores of deer wander. Here Sukarno began trying to bluster and cajole a tense, confused Indonesia back into the contrived balance of his Guided Democracy.

The morning after his arrival from Halim on 2 October, Sukarno summoned an emergency conference of the armed forces leadership, which included Suharto. In the first of a series of studied gestures, Suharto sent word he was too busy to come immediately. Then, when the Kostrad commander had finally appeared around mid-afternoon, Sukarno repeated his command of the previous day appointing General Pranoto as the 'daily caretaker' of the army. In what Anderson and McVey called a 'gem of Javanese sarcasm',[1] Suharto offered immediately to revoke all the measures he had taken to crush the *coup d'état* under his self-assumed powers. Sukarno backed off, agreeing to a wording of Pranoto's appointment that left him in charge of only the more mundane side of army administration and authorizing Suharto to restore 'security and order in connection with the 30 September affair'.[2] The next day Sukarno made his first broadcast since the coup, announcing that he was safe and well, calling for calm, and confirming the appointments of Suharto and Pranoto. Later that day, however, he came on the air again to absolve the air force of blame for the coup, perhaps after listening to Omar Dhani who had flown to a military airfield near Bogor late on 2 October and rejoined the president.

Suharto met this challenge head on. On the night of 4 October he told radio listeners that 'it is possible that there is truth in the statement by our beloved President that the Air Force is not involved in this affair. But it is not possible that there is no involvement in this affair of elements of the Air Force.'[3] By then Suharto's forces had discovered the bodies of the murdered generals at Lubang Buaya, exhumed them in front of television cameras, and published details of alleged cruelty and mutilation carried out on them by the communist women and youths. On 5 October the planned Armed Forces' Day ceremonies were replaced with an elaborate military funeral for the seven dead men at the Heroes' Cemetery in Jakarta. General Nasution, whose small daughter was near death, delivered a bitter oration. The emotional upsurge was quick to turn against elements who ignored or played down the loss. These included Sukarno and the diplomatic representatives of China. The army had found its martyrs and a cause for a purge of the entire PKI.

The president had summoned his huge Cabinet to Bogor on 6 October. Two PKI leaders, Njoto and Lukman, attended. Sukarno was reported by Foreign Minister Subandrio to have said of the coup attempt that 'these things could always happen in a revolution' and the important thing was now to maintain unity, not only of the armed forces but also political organizations and trade unions. The military had also spoken, Subandrio told the press, but they had been 'very much excited by the happenings, and their emotions may sometimes have been out of control'.[4] By then the army was setting out to stir up emotions even further. Mobs attacked and reduced to rubble the homes of prominent PKI figures, while

Suharto's security units began a wave of arrests in the capital. In the provinces local military commanders intensified their own purges which in some cases had preceded orders from Jakarta.

In Central Java the situation was more fluid. Suryosumpeno, Diponegoro commander, had gained the upper hand, but with many of his more trusted battalions away in Sumatra to pursue Confrontation he was unable to move against military and civil elements sympathetic to the 30 September Movement. In mid-October Suharto dispatched a force of the RPKAD commando regiment, under Colonel Sarwo Edhy Wibowo, to assist. The 'Red berets' arrived in Semarang on 17 October where two days later they staged a show of force. With mobs already attacking PKI-occupied premises and Chinese shops, the troops smashed a strike among PKI-led railway workers. By 21 October the RPKAD were moving south into one of the great heartlands of support for the PKI, the plain around Solo and Klaten where extensive plantations and dense population had turned many villagers into a virtual rural proletariat, and the drought-prone, deforested land around Boyolali on the slopes of the volcano, Merapi. On 22 October the RPKAD drove into Solo with a massive display of weaponry.

Suryosumpeno's men had gained nominal control of the city, but had been unable to take action against armed communist youth groups who were supported by some local army units. Townspeople were staying off the streets and hoarding food, while known anti-communists had moved away from their homes. The PKI Chairman, Aidit, who had arrived in Jogjakarta early on 2 October, had been moving quite freely between the party's strongholds near Solo and towns further east, although he had made one attempt on 5 October to get back to Jakarta in time for the next day's cabinet meeting. The RPKAD had driven off communist youth groups in Boyolali and had dealt ruthlessly with any sign of opposition, on at least one occasion turning the machine-guns of their armoured cars against villagers armed only with parangs and sharpened bamboo poles. Their arrival in Solo was the signal for anti-communist groups to begin a counter-attack against the PKI. As it became apparent that the advice of Aidit to stay quiet would not keep them out of trouble, PKI-dominated villagers began organized resistance. They were quickly crushed by RPKAD and Diponegoro units. Then, as in the 1948 Madiun affair, political conflict became a war between the cultural streams of *abangan* villagers and *santri* Muslim neighbours, the latter of whom had the active encouragement of Sarwo Edhy's RPKAD. 'We decided to encourage the anti-communist civilians to help with the job', he said later. 'In Solo we gathered together the youth, the nationalist groups, the religious organizations. We gave them two or three days training, then sent them out to kill the communists.' [5]

In Java it is hard to find a place where one is out of the sight or hearing of another human being. In the little hamlets that lie under their fruit trees between the rice paddies, everyone knows the business of everyone else. For a Westerner such a life would be claustrophobic, but for a Javanese it is reassuring and a basis for traditional patterns of co-operation and mutual assistance. The PKI had not disguised its membership. The teachers, officials, craftsmen and farmers who attended its meetings were as well marked in their allegiance as the *santri* men and boys who walked through the village in their green sarongs and black fezzes to the mosque. The growing militance of the PKI had strained the customary tolerance. Now with the encouragement of the army, communal groupings slid into violent attack and reprisal. Islamic and conservative youths formed gangs, carrying off known communists to mass execution. A character in one thinly fictional short story set in this time says:

> The people don't discriminate at a time like that. They have borne their anger and bitterness a long time. When it finally explodes, one cannot expect them to be rational . . . when anger and bitterness are king, intellect goes under.[6]

From Jogjakarta across to East Java the killings included known communists and mere suspects. In many cases whole families were slaughtered. Often aggrieved people took the opportunity of denouncing enemies who had no real communist links. Although PKI branches occasionally organized resistance and began their own reprisal killings, most went passively to their massacre. The rivers became a favoured dumping place for the huge number of corpses and in some parts became clogged with bodies. Among Muslims the killings took on the urgency of a Jihad, a holy war, with enormous community pressure brought to bear on young men to take part. At Jogjakarta, Roman Catholic students would leave their hostels at night to take part in the execution of truckloads of communists already taken prisoner. On the island of Bali, Indonesia's only overtly Hindu province, the killings developed just as fervently, with priests calling for fresh sacrifices to satisfy vengeful spirits over past sacrileges and social disruptions.

No accurate or closely approximate figures exist for the number killed during this frenzy. At the time, estimates ranged from 78 000 to 1 million. In December 1976 the armed forces security commands put the figure between 450 000 and 500 000. The killings continued into early 1966, until the fund of victims was exhausted or authorities stepped in to control the situation. Residents in Solo say the unprecedented severity of the flooding of the mystical Solo River in March of 1966 was generally taken as a sign that it was all over.

In Jakarta the battle of wits intensified between Sukarno and Suharto, who was made Minister and Chief of Staff of the Indonesian Army on 16 October. The army leader became the rallying point for groups who had nursed a silent opposition to the Old Order, as the pre-October days were to become known. These included the more right-wing elements of the armed forces, particularly officers of the Siliwangi Division who had been strongly influenced by the ideas of the banned Socialist Party (PSI), and the like-thinking of the Army Staff and Command School in

Bandung, although the Siliwangi commander himself, General Adjie, held a strong emotional commitment to Sukarno. The hawkish ex-Siliwangi officer, General Kemal Idris, was brought down from North Sumatra to replace Suharto in Kostrad. His troops (who included the RPKAD) remained the spearhead of Suharto's forces around Jakarta. Muslim organizations such as the Ansor Youth Movement, attached to the Nahdatul Ulama (Muslim Scholars' League), which were playing the major role in the massacres of East and Central Java, also became active demonstrators in Jakarta. But a new element arose in the thousands of university and high school students enthused in the full stormy tradition of Indonesian youth action. The University of Indonesia, whose crowded campus at Salemba faces a busy street not far from Jakarta's centre, became headquarters and even living quarters for thousands of young activists. Many of their leaders, if not former adherents of the PSI and the also banned progressive Islamic party, Masyumi, were attuned to the pro-Western, modernizing ideas of university professors who had struggled to maintain the institution's intellectual standards against the inroads of Sukarnoist ideologues. These teachers, as we have seen, had been in contact for some years with the army's thinkers in Bandung. Other more covert links had been established around 1963 between students and junior staff on one hand and army officers on the other. Now these contacts were activated, with the students planning their demonstrations to complement Suharto's ploys at palace level.

Sukarno usually lived at Bogor. The palace there was the domain of his leftist-inclined second wife, Hartini, and he defended and offered refuge to those who had flourished under his pre-October rule. His strength lay in his constitutional position as head of state and government and also in his enormous personal following which, as Suharto well knew, extended into the armed forces. Suharto could not afford to be seen contradicting too strongly the president's will in case he weakened his own tenuous hold by being cast as a usurper. In East Java, where Sukarno was born and spent his childhood, strong Sukarnoist feelings among the population spread into the navy, especially its marine corps, which tends to dominate the great port city of Surabaya, and into the province's Brawijaya Division.

A combination of mass protest and tough talking by senior army officers whittled away the position of Sukarno's followers towards the end of 1965. In mid-December Subandrio lost his posts in Sukarno's 'supreme command' council and as head of the Central Intelligence Body (BPI). In December a drastic money reform, the introduction of a new rupiah valued at 1000 of the old unit, failed to convey an impression of responsible government. It has been calculated that by the end of 1965 the price index stood some 363 times higher than in 1958 and that prices had risen about seven times during the previous twelve months. A labourer in Jakarta was estimated to have earned in real terms about 40 per cent of his earnings in 1958.[7] During January 1966 students milled around the State Secretariat close to the presidential palace under the watchful eye of the RPKAD's Colonel Sarwo Edhy, who had made the gesture of enrolling himself as a student at the University of Indonesia. Later the commando leader addressed students discussing their Tritura (Three Demands) to ban the PKI, purge the cabinet of leftists and incompetents, and lower prices of essential commodities. As the protests continued the intellectuals, politicians and soldiers who were to found the New Order came together for a seminar to discuss an economic strategy. It was held at the university and lasted several days. Participants included the American-educated economists, Widjojo Nitisastro, Radius Prawiro, Emil Salim, Mohammad Sadli, Ali Wardhana, and Subroto, and the social scientists, Selosoemardjan and Fuad Hassan. The politicians most prominent were Sultan Hamengkubuwono, the wily Adam Malik, who had gravitated from a tumultuous role with the left-wing Partindo and Murba parties towards a strongly anti-communist stance (although he had become prominent under Sukarno as a diplomat and later Trade minister), and Frans Seda, an economic administrator who was chairman of the small but influential Catholic Party. General Nasution represented the army. A message from Suharto was read out.[8]

Sukarno presented his major challenge on 21 February when he announced a new cabinet of a hundred members. Although Suharto retained his army post and the three PKI ministers were dropped, the list abolished Nasution's armed forces portfolio and included a large group with 30 September Movement associations, among them Air Marshal Omar Dhani. Subandrio was among the many old faces. As installation day on 24 February approached students mounted a siege on the Merdeka Palace in Jakarta. Youths sacked nearby government offices and immobilized traffic. The ministerial candidates had to slip in disguised, or be flown into the palace grounds by helicopter, as the Cakrabirawa guard held the howling mob behind barbed-wire barricades. As the ceremony proceeded inside the troops fired on the demonstrators, killing a medical student named Arief Rachman Hakim. His funeral, attended by 50 000 people, became another rallying point. Sukarno ordered a ban on the main student 'Action Front' (KAMI) and began privately urging left-wing nationalist youth to take counter-action. Although the army quietly defended the University of Indonesia campus, destructive and violent rioting by both sides spread through the city the following days, and the army was positively encouraging the anti-Sukarno groups. On 8 March students broke into and pillaged the Foreign Ministry, while a counter-demonstration later damaged the US Embassy. Attacks on Chinese representative offices followed in the next two days.

With the city brought to a standstill, Sukarno summoned party leaders to the Merdeka Palace on 10 March for a tongue-lashing during which, according to one report, he smashed a chair against the wall.[9] But during a meeting of the Cabinet the next day he was slipped a note by an officer of the guard that 'unidentified troops' had surrounded the palace. Sukarno abruptly rose and dashed for his helicopter, followed by Subandrio who did not even have time to put back on the shoes he had eased off under the table. Within minutes they were on their way to Bogor. The mysterious troops were in fact three companies of RPKAD who had removed their red berets and unit badges.

The later events of 11 March remain clouded. By his own account ten years later, made in order to clear up diverse interpretations, Suharto was at his home recovering from an allergy. Three generals – Amir Machmud, then Jakarta commander, Andi Mohammad Yusuf, then Industries Minister, and Basuki Rachmat, Veterans Affairs Minister – called for consultations, then drove to Bogor 'to report Suharto's illness and his preparedness to overcome the (security) situation'.[10] Sukarno had then volunteered his famous 'Supersemar' order transferring executive powers to Suharto. No draft had been presented. But whether or not Suharto dictated a draft to the three generals, or whether they prepared it on the way, it is generally accepted that some tough talking occurred during the several hours of discussion at Bogor. Calling Supersemar a 'disguised coup', the Australian political scientist, Harold Crouch, says that the move had been precipitated by Sukarno's new Cabinet. By giving free rein to strongly anti-Sukarno generals to stir up the students, Suharto had then been able to present himself as the defender of order.[11]

Suharto moved quickly with his new powers. The RPKAD staged a victory parade through the streets of Jakarta in which students mingled with the troops, while Sukarno flew down briefly to give a curt confirmation of the 11 March Order to officials. On 13 March Suharto formally banned the PKI (although many regional commanders had already applied effective local bans), and on 18 March announced the arrest of fifteen ministers including Subandrio, who was arrested in Sukarno's presence. Later that day Suharto announced that Sultan Hamengkubuwono and Adam Malik would join him in an interim triumvirate. Although he soon broadened his Cabinet by adding two Old Order figures, Ruslan Abdulgani and Johannes Leimena, Suharto was able to initiate sweeping changes to government policy. Malik became active restoring links with the region and with the Western powers, building in part on the efforts of Suharto's confidant, Ali Murtopo, who had spent much of the early post-coup period in pro-Western Asian countries, both introducing the new leadership's aims and tapping desperately needed funds, particularly from overseas Chinese sources in Singapore, Hong Kong and Taiwan. In June 1966 Malik reached a tentative agreement to call off the Confrontation against Malaysia, although this could not immediately be formalized given Sukarno's continuing truculence.

Overwhelming public and army pressure forced a reluctant Sukarno to convene the Peoples' Consultative Assembly (MPRS) which, theoretically at least, is the highest power in the land but which in practice meets rarely, does not deal with detailed policies, and tends to follow the chief executive's arrangements with little demur. The MPRS was still dominated by Sukarno's appointees in anticipation of a long-postponed election (and therefore had an 'S' for Sementara (Temporary) tacked to its usual initials, MPR), but in a sitting from 20 June to 6 July did Suharto's bidding after hearing an unusually contrite Sukarno. The Supersemar order was confirmed, Sukarno was asked to authorize Suharto to form a new cabinet aimed at improving the people's living standards, elections were to be held within two years, and Suharto was to take over the presidency if Sukarno was indisposed. Humiliatingly the MPRS ruled that Sukarno's appointment as President for Life be revoked and that his title of 'Great Leader of the Revolution' was merely honorary. Suharto appointed his first full Cabinet on 25 July with Hamengkubuwono as Economics Minister and Malik as Foreign Minister. Again Sukarno proved uncooperative, stunning Suharto three days later by appointing Ruslan and Leimena back to the Cabinet, and on 17 August delivering a full-blooded Independence Day speech in the old style. But events were running very quickly against Sukarno. An agreement with Malaysia was announced on 11 August and the RPKAD major, Benny Murdani, was sent to Kuala Lumpur as head of a new Indonesian liaison office. Through the rest of the year well-managed trials of Yusuf Muda Dalam, Subandrio and Omar Dhani took place in military courts. The prosecution drew out in great detail allegations of how the Governor of Bank Indonesia, Yusuf Muda Dalam, had manipulated licences to pay off Sukarno's girlfriends, as well as numerous other instances of corruption. Prosecution 'evidence' heavily implicated Sukarno in the 30 September Movement. An orchestrated outcry from the public greeted each attempt by Sukarno to shake off the new relationship between himself and Suharto approved by the MPRS.

Meanwhile Suharto's political strategists had been carefully paring away support for Sukarno. Thousands of arrests were made in the armed forces and civil service. However, it was some time before a move could be made against entrenched Sukarnoists in the navy and marine corps. Suharto installed a trusted officer, Air-Commodore Rusmin Nuryadin, as Air Force Chief of Staff soon after the Supersemar declaration. The Sukarno-loyalist Ibrahim Adjie had been sent overseas as Ambassador to Britain, and replaced as Siliwangi commander by Major-General H. R. Dharsono, who gave overt support to the students in Bandung. When an anti-Sukarno student named Julius Usman was killed in mob fighting, Dharsono gave him a hero's funeral and then defended the gesture to Sukarno's face. In the East Java Brawijaya Division the tough German-trained General Sumitro put down attempts among his officers and division veterans to rally support for Sukarno late in 1966. In the Nationalist Party (PNI) Suharto's men moved early against the left-wing whose leaders, former Prime Minister Ali Sastroamidjojo and Surachman, held the senior party positions. A conservative faction controlled by Hardi and Suharto's old friend in Semarang, Hadisubeno, persuaded the left-wing group to agree to a meeting in Bandung in April 1966 to discuss 'reunification' of the party. With the army closely watching transport into Bandung, and a joint force of Siliwangi officers and student leaders controlling credentials, the selected meeting forced the left group out of office.[12]

When Sukarno issued a final, provocative statement on 10 January 1967 in answer to calls for an explanation of his conduct during the coup attempt, Suharto was able to rally the support of all the services, although the navy was still reluctant, for a showdown. For several days during February, according to many accounts, Suharto and his colleagues wore down Sukarno's resistance to a formal transfer of power under the terms provided six months before by the MPRS. On 22 February the Information Minister, B. M. Diah, announced that Sukarno had agreed to the move two days before. The threat held over Sukarno had been that of public trial for involvement in the coup movement. Early in March Suharto appeared in a heavily guarded MPRS to be sworn in as Acting President. Sukarno retained the title of president, but was stripped of his powers and ordered to refrain from political activity until after the forthcoming elections. The New Order had begun, but even before Sukarno had fallen the first presage of an end to the army–student alliance had come: in October 1966 Kostrad troops had used rifle-butts and bayonets to disperse students impatient at Suharto's protracted manoeuvrings against Sukarno.

Parallel, and to some extent interwoven, with Suharto's accession to full power came the last major attempt by remnants of the PKI to rally. Throughout 1966 had come reports of PKI groups forming themselves into a People's Liberation Army along Maoist lines, and establishing surreptitious organizations with names like 'Iceberg' and 'PKI of the Night'. The Indonesian Army alleged communists had infiltrated or even set up a number of groups ostensibly aimed at preserving the position of Sukarno. Clearly many of the sensational announcements about a PKI resurgence made during this period by Suharto's army officers have to be discounted, since it was part of the pressure tactic against the president to link him and his followers as closely as possible with dangerous elements. But it is widely accepted that during 1966, with Aidit killed the previous November, a new PKI Central Committee was set up under or with the hunted politburo member, Sudisman, who apparently managed to spend much of his time in Jakarta. In September a document of 'self-criticism', usually attributed to Sudisman, attacked the party for having grown soft and compromising under Sukarno. The paper urged formation of a tightly disciplined party on pure Marxist–Leninist lines, and the pursuit of an armed 'people's struggle' in the countryside with the peasantry led by proletarians. This policy came to be supported by a PKI group in Peking (with associated emigrés in Albania) under the leadership of Jusuf Adjitorop, a PKI politburo member who had been in China when the coup attempt was made.

Although Sudisman was arrested in Jakarta in December 1966, PKI activity continued to be reported throughout Central and East Java and also in Bali. With the guidance of some of about fifteen PKI cadres who had visited North Vietnam in 1964 to study methods of revolutionary warfare, the PKI underground was said to be establishing bases in the more sparsely settled, economically backward areas including the slopes of the volcanoes Merapi and Merbabu near Boyolali and the rugged mountain country south of Blitar in East Java. The PKI was said to have marked out their operating areas in red, pink, white or green according to the balance of control between the party and pro-Suharto forces. The choice of green as the mark for enemy territory seems to indicate a pre-occupation with Muslim influence. Winning the support from a desperately poor local population who regularly suffered severe food shortages each dry season, the PKI had begun waging a war of terror against opposing figures, particularly those prominent in the Muslim Nahdatul Ulama.

Army operations through 1968 broke up this organization within a few months, uncovering a network of food and munitions dumps and even turning up Viet-Cong-style underground bunkers linked by tunnels near Blitar, the base for the PKI's revival since the capture of Sudisman (who was executed in October 1968). The new leadership of Olean Hutapea, Rewang and Ruslan Widjajasastra were all said to be among the hundreds captured or killed.[13] Although army commanders issued frequent and often contradictory warnings against PKI resurgence after the South Blitar affair, the undoubtedly numerous remnants of the PKI's former 3 million members appear to have made little attempt to reorganize. Blitar showed the party to be thoroughly infiltrated and the army's presence pervasive in the countryside. The communists may have decided to postpone armed struggle until a more favourable climate emerged. They saw this as inevitable because they believed the army was inherently unable to solve Indonesia's basic socio-economic problems. The government had not been able to cite any widescale or lasting PKI effort. In its study on the coup attempt written in 1973 and released in 1978 it claims that a 'PKI of the Night' meeting at Madiun in 1969 conferred leadership on a Dr Sugiyono, who was arrested in 1970. Incidents it attributed to PKI agitation included the anti-Chinese riots of 5 August 1973 in Bandung and a brawl between Jakarta bus employees and *becak* (pedicab) drivers on 21 March that year. The PKI was also claimed to have infiltrated and manipulated several mystic sects in Java, and to have been behind discussion groups set up at Gajah Mada University in Jogjakarta and broken up in July 1973.[14] This may only show that the PKI has moved from real threat to convenient scapegoat.

The drawn-out change of regimes was largely enacted on the islands of Java and Bali, with the people of the Outer

Islands struggling to keep themselves informed of events. The quick action of regional commanders, such as Kemal Idris in North Sumatra, in suppressing local branches of the 30 September Movement and banning the PKI gained an immediate initiative that was never lost. In the strongly Muslim province of Aceh, on the northern tip of Sumatra, the anti-communist pogrom had begun even before that of Java. There and in some other regions news of the coup attempt sparked off fresh agitation and violence against Chinese minorities, sending a flow of refugees to nearby cities. At the most normal of times, news reached the provinces slowly and scrappily, mainly through the government's radio network and the national newsagency, Antara. The time-lag in news transmission gave military authorities plenty of time to start counter-measures and, on occasions when it suited them, they could arrange for the news to be augmented, for example by flying in large supplies of Jakarta newspapers during the Subandrio, Jusuf Muda Dalam and Omar Dhani trials.[15] But in two areas, West Kalimantan and West Irian, the after-effects of Sukarno's foreign adventures brought local uprisings.

During Confrontation against Malaysia the Indonesian Armed Forces had recruited, trained and armed some 1000 young Chinese from Sarawak to fight against the British, in line with a common Indonesian strategy of raising local volunteers in its military campaigns. The Chinese were mostly members of the communist 'Organization' as it was simply known in Sarawak. For some months after the coup attempt in Jakarta they carried on a guerilla struggle against Malaysian forces, aided for a while by some regular Indonesian troops who had not heard or chosen to hear their recall. As the purge developed in Java, the guerillas attracted a number of PKI refugees. In mid-1967 they launched a fierce offensive in West Kalimantan itself, attacking an air force base to seize a large quantity of weapons. Three months later an army patrol was all but wiped out. The army's response was to launch a counter-insurgency operation in co-operation with the Malaysian forces in Sarawak. It has since been admitted by authorities involved that they helped stir an uprising among the Dayak population who live by slash-and-burn agriculture in West Kalimantan's jungle and river interior. The West Kalimantan's large Chinese community, descendants of migrants who had flocked to its gold fields last century, predominated in the towns and ran a profitable trade in rubber and timber. Mostly they had lived quietly among the Dayaks. Now the Dayaks, who traditionally had been headhunters and who at that time still kept to their old lifestyle in longhouses, launched a savage massacre of the Chinese. Hundreds were killed, and up to 50 000 forced to flee to the big towns on the coast. The economy of West Kalimantan was disrupted and thousands of Chinese were forced to live in miserable refugee settlements. But the aim had been achieved: the removal of the environment that sheltered the guerillas. The military campaign was to occupy some of the army's best troops for years to come. By 1969 the army was claiming that the worst was over, but it was not until 1977 that travel restrictions were lifted in the province.[16]

In November 1966 a delegation came to seek help from Suharto from a West Irian that was in a desperate condition. Jakarta had been unable to spare much for its new province after the transfer of sovereignty in 1963. The Netherlands' legacy had been a small Westernized elite and an awakened political consciousness attuned to the idea of independence and close links with the eastern half of New Guinea, then administered by Australia. The Dutch had sharply raised development spending by the early 1960s. Local political groups were being encouraged in the Nieuw Guinea Raad (Council) for which some elections had been held. The Indonesian leaders who had stirred up the wave of sympathy for oppressed 'brothers' in Irian soon lost interest. Even before the end of the six-month United Nations interim regime Indonesian officials were querying whether the promised 'Act of Free Choice' by 1969 was really necessary. Demoralized and impoverished officials, who regarded their assignment in West Irian as the bottom of the barrel, stripped the territory of moveable assets.

By 1966 armed rebellion was widespread under the flag of a 'Free West Papua'. Emerging Irianese leaders began agitating from exile, like Nicholaas Jouwe who had been Vice-Chairman of the Dutch Nieuw Guinea Raad, or like a number of local figures in the main towns of the Bird's Head Peninsula and the north coast. Refugees continually crossed the border into Australian New Guinea. The rebellions were put down by punitive raids, which often involved aerial strafing and rocketing of villages. Indonesia came under international pressure to honour its pledge to hold a plebescite, a promise casually abrogated by Sukarno in 1964. Yet at home Suharto was attacked by nationalist and Muslim groups for even considering such a move which might result in West Irian leaving Indonesia.

The path Suharto chose was to affirm during 1967 and 1968 that an Act of Free Choice would indeed be held. But as the time drew closer he began to add that this did not mean 'we are going to abandon the principle of the unitary state of the Indonesian Republic with a territory extending from Sabang [an island off North Sumatra] to Merauke' [in the extreme south-east of West Irian].[17] In February 1969 he proclaimed that any decision to withdraw from Indonesia would be regarded as 'treason'. Politically, Suharto had few options.

As the Act of Free Choice approached, resistance by the Irianese spread to the Central Highlands where much of the population is concentrated, away from the unhealthy coastal areas. Some 6000 troops under Brigadier-General Sarwo Edhy, who had been appointed regional commander in mid-1968, mounted frequent pacification sweeps. Irianese hopes for independence were now aligned under a 'Free Papua Movement' (Organisasi Papua Merdeka, OPM), although co-ordination above local level seems to have been slight. The original agreement with the Dutch in 1962 had not specified any particular form of plebescite. Foreign Minister Malik now made it clear that the idea of a 'one-man, one-vote' referendum would not be entertained because of its claimed impracticability. Instead a process of 'consultation' considered more appropriate to traditional ways would be carried out, via local assemblies. The results were never in doubt. The often carefully selected local assemblies rarely gave anything less than unanimous votes to stay with Indonesia throughout 1969. Ali Murtopo and his Opsus (Special Operations) team had been placed in charge of the 'project' of winning over waverers. Through two Opsus-owned trading companies hitherto unobtainable consumer goods were lavished on Irianese assemblymen and traditional chiefs. Wholescale bribery, accompanied by the arrest of several hundred outspoken opponents of Indonesian rule, succeeded.

Foreign criticism of Indonesia's conduct was to some extent deflected by the announcement early in 1969 of a $US230[18] million long-term development plan, along with a $30 million programme by the Fund of the United Nations for the Development of West Irian (FUNDWI) then getting under way. The extreme economic backwardness of West Irian was also widely acknowledged. Even so, a large group of thirty nations, mostly African, abstained during the United Nations General Assembly vote on the outcome of the Act of Free Choice which endorsed by eighty-four votes to nil a Dutch–Indonesian resolution to accept it. Physical resistance subsided after the confirmation of Indonesian sovereignty, but West Irian continued to pose special difficulties for Jakarta, and as we shall see in Chapter 11, erupted in a series of clashes that has had an important bearing on relations with the Oceanic region.[19]

After Suharto's election as Acting President in March 1967, pressure continued for an end to the 'dualism' in the national leadership. This was finally resolved by a vote of the MPRS a year later appointing Suharto as full President. Declining health and tighter surveillance increasingly restricted Sukarno's activities. As if to emphasize that his struggle with Sukarno was all but over,

Suharto began appearing in civilian clothes. He saw his task now to stabilize the economy and to begin a programme of rehabilitation and development. Issues of military rule and corruption had eroded the easy civilian–military alliance of the previous two years. Disillusionment had led to divergence. The soldiers, the Muslims, the Westernized students and intellectuals, and the traditional conservatives found they held quite different aims for Indonesia's New Order.

NOTES

1 Benedict Anderson and Ruth McVey, 'A Preliminary Analysis of the 1 October 1965, Coup in Indonesia', *Interim Report Series*, Modern Indonesian Project, Cornell University, 1971, p. 54.
2 Ibid., p. 54-5; and John Hughes, *The End of Sukarno*, Angus & Robertson, London, 1968, p. 122.
3 Hughes, op. cit., p. 123.
4 Ibid., 128.
5 Ibid., p. 151.
6 Martin Aleida, 'Dark Night', in Harry Aveling (ed. and trans.), *Gestapu*, South-East Asia Working Paper, University of Hawaii, 1975, p. 92.
7 *Far Eastern Economic Review*, 13 February 1969.
8 Harold Crouch, *The Army and Politics in Indonesia*, Cornell University Press, 1978, p. 301.
9 Hughes, op. cit., p. 232.
10 *Antara*, 3 March 1976.
11 Crouch, op. cit., p. 237.
12 Ibid., pp. 365-7.
13 See Justus M. van der Kroef, *Indonesia after Sukarno*, University of British Columbia Press, 1971, ch. 5.
14 *Tempo* (Jakarta), 5 August 1978.
15 van der Kroef, op. cit., p. 42.
16 Ibid., pp. 110-13 and David Jenkins, 'The Last Headhunt', *Far Eastern Economic Review*, 30 June 1978.
17 van der Kroef, op. cit., p. 135-6.
18 American dollars are used throughout this volume.
19 van der Kroef, op. cit., ch. 6, gives a detailed account of West Irian developments until about 1970.

4. The Technocrats

The accession of the Suharto Government changed Indonesia's operational motto from 'Revolution' to 'Development'. During his methodical sapping of the Sukarno camp, Suharto had often been compelled to blur the transition. But as the Old Order was undermined the strident slogans of Guided Democracy were replaced by a new jargon: 'stabilization', 'rehabilitation' and eventually 'dynamic stability' and 'twenty-five years of accelerated modernization'. Suharto promised a new era of constitutional government and a disciplined economic management aimed at rapid improvement in general welfare.

Sukarno's economic policies, viewed from an ideologically sympathetic standpoint, had failed because they were not revolutionary enough. Private enterprise had been left to sink or flounder amid persistent high inflation, decaying infrastructure, bureaucratic parasitism and regulatory harassment. Yet the state sector remained essentially the static, paternalistic structure inherited from the Dutch, who themselves had built on earlier Indonesian feudal systems. In the words of one foreign economist, Sukarno failed to establish a 'dedicated cadre class' to carry through his plans, nor did he sufficiently support radical reallocations of resources such as land reform.[1]

Often a dilettante in economic policy, Sukarno moved progressively further from reality under Guided Democracy. Talismans and incantations were his response to the abrupt downward slide of all economic indicators from 1964. A three-year plan to achieve self-sufficiency in rice between 1959–60 and 1961–2 had seen rice imports increase over that period from 935 736 tonnes to 1 027 176 tonnes, despite some increase in local production. Indonesia's foreign payments position became calamitous. From the early 1960s exports had run down steadily from the level of around $900 million prevailing in the 1950s, largely because of falling prices. Imports had also fallen so the trade surplus continued, but heavy invisible costs such as transport charges and repatriation of foreign oil company profits created heavy deficits on current account. These had to be met by foreign borrowing and run-down of reserves averaging in total some $300 million a year. By 1965 the reserves were almost gone, and the Soviet bloc nations who had provided much of the credit were reluctant to extend themselves further.[2]

In his 1964 Independence Day speech Sukarno announced that Indonesia was to embark on a 'Year of Living Dangerously' which involved a ban on all further imports of rice and consequently withdrawal in part of the civil service rice ration, an established method to help inflation-proof incomes. But by early 1965 orders for rice were again being placed in Bangkok, and Indonesia seemed no closer to achieving the cutbacks now necessary on already lean imports despite a reported rescheduling of Soviet loan repayments. Indeed, the list of projects classed as essential for import purposes included an ambitious complex of buildings to house Sukarno's proposed alternative to the United Nations, the Conference of New Emerging Forces (Conefo), and the National Monument at the centre of Jakarta's Merdeka Square, a gigantic pillar capped with a gold-plated flame consciously modelled on the lingga or Hindu phallic representation. (The monument is now known with ribald affection as 'Sukarno's Last Erection'.)

Two initiatives that were later to achieve results under Suharto had begun. The Army-run oil corporation under Colonel Ibnu Sutowo was starting to attract new petroleum explorers under a novel 'production-sharing' contract. Students from the Agricultural Institute at Bogor had run a highly successful pilot extension programme to intensify rice production. Yet generally the economy was stagnant, and the government was far from being able to pay its bills. Production of principal commodities such as rice, rubber and vegetable oils had levelled off or declined. Tin output was down and the textile industry, according to some contemporary estimate, was running at 5 to 10 per cent of capacity. Transport and communications were run down. Bus owners, for example, typically had more vehicles immobilized for lack of spare parts than they had on the road. The Jakarta cost of living index rose 160 per cent between September 1964 and February 1965, and was to rise by some 500 per cent during 1965. Immediately before the Untung coup attempt in September 1965, a further sharp decline in exports was reported. No foreign reserves were left, and the country owed $230 million in debt servicing for the year. No plans had been announced to preserve Indonesia's international solvency.

Following the 30 September attempted coup Sukarno's ministry made desperate efforts to bring the economy under control: new taxes were introduced and an attempt made to begin removing the heavy subsidies from public enterprises; the exchange rate was depreciated; a currency reform was initiated by the issue of a new rupiah worth 1000 of the old; and subsidies were removed on staple commodities. The measures were quickly revealed to be both doctrinaire and desperate. The currency reform, for example, had to be made because a large increase in civil service salaries made to restore some measure of purchasing power presented a demand for currency beyond the capacity of the Government Mint. The opportunity was thus taken to use surplus stocks of notes that had been printed in 1960 but never introduced. The removal of subsidies vastly increased the living costs of ordinary householders. Rising prices helped fuel the student action fronts who took to the streets in January

1966, and backed the eventual Supersemar transfer of power.

From December 1965 the central bank (Bank Indonesia) had been unable to meet foreign exchange commitments, and could not even honour cash letters of credit. A few small credits trickled in, enabling the limited purchase of materials for domestic industry. Sultan Hamengkubuwono, who became the economic co-ordinator in Suharto's new triumvirate, added up Indonesia's total foreign debt and broke the news in a soberly worded statement on 12 April 1966. Indonesia was expected to earn a total of $430 million in foreign exchange in 1966. Yet her debt service obligations alone that year would amount to $530 million. The country owed $2 358 million abroad. Of this, $1 404 million was owing to communist nations: $13 million to China and $990 million to USSR and its allies. Much of the Soviet block credit had financed arms purchases, such as supersonic Mig-21 fighter aircraft, which did not represent a productive investment for Indonesia and which soon became immobilized for lack of spare parts because of the unwillingess of the USSR to supply the new anti-communist regime. Western countries accounted for $587 million of the total debt, among them the USA with $179 million, West Germany with $122 million, France with $115 million and Italy with $91 million. Japan was owed $231 million and the International Monetary Fund (IMF) $102 million. 'Any person who entertains the idea that Indonesian society is experiencing a favourable economic situation is guilty of lack of intensive study', Sultan Hamengkubuwono commented bitterly.

Clearly Indonesia needed to delay repayments and obtain a rescheduling of its debts. In the short term at least, it also needed new credit to cover vital imports. A dialogue began between Jakarta and lending nations. The Sultan himself went to Tokyo while Adam Malik, formerly Ambassador to Moscow, went to the USSR and other East European countries, and senior officials lobbied the

Western lenders. A mission from the IMF arrived in Jakarta in June 1966 to set up an office in the central bank to assess Indonesia's foreign exchange position. Late in September the Indonesians met their non-communist creditors in Tokyo, where the sultan laid out the Suharto Government's strategy for economic recovery. On his return to Jakarta Hamengkubuwono announced a drastic stabilization policy, giving priority to control of inflation which for the whole of 1966 was to reach a peak of around 640 per cent. By late October Indonesia had secured commitments of new credit totalling some $174 million.

In February 1967 Indonesia held a more formal meeting with Western and Japanese creditors (and possible new lenders) in Amsterdam. This meeting, the first of an informal arrangement that came to be known as the Inter-governmental Group on Indonesia (IGGI), was attended by delegations from Australia, Belgium, France, West Germany, Italy, Japan, the Netherlands, the United Kingdom and the USA, with observers from Canada, New Zealand, Norway and Switzerland. International agencies present were the IMF, the World Bank (IBRD), the United Nations Development Programme, the Organization for Economic Co-operation and Development, and the Asian Development Bank. Supported by the IMF delegation, which presented a report on the Indonesian economy, Indonesia submitted a request for aid totalling $200 million in 1967.

This help was slow in coming. It was not until a second IGGI meeting in June that the aid request was fully agreed to, with the USA and Japan each meeting one-third of the total. By the time it was disbursed late in the year Indonesia was undergoing increased economic strain partly as the result of a drought which had badly damaged the end-of-year rice crop, but also because public uncertainty about future assistance had fed speculative purchasing of foreign exchange. The $35 million requested from IGGI for 1968 at a meeting in November 1967 was still not finally endorsed by the next meeting in April 1968, a pattern that did little to help confidence within Indonesia.

At the beginning this foreign aid was very much an emergency affair. It covered essential imports including both consumer goods and the raw materials and equipment needed for domestic industry. Most of the aid was not allotted to specific projects, but sold as foreign exchange by the central bank on the free market within Indonesia: rather to the apprehension of its lenders but justified by the Indonesians on the plausible ground that the country's bureaucratic apparatus was not yet up to handling a planned allocation. With the eventual rescheduling of the Sukarno debts (mostly on thirty-year repayment terms with long grace periods), and with the steadying of the economy, foreign assistance was geared more closely to long-term development strategy than to such economic first-aid. But the heavy reliance on foreign aid was to become a persistent, intensely controversial issue throughout Suharto's rule.

As the economic situation grew less of an emergency the IGGI aid package shifted its emphasis from unspecified 'programme' aid or food contributions to funds designated for specific projects. In 1968 commitments of programme aid were augmented by a heavy use of export credits whereby, say, a Norwegian Government credit is extended for the purchase of Norwegian-made ships. Of the $1823 million in aid realized in 1976–7 all but $147 million came in project aid. By 1978, some twelve years after Suharto took power, such foreign assistance accounted for 18 per cent of government revenue in a budget still officially described as 'balanced'.

This reliance has undoubtedly resulted in some surrender of the Indonesian Government's autonomy over economic planning. It is a willing and conscious policy, but it cost Suharto much political support in his intensely nationalistic country. Foreign aid donors are naturallly anxious to assure themselves their funds are being used to proper ends, particularly countries like the USA, the Netherlands, Australia and Britain which have strong domestic lobbies critical of the Suharto Government. The foreign supervision is a highly visible one. The IMF has maintained its office within the central bank building since 1966. The World Bank, which has accounted for an increasing proportion of aid to Indonesia, established a local mission in 1968. Its large expert staff has become deeply involved in the planning of key economic sectors. The two agencies assist in preparing Indonesia's annual submission to the IGGI, which usually meets once a year in the Netherlands at the beginning of the Indonesian financial year in April. Although under more criticism in recent times than in the early post-1965 days when little else was available, reports by the IMF and the World Bank, based on inside information and data not always accessible to other observers, have tended to be the basis of current economic evaluation of Indonesia for many foreign government aid agencies. The IGGI meeting is widely covered in the Indonesian press. Within a few weeks the 'confidential' World Bank report is almost routinely leaked to foreign journalists. For many educated Indonesians these are examples of undue deference to foreign interests in the vital affairs of their country, and of unwillingness by Indonesian leaders to trust their own people.

Along with the question of control is the issue of dependence and vulnerability. Even with the greatly expanded, unforeseen debt loads of the late 1970s, servicing has remained within recognized dangerlines. It is simplistic to compare the Sukarno and Suharto era debts without reference to the size of the economy or trade figures and to conclude that the New Order has made Indonesia more 'dependent'. Even so, many economists not unsympathetic to the Suharto Government believe the level of foreign backing to be somewhat imprudent. Moreover, the choice has discouraged other national investment policies, particularly development of an efficient and equitable taxation system. Personal income tax provided only 3.5 per cent of domestic revenue in 1978–9 budget estimates and non-oil company tax provided 4.9 per cent. A maze of taxes is applied to movement of goods and services, some acting as direct disincentives to stated government objectives such as export promotion. Many experts regard the taxation system as it now stands as unenforceable, even if there were enough honest and competent people to run it. The result has been a loss of stable, domestic revenue sources, as well as some exacerbation of inequalities. An alternative was urged by some Indonesian economists, such as Professor Sarbini of the University of Indonesia, from early in the New Order. Perhaps with too much optimism Sarbini suggested in 1967 a fiscal strategy based on greater internal savings, one element of which was training of a nucleus cadre of tax officials whose influence would spread outwards in geometric progression.

Similar criticisms have frequently been attributed to the alleged intellectual predisposition of the men Suharto chose to direct the economy. Almost as much as the Kostrad group of army officers, these economists have drawn the attention of New Left conspiracy theorists abroad. Within Indonesia they have come under attack during bouts of military infighting and flare-ups in the country's development debate. Practically to a man at ministerial level they come from the Faculty of Economics at the University of Indonesia (although some key economic positions went to other hands, particularly the Industries portfolio under the reclusive General A. M. Yusuf, and, as we shall see in chapter 7, petroleum was virtually beyond their jurisdiction). The chairman of the economic advisory group to Suharto and Hamengkubuwono in 1966 was the Dean of the Faculty, Widjojo Nitisastro, who was thirty-five on his appointment. East Javanese by birth and a Muslim, Widjojo fought in the irregular 'Student's Army' in the 1940s before taking up teaching and economic studies. After gaining a PhD from the University of California, Berkeley, he returned to the University of Indonesia. Two other members of his team also gained doctorates at

Berkeley: Ali Wardhana, a Central Javanese and Muslim, and Emil Salim, a West Sumatran and grandson of the nationalist pioneer Haji Agus Salim. Others with North American doctoral qualifications are Subroto, a Central Javanese, and J. B. Sumarlin, a Roman Catholic from East Java. One associate, Mohammad Sadli, also studied in the USA before gaining a doctorate at the University of Indonesia. However, two of the Technocrat team, Radius Prawiro, a Protestant from Jogjakarta, and Frans Seda, a Catholic from Flores, did their formal training in Holland, earning the Dutch qualification of Doctorandus (roughly equivalent to a Masters degree). Less in the limelight but highly influential in policy-making has been Rachmat Saleh, an economics graduate of the University of Indonesia who took over the governorship of the central bank (Bank Indonesia). Finally, they were joined in 1967 by Dr Sumitro Djojohadikusumo, the brilliant and iconoclastic economist who had figured prominently in Indonesia's early political and academic life before joining the 1958 rebellion in Sumatra and then moving to exile in Malaya and Singapore.

These younger economists had made contact with Suharto and his generation of army officers some years before at the Army Staff and Command School in Bandung where they had been part-time lecturers. For some New Left writers the early cultivation of the University of Indonesia economists by American institutions, such as the Ford Foundation, and their link with the army are seen as part and parcel of a broad, twenty-year strategy by the US political establishment to influence and intellectually dominate Sukarno's successors. While the US Army was indoctrinating Indonesian officers at Fort Leavensworth, Berkeley was allegedly deputized to 'train most of the key Indonesians who would seize government power and put their pro-American lessons into practice'. Hence the epithet 'Berkeley Mafia'.[3]

More often, Widjojo and his colleagues are known less rancourously and more appropriately as the 'Technocrats'.

Pursuing policies that have at times made them extremely unpopular with sections of the public or, more dangerously, with groups in the Jakarta elite, they have maintained a policy of closeness under attack. Their headquarters is in a cool, two-storey building facing a neat park in the wealthy suburb of Menteng, the offices of the National Development Planning Council (Bappenas) which is chaired by Widjojo. Here and in their other departments the Technocrat ministers set a cracking working pace, surrounded by bright young graduates. In-house experts from foreign academic backgrounds are frequently installed close by for consultation or work on long-range plans.

From another viewpoint the label is rather misleading. The offices run by the Technocrats tend to be enclaves of efficiency in a drowsy, tea-sipping world of endless, meaningless paper-shuffling. In some cases the Technocrat minister does not control his senior officials who owe their appointment and allegiance to other power-centres. He may have only a handful of staff whose abilities he can trust. Resources at his disposal are far below the level really needed to implement policies or to ensure the probity of civil servants down the line. Such limitations of power may have been conscious and persuasive in determination of policies, such as in fiscal strategy, even before the question of hostile vested interest is raised.

Their basis of power has always been the support they receive from Suharto. When he has favoured their rivals, as in the early skirmishes for control of the state oil company Pertamina, the Technocrats have had to submit quietly and do the best they could in less than ideal circumstances. One tactic for self-preservation has been a kind of team ethic: when Suharto was under strong pressure before his 1978 cabinet reshuffle to drop Ali Wardhana and Radius Prawiro he was told by Widjojo it was all or nobody who stayed on. But on earlier occasions two of their more vulnerable allies could not be saved. Finance Minister Frans Seda, a Christian, met strong hostility from Muslim commercial interests, and had to be moved to a less sensitive portfolio. The prickly Dr Sumitro was shifted from the key Trade Ministry into a new post as Research Minister in 1974 after Socialist Party (PSI) influence became a *cause célèbre* and Sumitro himself had aroused antagonism within ruling circles.

Certainly the Technocrats move in a world of seminars and conferences, rather than inspection tours, public meetings and detailed business haggling. Having come into politics directly from the university their outlook is certainly different to that of, say, the former air force officer, engineer and entrepreneur A. R. Suhud, who became Industries Minister in 1978. The Technocrats have been accused, among other indifferences, of a 'basic contempt for productive enterprise and commerce, unless it came in the well-heeled super-technology form of foreign investments'.[4] They have also been attacked for regarding the private sector with 'distaste'.[5] The charge probably has some truth, but squares rather oddly with the supposed 'Western orthodox' biases imparted by the philanthropic arms of the Ford and Rockefeller empires.[6]

In 1966 the priorities for economic management were clear cut: to kill hyperinflation, overcome the balance of payments problem, and restore production especially in the export industries. With a high degree of public support, including the agreement of some of the economists who later parted company, the Technocrats introduced stringent measures. To attack inflation a highly selective credit policy brought the growth of money supply closer to reality, pulling it down from an increase of 764 per cent in 1966 to 132 per cent in 1967. Government expenditure was more closely tailored to revenue, while the massive foreign credits provided by the IGGI helped revive domestic production in many sectors. Certain enterprises previously reliant on quotas, monopolies and selective extension of subsidized credit found themselves out in the cold. Some industries, particularly the limping textile industry, found credit hard to find and encountered new import competition since the freely sold foreign exchange had been used to import commodities. When conditions later improved it was not always the old producers who were in a position to take advantage but newcomers from overseas bringing more sophisticated packages of technology, finance and marketing.

But the Technocrats were highly successful in achieving their immediate objective of stabilization. In 1966 those who spoke of bringing inflation to a halt within two or three years were described as optimists. Inflation, which in Jakarta had been 839 per cent in 1966, dropped to a 'mere' 113 per cent in 1967, and the following year to 85 per cent with little increases in prices during the last quarter of 1968. From 1969 Indonesia entered a period of price stability in which the Jakarta cost of living index rose by only 22 per cent over three years. This occurred even though money supply continued to rise at around 30 per cent a year, indicating that real money stocks were being rapidly increased to regain lost ground.

By the time inflation had receded Indonesia was embarked on accelerated economic growth. In the last half of the 1960s the country won back what had been lost under Guided Democracy. According to one estimate real national income per capita surpassed the best pre-1965 levels (attained in 1952 and 1957) by 1969. By 1970 exports had regained the share of gross domestic product held ten years previously.

With comparatively little domestic debate the Suharto government had adopted a policy of high reliance on imports, financed by foreign aid and private capital inflow, to further its development programme. This strategy was reinforced early in 1969 when the government introduced the first Repelita (an anagram from the Indonesian for Five Year Development Plan) setting out steps to consolidate the economy before further five-year plans took the country into higher stages of industrialization. Repelita 1 set a target of rice self-sufficiency by 1973, involving a 47 per cent increase in output over five years. Industrial expansion was to be oriented to agricultural support materials and basic import replacements such as fertilizer, cement and textiles. It was based on Indonesia's current account deficit rising from around $400 million to $876 million, to be covered by the flow of aid rising from about $400 million to $700 million and private capital inflow from $60 million to about $170 million. The plan was hastily put together. It was quickly criticized as over-ambitious, mainly because of the rice target, and excessively dependent on foreign inputs. And for one contemporary commentator it met 'disappointingly little informed comment' in Jakarta before adoption.[7]

A new foreign investment law introduced in January 1967 and active courtship by foreign oil explorers opened up Indonesia to a rush of foreign business interest which quickly gathered Klondike overtones. In contrast to the uncertainties before 1965 foreign companies were given pledges against nationalization and their freedom to repatriate capital was guaranteed. Exemptions from taxes and charges were liberally awarded, and the few provisions for local equity and recruitment were not rigorously applied. In the petroleum sector the new style of production-sharing contract offered by General Ibnu Sutowo, head of the state oil enterprise soon to grow into Pertamina, found a score of takers, mostly American. By the end of 1969 the government had approved foreign investments outside the oil sector totalling $1226 million, of which the largest shares were held (in order of size) by mining, forestry and manufacturing.

Again excluding the oil sector (which will be discussed in chapter 7), foreign investor interest showed a tendency to move away from the extractive sectors of mines and timber towards the manufacturing area, a shift that has meant increasing attention to internal markets. The change may also indicate that perspectives lengthened as investors grew accustomed to the Indonesian environment, and began to place more faith in the political and economic stability engineered by the Suharto Government. Another factor might have been that the resources involved in the initial spurt of mining and forestry ventures were already well known and waiting only a change in the political climate for development.

Two of the big mineral deposits to attract early attention, the copper mountain called Ertsberg in West Irian and the lateritic nickel of Central Sulawesi, had been identified by Dutch explorers and were virtually touted around the mining companies of the world by the new Suharto Government. Dr Mohammad Sadli, who chaired the government's Investment Co-ordinating Board before becoming Mines Minister, said in 1971:

> When we started out attracting foreign investment in 1967 everything and everyone was welcome. We did not dare to refuse; we did not even dare to ask for bonafidity of credentials. We needed a list of names and dollar figures of intended investments, to give credence to our drive. The first mining company virtually wrote its own ticket. Since we had no conception about a mining contract we accepted the draft written by the company as basis for negotiations and only common sense and the desire to bag the first contract were our guidelines.[8]

This earliest mining venture was the Freeport Minerals copper venture at Erstberg, based on an agreement reached in April 1967, only three months after enactment of the first investment law. The Freeport project came to symbolize the 'new frontier' image Indonesia was quickly gaining in Western and Japanese business circles. Involving an input of technology and capital far beyond Indonesian resources at that stage, Freeport was to set about mining a rich copper outcrop 11 500 feet above sea-level in one of the least accessible parts of West Irian. At a cost that quickly rose to $175 million, some $55 million above original estimates, the company and its American contractors built an aerial tramway system spanning 4800 feet to bring ore down to a mill and township constructed at 9000 feet above sea-level. A road and slurry pipeline were pushed across 116 kilometres of mountains, jungle and coastal swamp. A new port, airstrip and power plant were among the infrastructure the company had to provide. The technical problems and financial risks had been great, but so were the rewards: in the first two years after production commenced in 1973 Freeport earned over $60 million net of taxes, according to reports.[9]

Other foreign mining companies followed Freeport, although the Indonesian Government had within a year tightened up the tax and other concessions in a new 'second generation' mining contract. Principal among them was the Canadian firm International Nickel (Inco) whose project in the centre of Sulawesi, where Islamic rebels had held out until 1965, eventually grew into an $850 million investment. In forestry, dozens of foreign companies took up concessions in the jungles of Kalimantan to supply hardwood lumber to East Asian mills.

Investment in manufacturing became more substantial in the early 1970s. By the end of 1975 when the investment boom had tailed off, total approved foreign manufacturing investment was near $2000 million, with the heaviest concentration (mostly Japanese) in sixty-five textile projects worth a total of $708 million. Forestry attracted $568 million, the real estate, tourism, construction and contracting sectors a total of $440 million, and the agriculture, land development and fisheries areas $106 million. Of the $4488 million total approved investment (non-oil), Japanese firms accounted for nearly half with the USA ($520 million), Hong Kong ($423 million) and the Philippines ($302 million) next most prominent. Significant investment also came from Canada (to be swelled later by the single massive Inco project), Australia, West Germany, France, Korea, Malaysia, the Netherlands, Singapore, Switzerland and Britain. A total of 790 projects were involved.

By contrast those domestic capital projects processed by the government over the same period were much smaller: almost the same approved total investment was accounted for by three times the number of projects. Manufacturing industries were the main field, with 1771 ventures capitalized at $2679 million, while other large concentrations were in forestry ($428 million), housing and real estate ($22 million), hotels and tourism ($192 million), agriculture ($213 million) and mining ($213 million).

It should be noted that perhaps only one third of foreign investment approvals were realized. On the other hand domestic investment has been understated. Many local businessmen choose not to commence their ventures through the Investment Co-ordinating Board because they feel the advantages gained in the way of taxation concessions and other incentives are outweighed by bureaucratic obstacles. Many businessmen in the large Chinese–Indonesian community also invest in an informal way, often using unregistered foreign investment by way of loans from family or clan associates in Hong Kong, Singapore, Taiwan and other overseas Chinese commercial centres. Such loans are simply disbursed and repaid as remittances through Indonesia's free foreign exchange system.

The boom in the modern sectors of the economy rapidly transformed the face of Jakarta and a few other big cities. The ambitious central Jakarta boulevard, Jalam Thamrin, became lined with new office blocks and filled with new cars and motor-cycles, while the previously ubiquitous *becak* (pedicabs) were pushed to the side-streets by regulations aimed at complementing this 'modernization'. New luxury hotels began to compete with the Hotel Indonesia, which had been completed with Japanese war reparations money in 1963. Foreign businessmen struggled to work with the run-down physical and administrative infrastructure. Rents for Western-style houses had climbed by 1970 to over $1000 a month, payable three years in advance. The cost of installing a telephone connection became about $1500 on the black market. The price reached a peak of about $3600 in mid-1976 before new capacity brought illicit rates down to $1800.

By the early 1970s Suharto's development strategy had plenty of critics. They took exception particularly to the level of corruption and conspicuous consumption among the better-placed city dwellers and the concurrent rash of nightclubs, massage parlours and casinos opened to pander to cosmopolitan tastes. It was fairly plain, too, that the new development remained largely confined to Jakarta and two or three other cities. The traditional sectors of the economy, the small traders and cottage industries, were at best enjoying a modest rate of growth and at worst being ruthlessly pushed aside.

For many observers these were inevitable though painful adjustments which would eventually be overcome by the greater benefits that would trickle through from the more rapidly progressing sectors. Nor had the traditional sector, the greatest part of which is peasant agriculture, been entirely by-passed. In agriculture the average rate of growth had increased from 1.4 per cent a year in the first half of the 1960s to 3.8 per cent in 1965–70, with the rise highest in food crops. As the government proceeded with its rice intensification programme to bring new inputs of improved yield varieties, cheap fertilizers and extended irrigation the rate of agricultural growth was sustained at 3.7 per cent from 1971 to 1975.[10] By mid-1972 after several good seasons the Repelita 1 target of self-sufficiency looked possible with continued luck. In 1971 rice production had been comfortably over that year's target. And despite periodic setbacks Indonesia was in fact to enjoy one of the highest and steadiest improvements in rice output of all South Asian countries in the ten years after 1965, even though the goal of self-sufficiency remained elusive and there occurred a decline in certain other important food crops that substituted for rice.

The degree of change from the situation a few years earlier led to talk of another 'economic miracle' in the making. With a high degree of foreign business interest, apparent good progress in meeting five-year plan targets, inflation almost completely halted, and rapidly expanding resource industries, Indonesia was looking like another Brazil and, in the words of one commentator, was virtually writing its own ticket for aid from the IGGI nations.[11] After several devaluations and uncertainties due to multiple exchange rate, the rupiah had been successfully fixed from August 1971 at a steady rate to the US dollar. The one worrying feature was a continuing high deficit on current account as a result of the Suharto Government's deliberate choice to rely so heavily on foreign capital inflow. But there was cautious optimism that the increasingly confident economic management by the Technocrats would steer the country to a more soundly based stage in what was now officially seen in a 25-year perspective.

A poor harvest in 1972 and the multiplication of world oil prices in 1973 were to knock this pattern completely awry. From 'export pessimism' Indonesia abruptly gained an abundance of foreign income. For the first time in its history the country seemed to have money to spend. But it was not the Technocrats who spent it. Indonesia was to have a dizzying two years when it appeared to have shaken off its dependence on foreign bankers and aid evaluators. Then the Technocrats and their sober-suited foreign friends moved back into influence to rein in a careering state enterprise that had brought Jakarta's solvency, once again, into question. Another shock, with fewer international ramifications but of profound significance, had hit the Suharto Government. After its promising start the new rice technology and agricultural extension packages were failing to greatly increase output.

Yet despite these great tests the New Order economic structure was soon to undergo, the momentum started in the late 1960s appears to have been sustained through the 1970s. An Australian economist, Peter McCawley, who has pieced together economic data covering the life of the Indonesian Republic believes that these suggest steady high progress. The data indicated that between the early 1950s and 1960 real national income per capita fell by perhaps five or six per cent per annum, remained constant during the first half of the 1960s, and then grew by perhaps eight to ten per cent per annum during the next decade. Judgements of this sort are rather dependent on the precise time periods chosen for comparisons, but the data do suggest that in conventional terms, there has been sustained economic growth during the Suharto era after a long period of stagnation up to 1965.[12]

NOTES

1 Ingrid Palmer, *The Indonesian Economy Since 1965*, Cass, London, 1978, pp. 14–15.
2 Unless otherwise cited, figures and contemporary observations in this chapter are drawn from the *Bulletin of Indonesian Economic Studies (BIES)*, published three times a year at the Australian National University, Canberra. Its regular 'Survey of Recent Developments' is widely regarded as an authoritative running commentary on the Indonesian economy.
3 See David Ransom, 'Ford Country: Building an Elite for Indonesia' in Steve Weissman *et al.* (eds), *The Trojan Horse, A Radical Look at Foreign Aid*, Ramparts, Palo Alto, 1974.
4 Palmer, op. cit., p. 155.
5 Derek Davies, 'Taming the Technocrats', *Far Eastern Economic Review*, 20 May, 1974.
6 See Bruce Glassburner, 'Political Economy and the Suharto Regime', *BIES*, vol. XIV, no. 3, November 1978.
7 'Survey of Recent Developments', *BIES*, vol. V, no. 2, July 1969.
8 Quoted in Palmer, op. cit., p. 100.
9 See Lenny Siegel, 'Freeport Mines', *Pacific Research and World Empire Telegram*, January–February 1976.
10 Peter McCawley, 'The Indonesian Economy under Suharto: A Survey', Working paper, Research School of Pacific Studies, Australian National University, 1978, p. 3.
11 Benjamin Higgins, Professor of Economics at the University of Montreal, in *BIES*, vol. VIII, no. 1, March 1972, p. 4.
12 McCawley, op. cit., p. 2.

5. The Politics of Order

Two weeks before Indonesia's third general elections on 2 May 1977, politics came to the village of Pranggan in East Java. A rare enough occasion, one to warrant a full turn-out among Pranggan's 3000 people. A dutiful, respectful attendance, too, since Lieutenant-Colonel R. S. Chambali headed the list of local assembly candidates in the surrounding Kediri Regency. Officially he was representing Golkar, the military-backed political organization, although, in effect, he was representing the Suharto Government. Such a distinction had little relevance to the Pranggan or the other 343 villages in Kediri.

Chambali cut a dashing figure under the flare of kerosene pressure-lamps. He was wearing a long-sleeved batik shirt, glistening black moustache and sideburns, and a fez-type cap which, while attesting to his good Muslim and nationalist intentions, lent an impudent note by being light grey and furry, instead of the usual black velvet model. Tucked under his arm as he faced up to the microphone was his old military swagger-stick, tipped with a brass garuda.

Behind him rows of local dignitaries in safari shirts sat on chairs under a marquee. His audience sat on the ground, smoking tobacco loosely rolled in corncob-skins, drawing sarongs around their shoulders against the cool night wind: impassive, work-hardened men, placid-faced women and sleepy children as far as the circle of light reached across the grassy square. When horse-play among a group of youths threatened to disrupt the forceful flow of Chambali's speech, his response was unhesitating. He stopped, drew back his shoulders, and barked: '*Disiplin*!' The noise stopped. Pranggan had particular reason to know Chambali was a tough man.

Fifteen years earlier Colonel Chambali had been the Indonesian Army's territorial commander in Kediri. The Communist Party (PKI) then had an estimated 150 000 members in the area and had launched its 'unilateral action' campaign to force compliance with the 1960 land reform law, encouraging landless peasants to seize land from large holdings and plantations. In doing so, the PKI was capitalizing on and exacerbating traditional religious and economic differences. (This was just a few kilometres from where Clifford Geertz had made the field studies which resulted in his classic definition of Javanese cultural 'streams'.) Landless and poor moved against the army–civil service elite and the *abangan* little man moved against the *santri* Muslim landlord. The climax came when thousands of villagers from around Pranggan, at the urging of the PKI, marched on a state-owned sugar plantation near by at Jengkol. A detachment of Chambali's troops fired warning shots to disperse the mob. Then, when they themselves came under attack (losing one man), the soldiers opened fire on the crowd, killing twenty-one people and wounding eighteen.

After the attempted coup on 30 September 1965, the Kediri area became the site of East Java's heaviest massacre of communists. Chambali's successor was a brother of one of the murdered generals. A local Muslim leader, *Kyai Haji* Machrus Ali, launched a Jihad (Holy War) against the PKI. Together the army and squads of Muslim youths brought thousands of PKI supporters down to the wide, swift-flowing Brantas River which bisects Kediri, for execution and disposal in the waters. Others were put into detention. Many of these were soon released, but even in 1977 some 46 000 former members of banned communist organizations were still without rights of political participation (as against 654 000 qualified voters among Kediri Regency's 1.1 million population).

After retiring from the army in 1968, Chambali became a New Order stalwart in local politics, helping to turn the weak Functional Groups organization into an electoral bulldozer powered by the armed forces and government apparatus, which gained a 56 per cent win in Kediri in 1971 when the Suharto regime held its first general election. But in doing so, he and his military colleagues had effectively shattered the local Muslim–army alliance of 1965. Heavy-handedness in the 1971 elections caused lasting resentment, particularly among the Muslim groups. This bitterness pervaded the campaign period in 1977. The civil servants, armed forces and security men backing Golkar from their offices in Kediri now regarded the Pesantren Lirboyo, the big Islamic boarding school run by *Haji* Machrus Ali across the Brantas River, as an enemy stronghold. The hostility returned: the Jihad had now become the official bogey. Listing dozens of arbitrary arrests, beatings and threats the *Haji*'s assistants referred to the Golkar government forces as *orang mereka* (their people), corrupted by power to become the new dictators and violators of the law. The response of one Kediri civil servant when questioned about the minor compromise of his neutrality by wearing a Golkar windcheater typified the official attitude: 'Who cares, as long as we win?'

Kediri experienced a comparatively trouble-free election campaign. From other areas came reports of politically motivated gang attacks and one or two allegations of murder. Political 'dirty tricks' were prevalent. In the village of Patuk near Jogjakarta, for example, the headman obeyed orders by conducting a 'survey' of voting preferences a few weeks before polling day. All villagers had to state their choice: non-Golkar supporters were subjected to heavy discussion, usually on the lines that the whole village would suffer if Golkar lost. At government offices 'practice elections' were held. In South Sulawesi whole villages were declared 'free of political parties' by local officials, establishing in their minds a right to refuse access to party campaigners. Golkar, of course, was not a political party, but a 'functional group' organization, i.e. a coalition of professional and community associations who stressed their shared interests in national harmony.

The election was regarded in official circles more as an exercise in logistics and management than a consultation of the popular will. As one very influential Golkar adviser in Jakarta put it:

> Voting is still considered more of an obligation than a right. People want to participate because the Government wants them to participate. There are cases of over-acting by officials because they want to make it a success. They have been given their targets and it will be a black mark for their careers if these are not achieved. They have to do it. But there is no real need to coerce voters to choose Golkar. It is more like a stern parent disciplining a child to go to school. Instead of waking him up and slapping him, a wise parent will say: 'Go to school now and you will get your ice-cream later'. What are the issues? Nothing! It is a ceremony that you must fulfil. It is a token of participation and Indonesianhood. These people cannot imagine that their vote could change a government or influence a policy.[1]

This is perhaps a realistic belief in the Indonesia of 1977, although villagers were quite capable of perceiving rights or wrongs and, if questioned, of articulating their grievances. It was in any case extremely difficult for participants to proceed beyond the most anodyne level of public debate, given severe restrictions enacted by presidential decree a year previously. Participants were forbidden to blaspheme against or question any religion; to threaten other groups; disturb national unity; incite regional or racial feelings; to pass 'negative judgements' on foreign bodies, states and other parties or other party emblems; or to 'pass judgements on and take lightly government policies, civil as well as military authorities, and these authorities as individuals'.[2] But by election time few of the candidates would have been likely to feel this regulation a harsh restraint.

The crushing of the PKI and Nationalist Left in 1965–6 and the overthrow of Sukarno's Guided Democracy had given Suharto the opportunity to turn Indonesia in a new direction politically as well as economically, and in this he could count on widespread if diverse expectations among the triumphant sections of the country's elite. Up to 1970 the political format remained quite fluid, but in retrospect there is a certain inevitability about the form that from then on took shape and hardened.

Included in the political scene were the old political parties, including the nationalist PNI which became dominated by a paternalistic traditionalist elite of civil servants and professional people and a leadership thoroughly compromised by the horse-trading and patronage of the previous regime. The Nahdatul Ulama, deeply conservative and based on the rural strongholds of Islam in Java, was also concerned to preserve the social and economic balance and uphold its own empire of patronage built on its long-standing control of the Religious Affairs Ministry. Along with the new 'action fronts' of secular-minded, reformist students and intellectuals, and the pro-Western 'New Order Hawks' in the military, surfaced elements of the modernist Islamic Party, Masyumi, and the Socialist Party (PSI), both banned since 1960 and discredited as 'traitorous' after the involvement of prominent members in the 1958 Sumatra revolt.

In the Muslim community voices were raised again for adoption of the 'Jakarta Charter', a requirement that all espousing the Muslim faith be compelled to observe its rituals. This demand was something of a fall-back position for the Muslim community from the concept of a full Islamic state and, they argued, not incompatible with the Pancasila ideology. It had gained brief constitutional favour in 1945, but then had been successfully resisted by Javanist, secularist and non-Muslim elements as an opening for religious tyranny and obscurantism.

Among secular proposals came demands for such Western democratic ideals as 'human rights', 'rule of law' and even ministerial responsibility to Parliament. Underneath these opinions often ran a deep contempt for the old parties and for the multi-party system. Many New Order enthusiasts hoped the army could lead Indonesia towards a simplified party system or, alternatively, provide the nucleus for a coalition of modernist, development-minded groups against the squabbling idealogues of the past.

These Western-oriented political ideals appealed to several of the more powerful army generals promoted by Suharto during his running battle with the Sukarnoists: the Siliwangi commander, Dharsono, his own replacement as Kostrad commander; Kemal Idris; and the former RPKAD Commando chief, Sarwo Edhy, who had been made commander of North Sumatra. Dharsono, based in the university city of Bandung, was the most persistently and closely linked with the student action groups and Socialist Party thinkers seeking sweeping change. The 'New Order Radicals' like Dharsono used their positions vigorously against the PNI and other left groups, but were also linked with 'black lists' of 'corrupt generals' (including the state oil chief, Ibnu Sutowo, and the Presidential Assistant, Alamsjah, both powerful 'financial generals' from the South Sumatra Sriwijaya Division) which were being circulated. Dharsono eventually made an unsuccessful attempt to introduce a two-party system among the puzzled and highly reluctant members of West Java's provincial assembly on the basis of a pro-government side and a 'loyal opposition'. Within three years this group of 'corrupt generals' had all been shunted aside, either to diplomatic postings overseas or to military commands far away from the political limelight.

A basic strategy in the undermining of Sukarno had been to make the fullest possible use of 'constitutionality', requiring the maintenance and manipulation of the existing government institutions. Even if he had wanted a completely new start, Suharto would have risked acquiring a 'usurper' image. He would have also strengthened demands for early elections to replace the provisional Congress (MPRS) and Parliament (DRP). The authoritarian 1945 Constitution was as good a vehicle to install firmly the New Order as it had been to found Guided Democracy. Moreover, this constitution then provided, through decrees issued by Sukarno since 1959, much of the legal basis for the expanded role of the armed forces under the Dual Function doctrine. And as long as the 1945 Constitution was upheld the Muslims were denied an appropriate occasion to press for a return to the Jakarta Charter. As the 1966 overthrow of the former left-wing Prime Minister, Ali Sastroamidjojo, and his group in the PNI had shown, the parties could be brought round to supporting the New Order if necessary, without risking the alienation of substantial sections of the population by killing off their familiar political organizations.

Apart from these tactical arguments against radical institutional changes, Suharto and his group had not come to power free of political ideas. Nor, more obviously, had such influential military figures as Nasution or Suwarto. Suharto, from his mixed *abangan* and minor *priyayi* background, was typical of the 'small town Java' types the Australian political scientist Harold Crouch describes as dominating the Indonesian Army officer corps by the early 1960s.[3] As we have seen, Suharto's experience of the world outside Central Java was extremely limited, until his transfer to Army Staff and Command School in 1959, as had been his formal education. His only overseas visits (in 1961) had been to the Belgrade of Tito, the Paris of de Gaulle and the Bonn of Adenauer. His upbringing had been in the highly feudal environment of pre-war Jogjakarta and Solo. He had married a member of the *priyayi* (official) class. He had risen in the politicized Diponegoro Division of Central Java rather than the more 'professional' Siliwangi Division of West Java. As regional commander he had found his allies among the PNI-aligned civil servants whose paternal approach was reflected in their traditional job description: *pamong praja* or 'guardians of the people'. Although a man of austere tastes himself, he could be counted among the prosperous rulers of Sukarno's Indonesia.

As Crouch observes, the army did not bring new perceptions on political organization, but came to power as part of the old elite furthering their old objectives in a less entrammelled environment. By 30 September 1965, he adds, 'many officers had already become experienced and adroit politicians'. The army itself was already a political institution. Following the vast extension of army intervention in civil affairs after imposition of marital law in 1957 and the refinement of the territorial management concept at the Army Staff and Command School in the early 1960s (see chapter 2), the ambit of army interests had been extended in a formal way. To the conventional commands of intelligence, operations, personnel and logistics were added two new divisions: territorial affairs and 'functional groups'.

The territorial command supervised the activities of a network of military watchdogs running parallel to the civilian bureaucracy down to the *kabupaten* (regency) level, starting with the regional command or Kodam (in Java covering a single province, elsewhere often more than one) and reaching the district command or Kodim. At the provincial level the military commander chaired a 'four-in-one' committee including the civilian governor, the police chief and the chief prosecutor. While combat-ready troops were held in fighting formation other personnel were deployed in the 'territorial' structure, where they were supposed to monitor political and social developments and prod the civilian counterpart where necessary. Soon after 30 September 1965 Suharto extended this network in Central and East Java, setting up sub-district commands (Koramil) below the Kodim level and even stationing non-commissioned officers in the villages. After the coup attempt these military posts almost inevitably came to dominate local politics, given the need to secure military permission for travel, meetings, sermons and publications.

In the 'functional groups', a term first used by Sukarno in 1957 when searching for a new model of government, the army had adopted perhaps the most distinctive and pervasive political concept in Indonesia. A fascinating study by an Australian historian, David Reeve, has traced the functional group idea back to the early stirrings of Indonesian nationalism.[4] The founders of the Indonesian state, particularly those who had not studied abroad, often found Western political ideas and practice disquieting. The whole basis of the Western state, the liberal democracies as well as the socialist regimes, was, to their way of thinking, based on the unnatural attempt to dominate their environment, the exploitation of man by man, the exclusion of one class by another class. The Javanese 'soul' required a more 'organic' political body in which the contribution of each individual to the body corporate was recognized, in which each could participate according to his station. Their answer was a system that placed the collective above the individual good, one based on the 'family principle' and requiring a certain 'democracy with leadership'. Reeve found that for the Javanese these ideas were rooted in the island's Hindu–Buddhist past, a notion encouraged earlier this century by the Theosophical movement in the West. for the Dutch-educated West Sumatran, Mohammad Hatta, the model was more the village co-operative spirit.

Faith in the village *gotong royong* (mutual assistance) tradition, of decisions reached by *musyawarah* (consultation) arriving at a *mufakat* (consensus) is strong throughout Indonesia. But as the anthropologist Koentjaraningrat points out, this process of consultation requires a leader or strong personality who can help synthesize conflicting viewpoints, often through 'informal behind-the-scenes operations' so that a consensus is presented at the start of open discussion and thus comes under minor modification only.[5] To an extent that often baffles Westerners, the Indonesians, and particularly the Javanese, believe the most contradictory interests can thus be reconciled.

These corporatist arguments were raised in 1945 when the shape of the new nation was debated and emerged once more when the 1945 Constitution was reinstated in 1959. Like Sukarno, the army looked for new political forms, in its case to counter the PKI and indeed the whole party system for which its contempt had grown rather than diminished since independence. Successive experiments led Nasution and others to open links with civilian bodies, a prime target being the 'mass organizations' attached to the non-communist political parties. These organizations, covering youth professions and so on, were often more vigorous and in touch with rank-and-file supporters than the main party leaderships who, in the absence of frequent elections, had turned their attention to the spoils system of Jakarta. It was a natural step for the army to raise 'functional groups' into pillars of government, as also proposed by Sukarno. Perhaps because the army responded too enthusiastically, Sukarno stepped back to a compromise. Functional groups (representing the armed forces, workers, peasants and the religious) were appointed to the Guided Democracy institutions to embellish the more familiar party components of the Nasakom coalition, principally the PKI, the PNI and the Nahdatul Ulama.

Despite this setback Nasution and the army leadership continued to promote the functional groups. The biggest was the Union of Indonesian Socialist *Karyawan* Organizations, or SOKSI, a labour union umbrella organization, which deliberately set out to counter the PKI union movement, SOBSI. The word *karyawan* or functionary held a broader meaning than the term used by the PKI, *buruh* (worker). Covering both manager and labourer, who were seen as working for a common objective in their allotted tasks, the *karyawan* concept left no room for class conflict. The new union was to enlist much of the workforce in army-controlled plantations and enterprises. Other arms of the Golkar movement encompassed many figures from the turbulent Murba Party, such as the Trade

Minister, Adam Malik, the Kosgoro co-operative movement of former 'Students' Army', guerillas and groups of conservative intellectuals. The army move did not go unnoticed by the PKI and the left. After some initial success, the functional groups were fighting to hold their position from about 1963 onwards.[6]

Suharto was not closely involved with the Functional Groups movement. But from soon after the Supersemar declaration of March 1966 he included among his personal political advisers men such as General Daryatmo who had spent several years on the territorial or functional groups side of army staff work. As the preoccupation of Suharto and his Kostrad group turned from ousting Sukarno without starting a rebellion to reconstructing the political system without losing control, the corporatist idea grew more attractive.

A decisive period came over the nine months from July 1967 to the following March. The deadline of July 1968 set for general elections was approaching with little prospect of agreement on the electoral system to be used. Partly on the recommendations of an army political seminar in 1966, the more radical New Order elements sought drastic reform of the existing system of choosing elected parliamentarians by province-wide proportional representation. The ideas they put forward included an expansion of the functional group membership to half the DPR (Parliament) and the adoption of single-member constituencies at regency level. Not surprisingly the parties were opposed to this, especially the NU and PNI who drew the bulk of their support from Java where regencies held up to four times the population of those regencies in the Outer Islands.

For reasons outlined above, Suharto was reluctant to abandon the parties. He was increasingly irked also by the New Order Radicals who were clearly associated with the rising criticism of corruption within his own entourage and with impatience at his 'Javanese' style of government. In July 1967 Suharto's political team reached a consensus with the parties that the Parliament be expanded from 347 to 460 members, with seventy-five seats reserved for armed forces appointees and twenty-five seats for appointed civilians. The functional group component would henceforth compete with the parties for elected places. In the supreme legislative body, the MPR, which set basic policy and chose the president, the DPR component would be augmented by 460 military, regional and party representatives. While Suharto concurred with the prevailing idea that the parties needed to be reformed, he also indicated that at least one of the dispossessed streams, the modernist Muslims not formally represented since the banning of Masyumi, would be allowed to re-emerge. This occurred in 1968 with the government-sponsored formation of Parmusi, the Indonesian Muslim Party. However, former Masyumi leaders were not allowed to take up positions in it.

Even so, Suharto was still not ready to trust the parties in an election. He was advised by his Technocrat ministers that an early election could threaten economic stabilization. In Java a major attempt by the PKI to regroup, was being uncovered. Sukarnoists remained strong in the PNI, especially in East Java, and in the navy and police which had not been fully purged. From January to March 1968 Suharto assigned 'project officers' to carry out sweeping political changes. Under heavy military pressure, Parliament reconvened and decided immediately to recommend to the Provisional Congress (MPRS) that Suharto be appointed full president, that the government's new five-year plan be endorsed and that elections be postponed for five years.

This was a great blow to the student and intellectual activists, backed by army generals such as Dharsono, who still hoped for major changes. As the MPRS session approached in March 1968 student protest and bitter press commentary attacked the Suharto Government. Several student action front figures were arrested, and when the MPRS actually convened the Jakarta military commander, Amir Machmud, announced that thirty battalions of troops were available to maintain order. Soldiers stood guard at schools and universities in Jakarta, and transport was screened to prevent student activists arriving from other cities. Largely behind closed doors and heavily lobbied by General Ali Murtopo's political operatives, the MPRS agreed to Suharto's appointment for a five-year term. A deadlock occurred on the proposed Broad Outlines of State Policy document, into which the Muslims tried to insert a version of the Jakarta Charter. Despite the general heavy-handedness, some significant compromises had to be conceded by Suharto's men: the elections were postponed for only three years and certain emergency powers withdrawn from the presidency. But Suharto was required to give little in the way of undertakings to attack corruption at senior levels, curb the (by then) notorious influence of his personal staff, or reduce the military presence in civilian jobs. Discussion on guarantees of human rights also deadlocked.

Importantly, the 1968 MPRS session and events around it reassured the parties of their continuing place in the political system, even while demonstrating the intention of the army to dominate it. The mood of the New Order Radicals inclined to despair, but they continued to fight against the July 1967 consensus on the electoral system when election regulations came before Parliament in 1969. Their military supporters were picked off one by one, including General Dharsono who was sent as Ambassador to Thailand after his ill-received two-party system caused uproar in Bandung. The full potential of the 1967 consensus was not immediately grasped. Suharto and advisers such as Ali Murtopo did not appear completely convinced that the rather tarnished Functional Groups Organization was the right vehicle for enlisting mass support for military rule. The army's aims were not inherently opposed to those of the moderates of the PNI or of the modernist Islamic elements in Parmusi. Because of this the nationalist and modernist Muslim streams could be useful partners. But at the same time they contained a potential challenge as future alternatives to military rule. The solution eventually adopted by Suharto, planned and implemented chiefly through Ali Murtopo and Sujono Humardani, was a campaign of manipulation across the political spectrum. This achieved the precaution of emasculating political parties while creating an effective state party for the first time in Indonesia's history.

The attitude of Ali Murtopo and Sujono to politics has never been described as conventional. Ali Murtopo concealed an energetic, wide-ranging mind behind a mask of joviality and earthiness. He presented a broad, gap-toothed smile (until cosmetic dentistry later in life) as he ruthlessly pressured and enticed his opponents into meek alliance. His early life remains shadowy, but seems to have fitted Crouch's 'small town Java' model in some respects.[7] Born in Blora on the north coast of Central Java in 1924, he was the son of an impoverished *priyayi* family, his father trading in *batik* cloth for a living. His schooling in central and West Java was disrupted in his early teens. Towards the end of the Japanese occupation, he joined the Hisbullah, the Islamic force set up by the Japanese parallel with the PETA Army, before being absorbed into the regular Indonesian Army. Ali became a company commander in Achmad Yani's 'Banteng Raiders' unit of the Diponegoro Division in 1952. His working relationship with Suharto probably began when he became deputy chief of the Diponegoro's 'territorial' and political affairs branch in 1957. As we have seen, he followed Suharto into army Intelligence headquarters and from there into the Irian campaign and Kostrad, where he helped to organize a vast smuggling operation and to open secret contacts with Malaysia. Ali spent the early post-coup period outside Indonesia, arranging emergency funding for Suharto from Chinese business sources in Singapore, Hong Kong and Taiwan. On his return he spent several months in Central Java hunting down pro-coup elements in the Diponegoro Division before turning to politics in Jakarta.

As chief of Kostrad's Special Operations group (Opsus)

and then as a special adviser on Suharto's staff, Ali Murtopo built up a curious alliance of forces which was effective but not calculated to gain the trust of the Indonesian population at large. The military intelligence officers of the original Opsus organized a network of civil operatives and informers, working out of an unobtrusive house in the suburb of Menteng. Ali also became a deputy head of the new State Intelligence Co-ordinating Body, Bakin, an all-purpose intelligence organization that replaced the discredited BPI (Central Intelligence Body) run by Subandrio.

The Ali Murtopo forces were never integrated into one organization. Some branches are known to look with disdain upon the others. Perhaps the most influential has been a group of Roman Catholic intellectuals and activists, some of Chinese descent, who aligned themselves with Ali Murtopo in 1966. One of the best known is Liem Bian Kie. Raised in West Sumatra, he studied law and joined the teaching staff at the University of Indonesia before the coup. He remained influential among Catholic students, and in the tense pre-coup period had already made contact with Ali Murtopo and other Kostrad officers. Liem (who took the Indonesian name of Yusuf Wanandi) became Ali Murtopo's assistant in 1967. Another ally was Harry Tjan, son of a poor hospital worker in Jogjakarta, who had received early training in trade union affairs from the Murba Party and had then moved into the small Catholic Party. After working as a trade union organizer in North Sumatra in the 1950s (where he was awarded the additional name of Silalahi by the local Batak people), Tjan became Secretary-General of the Catholic Party. At some stage he too formed links with the army. During 1966 and 1967 it was often Ali Murtopo who waited outside the door of action front war councils before being told where to position troops to protect anti-Sukarno demonstrators.

One intriguing source of personnel and ideas lay deeper in Catholic political circles, in the person of Father J. Beek, a Jesuit of mixed Dutch and Indonesian origin who had taught in Jogjakarta since the early 1950s. Before the coup Beek had been urging Catholics to prepare for the eventuality of a communist takeover by developing a standby underground movement. This led to the institution after the coup of 'One Month Caderisation' courses for young Catholics at the Asrama Realino, a student residence on the outskirts of Jogjakarta. The cadres received intensive training in leadership skills such as public speaking, writing and 'group dynamics'. Beek was in contact with strongly anti-communist Catholic organizations overseas, such as the National Civic Council of B.A. Santamaria in Australia, and may have enjoyed their financial support.

Roman Catholic youths in Central Java played some part in the massacre of PKI suspects in 1965–6. But another target of Beek was Islam. While other Catholics argued that the church should build contacts with the Muslims, Beek took a militant, antagonistic approach. For him the church had a stark choice: embrace the new army regime, or go under to the Muslims. With the need to secure a pro-Indonesian vote in the West Irian 'Act of Free Choice' of 1969, and because Christianity was the prevalent religion in that territory, Beek became even more useful to Ali. Beek's cadres were sent to work to help win over the Irianese. However valuable for Ali Murtopo, the connection (which Beek has denied) aroused misgivings in both the army and the church. It came under strong attack at an Indonesian bishops' conference in 1971. 'In theory Beek's ideas are fine,' one of his colleagues comments, 'but in practice they are dirty.'[8]

The Suharto Government's intervention in the parties was a combination of threats against uncooperative leaders, bribery and persuasion, and ultimately the use by Suharto of his power under political laws to approve or disapprove of leaderships and candidate lists or even to 'recall' troublesome legislators.

The move against the PNI came in April 1970. A conference in Semarang had been called to choose a replacement for the party's chairman, Osa Maliki, who had just died. Despite Suharto's earlier support for Osa Maliki's running-mate, Hardi, during the overthrow of Ali Sastroamidjojo in 1966, the government now decided the automatic accession of Hardi to the PNI chairmanship would create a dangerous rival for the military, in that he represented a rational, modernist line of thinking which could easily become aligned with the Westernized Socialist Party elements and progressive Muslims. The government's preferred candidate was now Hadisubeno, the long-time associate of Suharto from Semarang, who was seen as representing a traditionalist stand in the PNI and unlikely to quarrel with the values that kept Indonesia firmly under its warriors and bureaucrats. Before the PNI conference began, delegates were summoned by their local military commanders. They were told they could expect a hot reception if they came home without Hadisubeno elected. In Semarang the delegates found Ali Murtopo and his operatives established in a 'command centre' near the conference hall, ready to hand out lavish hospitality or browbeatings as necessary. No vote was taken, but it was announced after a week of uproar that nearly all delegates had signed a statement in favour of Hadisubeno, who was then declared chairman.

In the new Muslim Party, Parmusi, the government's strategy was continually threatened by a resurgence of influential Masyumi leaders. Even the government-appointed interim leader, Djarnawi Hadikusumah, was eventually deemed too weak in his dealings with Masyumi. Late in 1970, an associate of Ali Murtopo, John Naro, was directed to convene selected executive members of Parmusi and have himself elected. Djarnarwi made an immediate counter-move, but Suharto intervened by appointing one of his ministers, Mintaredja, as a compromise chairman. Mintaredja, who had served a sentence in Surabaya's Kalisosok Prison for corruption, was an unpopular appointment. But he and Naro successfully proceeded to water down the party's policies, even abandoning

Parmusi's policy of support for the Jakarta Charter.[9]

A third important excursion by Ali Murtopo in 1970 involved the Indonesian Journalists' Association (PWI). The Jakarta press had become a battleground for the New Order. Some newspapers such as the socialist-oriented *Pedoman* and Mochtar Lubis's *Indonesia Raya* applied a Western-style scrutiny to government activities; others, a more traditional, consensual approach. At the PWI annual meeting, two rival executives emerged. One was led by the businessman and publisher of the nationalist *Merdeka* daily, B. M. Diah, who had earlier acted as Suharto's Minister of Information. Rosihan Anwar, editor of *Pedoman*, led the second. Despite lobbying by Ali Murtopo and Opsus, the Anwar faction narrowly won the election. When the Diah group protested and put forward their own executive, as duly elected, the government ignored Anwar, recognizing Diah.[10] Ali Murtopo's hold on the Journalists' Association has remained strong, and the influence of his 'consensual' ideas of press freedom were to become greater with the emergence of two semi-official daily newspapers controlled by his group: the Golkar-oriented *Suara Karya* and Opsus-based *Berita Yudha*.

These tactics caused widespread dismay among non-military Indonesians who had hoped for a more democratic open style of politics in the New Order. Even so, the army retained some potential as a progressive force for groups who continued to work for the emerging Golkar movement. Among these were the former Gadjah Mada University students who had graduated in the 1950s, such as Mashuri and Sugiharto, and the Bandung group of Rachman Tolleng. Both groups, in their different ways, nursed strongly anti-party attitudes. But preparations for the general elections on 3 July 1971 were soon to disabuse party politicians and New Order activists of many expectations about the degree of critical thinking the army was prepared to allow on display.

By then the armed forces were a far more monolithic force than they had been on taking power. Where a basic strategy of Sukarno had been to divide the four branches of the armed forces (army, navy, air force and police) and to promote the junior services as counterweights to the army, now the emphasis was on integration. Between 1967 and 1970 the four ministries serving the individual services were absorbed into the Department of Defence and Security (known as Hankam), which previously had wielded no direct control of troops. The service chiefs were down-graded from commanders to chiefs of staff. Political management also shifted to Defence headquarters, to be undertaken by the new Armed Forces Command for the Restoration of Security and Order, Kopkamtib, headed by the former East Java Brawijaya Division commander, General Sumitro. A new branch, kekaryaan, under General Daryatmo, was assigned to supervise political and social staff and the thousands of military men seconded to civilian duties. Two further changes reduced the independence of the troublesome regional commanders. First, Indonesia was divided up into four defence areas: the first covering Sumatra and West Kalimantan, the second and most senior covering Java, Bali and Nusatenggara, the third covering Sulawesi and the rest of Kalimantan, the fourth covering the Moluccas and Irian Jaya (the first three being under the army and the fourth a navy preserve). The commanders of these areas assumed many of the civil powers previously invested in the seventeen army regional commands. The effect of their appointment was also to integrate the three fighting services (the police retaining their own command structure). Secondly, a long-term expansion began of Kostrad, the army Strategic Reserve, by removing crack battalions from the Java commands to form new airborne brigades placed at the disposal of Hankam in Jakarta.

In the eighteen months before the 1971 elections this newly tightened machine, whose senior generals met twice a year at a 'Commander's Call' in Jakarta to discuss political developments under the chairmanship of the Defence minister, mounted an extensive operation to ensure the Golkar gained a majority vote. The security apparatus kept a tight hold on all stages of voting preparations, and at all levels kept the right to 'strike out' any candidate without saying why. If, as the Golkar adviser quoted on page 90 above claimed in 1977, the Indonesian people regarded voting as a duty to please those in authority, then all efforts were made to see that the authorities spoke with one voice. Especially after the blunt Sundanese (West Javan) General Amir Machmud took over the Interior Ministry (which supplies the core of the civil administration outside Jakarta) a series of regulations and informal commands applied a new doctrine of 'Monoloyalty' to Indonesia's 1.7 million government employees. Those who received their pay from the government owed it their undivided loyalty. That loyalty was to be expressed through universal membership of departmental employee associations which were linked to Golkar. Beginning with a decree in 1970 which gave senior civil servants six months to resign their party membership or quit their jobs, the Monoloyalty policy took hold. To the parties, who had relied on patronage and the prestige of having members in official positions, this was a savage blow, especially for the PNI which drew so heavily on the 'guardians of the people' in the Interior Ministry. The historian, Reeve, quotes the head of Bakin (the Intelligence agency), Major-General Sutopo Yuwono, telling Golkar leaders in September 1970: 'Golkar has now obtained everything that a government party could have, with, in addition, the support of the Armed Forces. What else could you want?'[11]

The 1971 elections duly took place in a calm but tense atmosphere. They had been preceded by months of harassment of non-Golkar parties by military and civil authorities, with numerous incidents of arrest and other acts of intimidation, including a final 'quiet week' which saw party campaigning halted while troops mounted 'exercises' through villages. While the intellectuals and activists around Ali Murtopo remained well to the fore in Jakarta, the military's role in Golkar increased in direct proportion to distance from the capital. The parties suffered grievously from the limitations placed on debate. The PNI and Parmusi were the worst hit, the nationalists gaining only 6.9 per cent of the national vote as against the 22.3 per cent in 1955 (when it was the biggest vote-getter) and the Muslim group only 5.4 per cent compared with the 20.9 per cent of its predecessor, Masyumi, in 1955. The nationalists had been unable to appeal directly to their traditional constituency, not only through Monoloyalty but by a ban on advocacy of Sukarnoism.

The old leader had finally died, aged sixty-nine, on 21 June 1970 after three years of virtual house confinement, during which his health deteriorated. Sukarno had wanted to be buried in the garden of his villa at Batutulis outside Bogor where he believed an ancient engraved stone supplied him with mystical power. Another version of his testament had him nominating a site under 'a shady tree' in the Priangan highlands near Bandung, the area where he had met long ago his archetypal Indonesian small man, a peasant called Marhaen.[12] Either way, Sukarno wanted only a simple headstone inscribed 'Sukarno, Mouthpiece of the Indonesian People'. Two of his wives, Hartini and Dewi, made a joint appeal in person to Suharto in favour of Batutulis, but Suharto wanted no such shrine established so close to Jakarta and Bandung. Sukarno was accorded a state funeral attended by massive, weeping crowds, but his body was airlifted to Blitar in East Java and buried in a grave beside his mother's.

In the election campaign, military authorities blocked PNI attempts to enlist Sukarno's eldest son, Guntur Sukarnoputra, and prevented a planned graveside commemoration of the first anniversary of Sukarno's death. PNI leaders also found themselves more vulnerable than most to sudden 'discovery' of evidence linking them with the coup. A final blow was the death of the chairman of PNI, Hadisubeno, in April 1971, shortly before campaigning reached its most active stage. The Semarang patrician had surprisingly turned out to be a stinging opponent for Golkar. He combined both a common touch and some appeal to the city cosmopolitans, and matched even the Golkar 'bulldozer', Interior Minister Amir Machmud, with hard-hitting pronouncements.

The Muslim Party, Parmusi, was similarly at a loss. With a docile despised leadership and the major point of its original programme, the Islamic State in its various guises, banned from articulation, Parmusi also suffered from the relative insolvency of its traditional source of funds, the Muslim entrepreneurs and traders who lagged behind other business groups under the New Order.

The strongest resistance to 'Golkarisasi' came surprisingly from the Nahdatul Uluma (NU), a party that never had any pretensions to modernity and was noted for its tendency to equivocate and horse-trade. This Muslim Scholars' League also encountered strong-arm tactics, but the Islamic elder in his *pesantren* (boarding school) or mosque with ready-made audiences and cadres was the one source of authority in the villages and kampungs that the Golkar machine was unable to diminish. In fact this authority had been vastly strengthened by the coup and its aftermath. The NU won 18.3 per cent of the vote, respectably close to its 1955 result of 18.4 per cent. In the 'horseshoe' around Surabaya which is closely settled by the devout Islamic people from the island of Madura, NU scored majorities in several regencies.

Golkar's vote was 62.8 per cent which, with nine appointed members for Irian Jaya, gave it 236 of the 360 elected seats in the Parliament (DPR), while the NU gained 58, the PNI 20, and Parmusi 28. When the 100 government appointees, most from the armed forces, were added, the Golkar–military dominance of the legislature was overwhelming. While protests were mounted over some aspects of the poll, particularly about the amazing speed with which votes were counted and the results relayed from certain remote provinces, the Suharto Government was quick to proclaim the result a massive affirmation of public confidence in its policies. Reeve, in his study of Golkar, points out that while restrictions and controls certainly played the major part in fixing Golkar's victory, there was also in 1971 'a measure of positive commitment to Golkar'. Among the educated elite there was still a general approval of the government's development programme. There was a wide distrust of 'politics' and parties since 1965 and a feeling that Golkar was safe, especially since it was endorsed by nationally respected figures like Sultan Hamengkubuwono. Reeve went on to observe, however, that Golkar's victory was 'more an end than a beginning' and that Golkar rapidly became an idea that appeared to have 'nowhere to go'.

Far from becoming an engine of 'dynamic stabilization', Golkar settled back to a passive role applauding the government and bureaucracy. It supplied little to the sharpening debate on the country's economic progress, and helped throw a protective screen around a spoils system in which it was an avid participant.

Meanwhile, the final cuts were made into the parties. Late in 1971 an enunciation came from the Central Java Military commander, Widodo, of the concept of the 'floating mass'. General Widodo maintained that party activity in the villages disrupted the hard work and unity necessary for development. Far better to let the population 'float' without party contact in the five-year period between elections. This call was taken up by the government, and given effect in a law on political organization enacted in 1975. The parties and Golkar were banned from organizing below regency level, virtually confining activities to big towns and cities. But Golkar was effectively represented right down to the villages by nearly every government office-holder.

A second attack came when the DPR was reorganized by government fiat into four 'fractions': Golkar, the armed forces, Development Democracy, and Development Unity. The Development Democracy fraction grouped the PNI with several smaller nationalist and Christian parties, while the Development Unity fraction comprised the NU,

Parmusi and a smaller Muslim group, the PSII. Early in 1973 these fractions were formally incorporated, again by direction from above, into the Indonesian Democratic Party (PDI) with thirty DPR seats on one hand, and the Development Unity Party (PPP) with ninety-four seats on the other. It was hardly a recipe for a harmonious 'simplification'. The PNI factions remained as mutually hostile as ever within the PDI, with further distrust and permutations imported by the junior partners. When the party held its first congress in 1976, a fist-fight marked the opening. In the Muslim-based PPP the government's favouritism towards the tame Parmusi component in awarding offices caused great dismay. An even more drastic twist came with the pointed removal of all religious overtones in the party's name, justified under the New Order's policy of transmuting political groups from the destructiveness of preoccupation with 'ideology' (which included religion) into the modern condition of being 'programme-oriented'. Perhaps more than in most countries names and symbols are important in Indonesia. In politics, party symbols, such as the crescent for Muslim groups, made a direct appeal to basic loyalties and beliefs. The loss was a severe one.

NOTES

1 Confidential interview by author, Jakarta, March 1977.
2 Government Regulation no. 1, 1976, Article 57.
3 Harold Crouch, *Army and Politics in Indonesia*, Cornell University Press, 1978, p. 26. Crouch's account of the Indonesian Army move into political control was a valuable reference for this chapter.
4 David Reeve, *An Alternative to the Party System in Indonesia: An Historical Evaluation of the functional Group Concept*, PhD thesis, University of Sydney, 1977.
5 Koentjaraningrat, 'The Village in Indonesia Today' in Koentjaraningrat (ed), *Villages in Indonesia*, Cornell University Press, 1967.
6 See Reeve, op. cit., for a detailed account.

7 Crouch, op. cit., p. 26.
8 From confidential interview by the author, Jogjakarta, May 1978.
9 For a superb account of the 1971 elections and participants see Ken Ward, *The 1971 Elections in Indonesia: An East Java Case Study*, Monash Papers on Southeast Asia, no. 2, Centre of Southeast Asian Studies, Monash University, 1974. See also Reeve, op. cit.
10 Peter Polomka, *Indonesia Since Sukarno*, Penguin, Harmondsworth, 1971, p. 200–201.
11 Reeve, op. cit., p. 423.
12 From the insight gained in this meeting Sukarno created his doctrine of 'Marhaenism' which idealized the typical Indonesian 'little man' owning his own means of production but not becoming an evil capitalist.

6. The Feudal State

As the independent bodies of Indonesian politics were brought into captive orbit around the army, a constellation of personalities and wealth concentrated on Suharto. His opponents and rivals were neutralized. Where Suharto had presented an image of shy charm, he now assumed an aura of authority. What was earlier seen as modesty now met criticism as remoteness. The Javanese element in Suharto soon tired of the turmoil and confrontation inherent in the open debate pursued by the action front students and the modernizing generals from Bandung. Moreover, both groups wanted such a forum to be institutionalized. Emergency arrangements settled into formal systems. Allies sought rewards and Suharto wanted his own men around him.

At one extreme the entourage encompassed the highly educated Technocrats. At the other, it shaded into a collection of old friends who seemed to fit, figuratively at least, into the category of 'albinos, clowns, dwarves and fortune-tellers' which Benedict Anderson found in medieval Javanese courts.[1] Indeed, the comparison often made of the Merdeka Palace under Sukarno with the Javanese *kraton* (sultan's palace) came within a few years to be made of Suharto's household (although this is not unique to Indonesia: similarities with royal courts are often drawn about presidencies elsewhere). Suharto himself consciously drew on the annals of ancient kingship for lessons in politics. In 1970 he reminded students who were protesting against corruption in high places about an old

Javanese form of lodging a grievance by dressing in white and sitting in front of the *kraton* from daybreak till dusk, when the king would grant an audience.[2] In 1977 Suharto attempted to emulate the mythical Prince Harun Al Rashid of the *Arabian Nights* who made incognito tours of his kingdom to discover the problems of his subjects. Suharto spent several days in rural Java travelling in a small caravan of unmarked jeeps.

On assuming power in 1966 Suharto moved to a more comfortable and secluded, but still plain, Dutch-built suburban house, saying he did not feel fit to move into the presidential palace. He drove around Jakarta in his army jeep. For two or three years he encouraged contact with outsiders: the foreign press found interviews quite easy to come by. On one occasion the Suharto family even invited the resident foreign press corps and local journalists for a picnic on one of the coral islands in the Bay of Jakarta. The elite in the city was an intimate, compact one, living in the two Dutch-established suburbs of Menteng and Kebayoran. The regime had an openness about it. In the absence of reliable telephones, private cars and taxis, people travelled by *becak*. An Indonesian tradition of making unannounced visits early in the evening remained an acceptable way of exchanging information.

But the outsiders came to ask less and less pleasant questions. The reaction of Suharto and his colleagues over a period of years was to close off contacts, and to claim that critical accusations from the universities and press mirrored only the ideals of a foreign-influenced elite. Far from cutting themselves off from the people they claimed to possess an arch of intuitive understanding to the common people which overrode the carping of newspapers and placards. What these intellectuals saw as wrong and even criminal was, according to Suharto, entirely appropriate to the ruler in the eyes of the ordinary Indonesian, who would have felt ashamed to see him behave otherwise. Resulting phenomenon created sharp disillusionment and a painful issue for Indonesia: the burgeoning of 'corruption' and 'bureaucratic capitalism'.

The line between government and commerce has always been a blurred one in Indonesia. As we have seen, the traditional states governed on the basis of appanage, by farming out monopolies and revenue-collecting agencies to favoured court clients. Personal enrichment from office was normal in the Dutch East India Company, and continued under Dutch rule. In Java especially, the civil service elite had maintained a continuous tradition right through until independence when patronage became the preserve of the parties, the presidency and the armed forces. The corporatist ideology of the common interest preceding individual rights and freedoms had its economic analogy in a general presumption in favour of state control and participation: business activities needed bureaucratic clearance before commencing, rather than there being an atmosphere of free enterprise.

To stay in business one needed friends in key sections of the bureaucracy to arrange speedy clearances and approvals. On the smaller scale of enterprise this meant cash payments to petty officials. For big business it required alliance with a minister or senior bureaucrat. During the 1950s this lead to formation of several business 'groups' aligned with the various parties. Party fortunes in gaining ministries were often directly reflected in the allocation of import licences, bank credit or distributive monopolies. In many cases these political favours were traded to others, so that measures to encourage indigenous businesses, for example, often passed on to Chinese or other non-*pribumi* elements. The Indonesiam *pribumi* business tycoon was often a wheeler-dealer whose major asset was his political connection. Only a few, such as the motor-vehicle importer, Hashim Ning, or the ship-owner, Sudarpo, built more firmly based empires. When the regime changed in 1965–7, many business fiefdoms also changed hands. For example, the assets of Jusuf Muda Dalam, head of the central bank under Sukarno, were simply taken over by the army's co-operative body,

Inkopad, and the Mercedes-Benz dealership passed from a former PNI-linked businessman, Suwarma, to an army trading company, Berdikari (itself formed from confiscated assets), and then, upon the collapse of the army venture, into the hands of General Ibnu Sutowo, the Pertamina chief.[3]

Such bureaucratic manipulation had been a principal grievance among the forces who supported the New Order. Suharto, however, appears to have accepted it from the start as an unavoidable part of government that could be isolated from the general economic processes of development. The size of the official military budget in particular had long been a delicate problem since it was proving less and less adequate to cover real needs. By the time Suharto took power it was an accepted fact that the armed forces had their own independent sources of funds. Suharto's need to unify the military vastly increased the demand. A basic strategy was to make soldiers rely as much as possible on Defence headquarters, rather than their regional commander, for their new uniforms, improved housing, pay and meal supplements. There were about half a million men in uniform to keep happy. Added to this were 1.7 million civilian employees (according to a special census taken in 1974 to see just how many were on the payroll, the first time a total had been determined), forming a comparatively small percentage of the population but in absolute numbers an enormous burden on Indonesia's revenue base. Indonesia's public servants were described in 1968 as

> the least well paid in the world. To pay a month's salary that would permit them to work full time at their designated jobs and/or to remove, or at least severely reduce, the temptation to corrupt would require the Government to collect $1,400 million in taxes for this purpose alone. This is over three times more than the total tax taken in 1967.[4]

Official rates of pay and conditions continued well below minimum needs. For selected groups, such as the Finance Ministry, these were topped up with extra official payments. Generally the civil service relied on cash for services rendered which resulted in a finer differentiation of bureaucratic procedures. For example in certain notoriously 'liquid' areas such as Customs or Immigration, formalities were stretched out to require up to three or four dozen signatures from officials, each one purchased by the fall of rupiahs into the ever-open top drawer of the relevant desk. Such monies were then pooled and divided on a hierarchical basis, with enormous group pressure placed on individuals who might attempt to resist the shared guilt this system imposed. The most consistently glaring of these operations became the Customs office at Indonesia's biggest port, Tanjung Priok in Jakarta, where one estimate in 1977 by the respected *Tempo* magazine placed the annual takings at around $20 million. Such spectacular exactions are perhaps less invidious in that they tend to fall on the more prosperous sections of the economy. But they form the peak of a pyramid of graft that stretches down to small levies imposed on street vendors, transport operators or even the ordinary man renewing his resident's card. For these people they are a substantial imposition and business disincentive.

A deeper infection is caused by the internal weakness of the state apparatus and absence of outside monitors. The country possesses only a few thousand fully qualified accountants. Outside the major cities privately practising lawyers are unknown. Legal requirements for auditing, tendering, and reporting are hazy at best. Indeed, a vast body of law derives from regulations made by bureaucrats, rather than from legislation. It is rarely compiled for easy consultation, or turns out to be vague and contradictory when it is. While the Technocrats introduced the first budgeting procedures that were regular and approximately correct, controls on how the money is spent, once allocated, are nowhere near so precise. Funds allocated for village works or paying schoolteachers are clipped by various 'administrative charges' or 'voluntary contributions' on the way to disbursement. Often funds are spent on purposes that directly benefit the official involved, or circulate back to him through contracts awarded to his circle of friends.

This is not a new phenomenon in Indonesia, but has been worsened in some respects by the political changes after 1965. The extension of the parallel military administration has certainly been one factor: by and large the officers chosen for senior 'territorial' jobs have reached the peak of their military careers and they tend to use their positions to provide financial security for retirement. The removal of countervailing forces at village level through the purge of the left-wing and the ban on political party organization below regency level, left few direct controls on district administrators. Individuals who pointed out irregularities were likely to meet a united front of administrators, security officers and other local notables, and to receive arbitrary punishment as troublemakers or even subversives. The only avenue of complaint tended to be the rumour or the anonymous pamphlet, a persistent feature of New Order politics. A regular event in Java in the lean period at the end of the dry season has been the uncovering by Jakarta newspapers of starvation in rural areas, and efforts by local officials to conceal the problem from superiors who could organize relief. According to traditional Javanese values, perhaps becoming more pervasive, the chief safeguard against the corrupt official lay in his peers, men of substance also, reacting to the popular unease or seeing an 'excessiveness' in his behaviour that required quiet action – where possible by reimbursing any lost funds.[5] Unfortunately this concept of 'excessiveness' has proved highly elastic. A consistent estimate through the New Order period has been that some 30 per cent of development expenditure is lost by such 'leakages'. Even a third of this loss would be a massive weakness in the development programme.

The Suharto Government soon proved its inherent inability to act in a decisive way against such corruption. Despite its ostensible sensitivity to frequent public outcries it was itself deeply pervaded by, and dependent on, 'irregular' financial arrangements. As discussed in relation to Pertamina in chapter 7, the oil sector became the major source of finance for the armed forces. The military also benefited from the second biggest export commodity, timber. Its holding company, Tri Usaha Bhakti, was given control over forest leases in Kalimantan, where in return for paper clearances it gained a 35 per cent stake in all lumber enterprises without laying out any capital. This was, in effect, a resource rent. Similar operations ran at service, corps, and regional command level. The navy, for example, located a major tractor assembly business on its land in Jakarta, the Strategic Reserve (Kostrad) gained the Volkswagen monopoly through its own business foundation, and the Siliwangi Division secured the spin-off from Pertamina activities in West Java through its contracting enterprise, Propelat. Business empires grew around several financially adept generals or around the military-controlled holding companies, foundations, and co-operatives.

As with Kalimantan timber, the contribution of the military partner was almost entirely political. Finance and management skills came often from foreign or Chinese investors rather than indigenous (*pribumi*) entrepreneurs. Prejoratively known as *cukong* to the indigenous Indonesian public, the Chinese partners were widely reviled as a sinister influence. Their good fortune made the plight of struggling *pribumi* commercial groups all the more sharply felt. While the Technocrats privately voiced unhappiness at the distortions produced by such 'bureaucratic capitalism', they were largely powerless to change it. In certain departments the Technocrat minister had little control over military personnel, in ostensibly subordinate jobs, who enjoyed protection from the Defence Department. Two Mines ministers lost their jobs trying to pull Pertamina into line. For their successors there was the compensation that Pertamina at least kept their staff contented by paying a 50 per cent salary supplement to the entire Department of Mines (until

April 1978 when Suharto ordered it to cease). To refuse Pertamina's generosity would have seriously impaired the running of the department and probably have introduced a more petty style of corruption. The budget 'leakages', illegal levies, and the diseconomies wrought by the unplanned growth of 'bureaucratic capitalism' have undoubtedly contributed greatly to Indonesia's place as a high-cost economy in Asia, despite its extremely low wage structure. When it is also considered that the financial operations of dozens of state corporations are never reported to Parliament (including Pertamina, the national airline Garuda, and many other large concerns), the pervasiveness of the bureaucracy and its cost is hard to over-emphasize.

The presidential office also needed money, since its official budget covered only a small proportion of running expenses, let alone any wider network of patronage. Suharto's advisers concluded at an early date that it would be unwise to change this arrangement. Soon after the 1967 transfer of authority, the Technocrat ministers sent an emissary to Suharto's chief administrator of Cabinet, General Alamsjah, offering to provide an adequate budget if unofficial sources were dropped. The offer was abruptly refused. Funds came instead in a multitude of ways. Often, the presidency received gifts from other centres of power, as with Pertamina's provision of a new building for the Cabinet. Another important source of patronage lay in the state monopoly on transportation of Muslim pilgrims to Mecca, which created a pool of funds for the president to disburse to mosques and Islamic schools as examples of his own generosity and concern.

Suharto himself rarely showed his hand in business dealings but became increasingly implicated, at great political cost, by the activities of his inner circle of advisers, his family, and certain Chinese businessmen known for their palace connections. These links were already in existence when Suharto took power. The nucleus of a business empire lay in the Diponegoro Division and

Kostrad enterprises which Suharto had played a large role in founding; the growing ambitions and confidence of associated 'financial generals' such as Sujono Humardani and Suryo; and the mutual trust of Chinese business leaders who were discreetly associated with the Diponegoro Division in Semarang.

The case of Liem Siu Liong, the *cukong* most closely associated with Suharto and probably in command of the greatest personal wealth of anyone in Indonesia, provides a classic example of the Army–Chinese business alliance under the New Order. From a poor family in the Fukienese port of Futsing, he set out in 1938, penniless and illiterate at the age of twenty, to join relatives in Kudus, Central Java, the centre of the *kretek* cigarette industry. During the revolutionary period he expanded his relatives' commodity trading business by smuggling cloves from North Sulawesi to cigarette factories in the town and, according to some sources, by running guns to the republican army through Singapore. During the disruption of the Indonesian clove industry in the 1950s by disputes over plantation ownership and the Permesta rebellion in North Sulawesi, Liem began importing cloves from Madagascar and Zanzibar. He met Suharto and other officers in the Diponegoro Division, forming a co-operative arrangement in setting up light industries and marketing their produce. Expanding out of Central Java, Liem founded two banks, Bank Windu Kencana and Bank Central Asia, with headquarters in the Chinese commercial district of Jakarta.

In 1968 under the New Order, Liem moved to capture the clove trade he knew so well. Indonesia took up to 90 per cent of the clove output of the two Indian Ocean islands, but through the entrepôts of Singapore and Hong Kong. The Trade Minister, Sumitro Djojohadikusomo, sought to create a direct trade link and enhance Indonesia's bargaining power by consolidating its buyers. He eventually granted a shared import monopoly to Liem's company, Mega, and to Mercu Buana, headed by Suharto's younger half-brother, Probosutedjo. The almost nationwide addiction to *kretek,* and a guaranteed selling price for imports double that paid in Zanzibar or Madagascar (set to encourage domestic clove production), created an enormously profitable enterprise. The importers were allowed to a 2 per cent commission, while the profit went to a fund administered by the president for contributions to hospitals and other personal philanthropy.[6]

In 1970 Liem fought off the Singaporean Prima group which sought to establish large-scale flour milling in Indonesia. A new company controlled by Liem, in which Suharto's cousin and foster-brother Sudwikatmono held a small share, gained exclusive flour milling and handling rights for Java, Sumatra and Nusatenggara, while Prima was relegated to sparsely populated eastern Indonesia. Liem's company, Bogasari, received lavish finance from the central bank five days after lodging its application. Liem went on to expand his empire to cover finance, textiles, car assembly, insurance, property development, timber, rubber processing, mining, retailing, and other trading. His Bank Central Asia became one of the biggest private banks in Indonesia. In 1977 one of Liem's most trusted lieutenants in the banking field, Mochtar Ryadi, made a brief appearance in Washington politics by offering to buy out the troublesome banking shares of President Carter's Budget secretary, Bert Lance. The offer was declined.

Although he owned many of Jakarta's pleasure traps, Liem kept to an unobtrusive life-style under a discrete army guard, and took the Indonesian name Sudono Salim. His name does not even appear in the official hierarchies of many companies he controls. In his stead are a collection of obscure associates and relatives with mostly junior partnerships held by relatives of Suharto or Mrs Tien Suharto.[7] Liem's alignments were paralleled by those linking the Suharto entourage with other Chinese businessmen such as Bob Hassan (see chapter 2) and Ong Seng Keng (alias Arief Husnie), who with presidential aide

General Suryo figured in a scandal over agricultural programmes in 1969. The Suharto group was by no means unique. The New Order saw business partnerships link such powerful figures as Ibnu Sutowo, Governor of Jakarta, Ali Sadikin, and Sultan Hamengkubuwono with various Chinese backers.[8]

In this scene of intertwined government and private business dealings, the greater political liability for Suharto tended to come from the social and business predilections of his wife. As well as encouraging a taste for luxury items (diamonds, orchids, Paris fashions) seen by many Indonesians as inappropriate to the country's economic position, Tien Suharto soon showed an embarrassing talent for fund-raising. Her Yayasan Harapan Kita (Our Hope Foundation) set up with General Ibnu Sutowo's wife for philanthropic purposes, and Kartika Chandra Kirana, a similar venture with army wives, soon became notorious for their methods of soliciting contributions from businesses anxious to remain on good terms with the government or from built-in shares of the profits from Bogasari flour and other family concerns. In 1958 Mrs Suharto, along with the wives of Mayor Hadisubeno and other local leaders, had handed over a 'social monument' to the grateful citizens of Semarang;[9] in 1971 she announced to a stunned Indonesia plans to build a Disneyland-style national cultural exposition on the outskirts of Jakarta at an initially estimated cost of $24 million.

Suharto's accession also saw a marked revival in the fortunes of the Mangkunegaran royal house of Solo, to which Madame Tien was related. The Mangkunegaran's financial dealings proved remarkably more successful than those of other Javanese royal families. The palace also provided another web of loyalty and patronage under Suharto, with the head of the Supreme Court, Professor Senoadji, and the Director-General of Forestry, Sadjarwo, being two prominent examples of Mangkunegaran family members who rose to key positions. Such phenomena tended to give weight to the accusations of 'feudalism' launched against Suharto. They appear to be mirrored in a wider integration of the military leadership and the Javanese aristocracy, and a burgeoning of the *keluarga trah* (literally 'pedigree family') among the newly wealthy of the New Order.

So entrenched became this form of capitalism, and so intimately was it related to the political system which nurtured and protected it, that the corruption issue had the highest political significance. At first it was commonly believed to be peripheral and possible to police. The action fronts and other groups supporting Suharto turned their attention to the corruption problem soon after Sukarno had been pushed aside. The excuses for inattention appeared less valid as the economy responded to stabilization efforts, and the activities of the prominent financial generals became more notorious. After two or three years as president Suharto himself had moved to a new house, or rather a series of houses, in Menteng's Jalan Cendana, an expensive neighbourhood. The name of his street, Cendana, was to lend its name in popular parlance to the group of companies controlled by Liem Siu Liong and Suharto's relatives. Around the corner Ibnu Sutowo occupied a large part of a block, where in 1969 he hosted a wedding reception for his daughter so vast and opulent that closed-circuit television was used.

In November 1969 this growing unease among reformist elements of Indonesia's elite came to a head with the launching of a withering exposé of corruption and irregularities by the journalist, Mochtar Lubis, in his Jakarta daily, *Indonesia Raya*. Lubis, a Sumatran whose novel *Twilight in Jakarta* (1963) captured the disillusionment of the 1950s, had spent most of the period 1956–66 in detention for his Western-leaning, social democratic views. In 1969 under the demand *Kami Ingin Tahu* (We Want to Know) Lubis detailed numerous violations of law by the state oil company, Pertamina, and a series of questionable dealings reaching into Suharto's office, including the exposure of a scandal involving one of his controversial personal assistants (*aspri*), General Suryo. In January 1970 budget increases in the prices of staple items brought thousands of high school students onto the streets of Jakarta again, this time bitterly parodying the lost ideals of the New Order.

Suharto reacted quickly the same month by appointing a 'Commission of Four' to report on corruption. Under a former PNI prime minister, Johannes Wilopo, who was now head of the prestigious though largely powerless Supreme Advisory Council, the commission comprised two former Catholic Party ministers, Kasimo and Johannes, and the Islamic politician, Anwar Tjokroaminoto. The former vice-president, Mohammad Hatta, was made an adviser, and most significantly the reform-minded head of the State Intelligence Coordinating Agency (Bakin), Major-General Sutopo Yuwono, became the commission's secretary. The investigation quickly got under way, delivering seven hard-hitting reports to Suharto between February and June 1970. The reports detailed loopholes and irregularities in the operations of the rice-purchasing agency, Bulog, and the state forestry corporation, Perhutani. They strongly criticized Pertamina for failing to pass on revenues collected on behalf of the government, operating illegal bank accounts and subsidiaries, making unauthorized donations, and generally operating under lax financial and political control. The commission urged the strengthening of the Attorney-General's Department to act against corruption; it supplied a list of cases recommended for early action, including the General Suryo scandal and another involving C. V. Waringin, a trading concern headed by Suharto's cousin, Sudwikatomono. Finally, the commission inveighed against secret non-budgeted funds, arguing that the president should have his own publicly accountable budget supply. 'This purging effort must be commenced from the top', its last report said. The reports might never have reached the public had they not been leaked to the Jakarta newspaper *Sinar Harapan*, which published them in full in July 1970. They were never officially released.[10]

Suharto and the critics of his government were still on speaking terms, even as *Sinar Harapan* began its exposures. One of the most prominent of the anti-corruption campaign leaders, the young psychologist and writer, Arief Budiman, gave an account of a cordial meeting of a small delegation with Suharto. The president, according to Budiman, gave characteristically cautious replies to the young delegation's suggestions for more aggressive public action against alleged corruption. While others sought sensations, to him the most important matter was to get things done. 'Maybe I am too modest. I do not like talking about things where there are as yet no results to be shown,' he said. On the lavish wedding for Ibnu Sutowo's daughter, Suharto said: 'I have repeatedly admonished Ibnu Sutowo, and I did when he was planning the wedding of his daughter. But he said that as a Javanese he could not reject the offer of his relatives to arrange a large wedding party, and I can understand that.' Suharto warned the delegation against manipulation by political interests, but said he viewed the student activity as 'positive' so far. Arief Budiman noted that:

> When we left Jalan Cendana, I felt there were many things, particularly concerning actions against corruption and *Pak* Harto's attitude of preferring to work silently rather than 'propagandize' what he is doing, that I did not agree with. But the impression that *Pak* Harto is a man of strong principles who knows what he is doing and where he is going was also strongly imprinted in my mind.[11]

This kind of optimism evaporated when Suharto used his annual speech to Parliament on 16 August, eve of Independence Day, to claim that the substance of the Commission of Four's recommendations had already been acted upon. The night before students had organized a 'night of meditation', during which the poet and playwright W. S. Rendra and several other intellectuals had been arrested as they sat on the grass centre strip of

Jakarta's main street. Troops patrolled the city. The recommendations of the Commission of Four were acted upon to the extent that minor officials in the Religious Affairs Ministry and the Telecommunications Corporation were prosecuted for petty bribery. Suharto claimed General Suryo's problem was settled privately by the repayment of moneys. Although Suharto affirmed his determination to fight corruption, and certain legal changes were announced to tighten administrative controls and monitor the personal wealth of officials, the results can be gauged by the subsequent performances of two key agencies criticized by the Commission of Four, Bulog and Pertamina. It took the rice crisis of 1972-3 and the Pertamina disaster of 1975 before real reform occurred.

Cynicism mounted during a series of scandals after the commission's report sank from view. In September 1971, the Chief of Staff of the Police Force, Lieutenant-General Hugeng, announced the breaking of a huge smuggling operation at Tanjung Priok, in which highly placed army officers protected the illegal importation of hundreds of Mercedes-Benz cars. Hugeng was replaced four days later by an older officer.[12] The conduct of the 1971 general election was another blow to the reformists who briefly formed an abstentionist movement known as the Golongan Putih (Blank Group). By the last months of 1971 the corporatist intentions of the regime had been unfurled and the concept of the 'floating mass' announced. In November 1971 the president's wife announced plans to construct her Indonesia in Miniature, which immediately came under attack by students and intellectuals as another showpiece comparable to Sukarno's monuments. The project was described as entirely private and self-supporting, yet the lack of satisfactory financial projections, doubts about the voluntary nature of many private contributions, and the compulsory resumption of small-holder farmland to clear a site at low rates of compensation fired the controversy. By this stage neither the critics nor Suharto doubted who was the real target. Suharto chose the opening of another prestige project, the lavishly appointed Pertamina Hospital in Jakarta, to make his point. Those present say they had never before seen Suharto so deeply angered, so biting, so far from his normal Javanese calmness. Speaking without his usual notes, although a transcript shows signs of deep consideration, Suharto said the critics were the 'same people' who had been set on discrediting the government since 1968, as were the 'people behind the screen'. Their tactics were to distort, antagonize and confuse.

> What was their real goal? We know what it is, and it is not the Miniature project. The real goal, in the short term, is to discredit the government, and also of course the person responsible, myself, as the head of government and President. And in the long run they want to kick the armed forces out of executive activities and eliminate the dual function of the armed forces. They want to chase the armed forces back into their 'stable', that is limit it to their security function. If that is the target, it is not up to the Miniature project to answer its critics. The answer must be given by the armed forces, and the armed forces answer is quite clear. As I have said repeatedly, the armed forces will not relinquish their dual function.

Stressing his concern for 'constitutional' processes, Suharto went on:

> I have been criticized for doing things too cautiously. I have been abused as a 'slow but sure' Javanese, as a Javanese who is like a walking snail, like a snail whose shell is too big and heavy for its body. Never mind. The main thing was to safeguard the state and the nation. For that reason, if there are now people trying to act in defiance of the constitution, I will go back to the attitude I took on 1 October 1965: quite frankly, I will smash them, whoever they are. And I will certainly have the full support of the armed forces in that.[13]

Soon after the speech, Arief Budiman and two students were arrested, as was Johannes Princen, a turbulent Dutch-born journalist and human rights activist who had deserted from the Dutch Army to fight with the republican forces. The Managing Editor of *Sinar Harapan*, Aristides Katoppo, and other staff members were detained and interrogated about news reports on two occasions. The arrests were forthrightly criticized in the more outspoken Jakarta newspapers. Within a month all had been released. But Suharto's warning was effective, and a more cautious mood began to settle on the political scene.

In the next few months, attention turned to the plight of the political parties as convocation of the People's Consultative Assembly (MPR) drew near. The government had announced its plans for the amalgamation of the Parties who were once more targets for General Ali Murtopo's Opsus team. Under the compliant NU General Chairman, Idham Chalid, and the officially favoured Parmusi leadership the Muslim parties fused into the Development Unity Party (PPP). The nationalist and Christian groups similarly moved together under the PNI veteran, Mohammad Isnaeni. The Muslims had suffered the demoralizing loss of their most vigorous leader, Subchan, a former leader of the Islamic Students' Association (HMI) who had joined the Catholic Party's Harry Tjan and several other youth leaders on the afternoon of 1 October 1965 to form a pro-army action front. Subchan had risen high in the Nahdatul Ulama, but early in 1972 was deposed in one of a series of interventions mounted by Opsus. A year later he was killed in a car accident in Saudi Arabia at the age of forty-two.

When the 920 members of the MPR gathered on 1 October 1972 to commence a session that would choose a new president and lay down the 'broad outlines' of policy for the next five years, it was a highly amenable chamber. The right of 'recall' and post-electoral candidate selection by the president had been employed to ensure that the 360 elected members of Parliament (who joined the MPR automatically) agreed with the government's aims. This included Golkar, which had lost its more critical members such as the Bandung intellectual, Rachman Tolleng. In addition were the 100 appointed members of the DPR, a further 207 appointed by the president (of whom 155 were military), 123 effectively selected by the government to represent the political parties and Golkar, and 130 chosen by the provinces (which usually meant by the regional military authorities). With Mintaredja as PPP spokesman and Isnaeni for the PDI, Suharto's election on 22 March 1973 for a five-year term was unanimous, as was acclamation for the government's 'Broad Outlines of State Policy'. Whereas office bearers in the earlier provisional legislative bodies had included independent minds such as General A. H. Nasution, the new DPR was chaired by Idham Chalid, with Naro and Isnaeni holding the vice-chairmanships given to the parties (the other two going to Sugiharto on behalf of Golkar and Domo Pranoto for the armed forces). The practice of having separate office-bearers for the MPR was dropped.

But the harmony engineered in the political institutions did not reflect the mood of Indonesia. A rice crisis started by an over-long dry season in Java at the end of 1972 caused a widespread privation in the villages in 1973. Corruption and inefficiency had been exposed in the unpreparedness of the military-controlled logistics body, Bulog, which controls rice markets. The tight hold on prices achieved by the Technocrats was lost. On the eve of the world oil crisis, the Pertamina oil empire was expanding and the 'We Want to Know' campaign of 1969–70 just a memory. The tensions broke in Bandung in August 1973 when a car driven by three young Chinese-Indonesians collided with a bullock cart. The Chinese were reported to have then beaten up the *pribumi* cart-driver. Wild rumours spread through the city. Mobs formed, overturned cars, and burned and looted hundreds of Chinese-owned shops.

The Bandung riot, with its racial and economic overtones, was followed by a more serious political event: a head-on confrontation between the government and Golkar on one hand and the Muslim *ummat* (community) on the other. The cause was the introduction of a new bill on marriage and divorce, but the antagonism behind the dispute went further back into the country's basic religious divergences. The Muslims had observed, with growing unease, a distinct encroachment on their claimed constituency of 90 per cent of the Indonesian population, as measured in official statistics. The rush to religion encouraged by the genuine trauma of 1965, and by a need for many people to show themselves as conspicuously not atheistic communists, had seen an unexpected number opt for Christian religions. The new orientation of Indonesia to the West had seen a rise in Christian missionary activity. Missionaries were often seen in the Muslim community as part of a Western plot to weaken Islam. Churches were burnt down in several parts of the country. One particularly heated case in 1969–70 occurred over the building of a new hospital by Baptists in Bukittingi, the heart of the devoutly Muslim Minangkabau homeland in West Sumatra. Because of strong local opposition the West Sumatra military command had provided some of its own land for the project, an unfortunate step in relations between the Muslims and the army. More widely, the influence of the Jesuit Beek and the prominence of Roman Catholics in both Opsus and Golkar drew similar unfavourable interpretations among Muslims. Also, the 'anti-ideology' bent of the regime clearly implied the secularization of politics, as evident in the merger of the Islamic parties under a variant of the 'Development' banner, and in the explicit renunciation by their imposed leader, Mintaredja, of traditional Muslim demands. The other great threat, slower to manifest itself and not so immediately involved in the Marriage Bill crisis, lay in the deep appeal of Hindu-Javanese ideas to the new Army–Golkar elite, many of whom were practitioners of the Javanese *kebatinan* (mystical sciences).

Suharto's personal commitment to Javanism is evident from study of his early career (see chapter 1). As with Sukarno, mystical influences on Suharto's behaviour quickly became a talking point as the Indonesian public learnt more about this reserved general. For the Westernized intellectuals this caused concern about the rationality of their country's governance. For the Muslims any encouragement of traditional beliefs among the ethnic Javanese could result potentially in a massive decline in the Islamic community. Suharto's mystic inclinations gained a more sinister overtone by the presence of General Sujono Humardani on his personal staff as *Aspri* (presidential assistant) for Economic Affairs. Sujono had moved from his positions in army financial administration to play a key role in the New Order's financial dealings, particularly in arrangements with Japan. A slim, elegant figure with a fine, aquiline face under a great bush of hair, Sujono epitomized the elegant conjunction of mystic, economic and political skills aspired to by the Javanese statesman and courtier. He soon became noted as a *guru* to Suharto, drawing on himself epithets ranging from 'Minister for Mystical Affairs' to 'Rasputin'. He was born in Solo in 1919. Later in life he forged connections with the Surakartan aristocracy by the marriage of one of his children to one of the thirty-four children, from six wives, of the present traditional ruler of Solo.

Under Suharto, the numerous *kebatinan* sects moved towards greater organization and recognition. An important driving force was the Solo-born official, Wongsonagoro, who after graduating in law became a regent under the Dutch in Sragen and took an active role in the early nationalist movement, Boedi Oetomo (Highest Endeavour). As 'Resident' in Semarang in 1945 he was involved in a near suicidal attack on the Japanese garrison in an attempt to gain arms, and later became the first Republican Governor of Central Java. In the early 1950s he briefly held the Interior, Justice and Education portfolios for the PNI before serving as Ali Sastroamidjojo's Deputy Prime Minister.

Wongsonagoro, who died in 1978 aged eighty-one, was a prominent mystic. In the 1945 constitutional debates he had successfully urged inclusion of the phrase 'and beliefs' in the article guaranteeing religious freedom. This was an important charter for *kebatinan* followers who later used it to press with partial success for official recognition (entailing various benefits and freedoms under the Ministry of Religious Affairs) along with Islam, Catholicism, Protestantism and Hindi-Buddhism. In 1970 Wongsonagoro organized a *kebatinan* conference in Jogjakarta, resulting in the formation of a new Joint Secretariat for Beliefs (Sekretariat Kerjasama Kepercayaan). Soon afterwards he pressed Suharto for official recognition, including creation of a new division in the Religious Affairs Ministry and, among other things, nomination of the first day of the month (Suro) in the Javanese calendar as *kebatinan's* official feast day.[14]

Security officials had their reservations about *kebatinan* sects. In 1967 in a remote hamlet in Central Java a mystic named *Mbah* Suro had gained a messianic attraction for peasants over a huge tract of territory. True to traditional form, *Mbah* Suro attracted a retinue of personal guards convinced of their invulnerability. The army claimed some evidence had emerged that PKI elements were using the sect to regroup. Determined to make a show of strength, the army sent in a unit of commandos and forcibly broke up the movement with the loss of more than eighty lives. This incident had led to the formation of a special office within the Attorney-General's Department to supervise mystic groups and schools. Nevertheless, Wongsonagoro's initiative appeared to find some official favour. The mystic viewpoint gained greater airing in the press and on the air. In the 1972-3 MPR session came another victory with the insertion of Wongsonagoro's phrase 'and belief' into the Broad Outlines of State Policy against strenuous Muslim opposition. Suharto was later to favour the *kebatinan* movement in 1973 by opening a congress of the Subud movement, a group led by the Javanese *guru*, Subuh, with a considerable international following, and in 1974 by lending financial and moral support to a second Indonesian *kebatinan* conference.

The congruence of the Golkar corporatist ideology and Javanese religious beliefs was reflected, perhaps unconsciously, in the choice as the Golkar symbol of the banyan tree, whose shade is a place of sacred or superstitious significance in South Asian villages. Signs of a more deliberate political tactic emerged before the 1971 elections, when government strategists revived a dormant organization called GUPPI (Union of Endeavours to Improve Islamic Education) as a Golkar-affiliated group to attract Muslim support and allocate patronage, and made Sujono Humardani its patron. After the elections the Nahdatul Ulama lost control of the Religious Affairs Ministry with the appointment of a non-partisan educationist, Professor Mukti Ali. Officials connected with Nahdatul Ulama fell out of favour and the new minister introduced more secular teaching in Muslim schools. Muslims saw a two-pronged attack forming: on one hand the regime would attempt to co-opt Muslim political activity into 'safe' channels and allay suspicions by rigorous observance of Islamic routines of prayer, fasting and pilgrimage; on the other it was moving to the point where millions of Javanese could either nominate themselves as *kebatinan* followers, or at least feel less uneasy in resisting Islamic political and social appeals, encouraged by the common observation among the Javanese elite that Islam was a 'foreign' or 'Arab' religion.

The old NU-controlled Department of Religious Affairs, with unanimous backing from the Muslim parties, had tried since 1967 to have passed through the DPR a new law on Muslim marriages which would have enforced Islamic law, with sanctions, on all Muslim couples. The threat of compulsion alarmed other groups, and the legislation was bogged down in the face of counter-proposals and delaying tactics. In August 1973 the government introduced a new bill, proposing a single marriage law for all Indonesians. The Islamic courts organized by the Department of Religious Affairs were to be given a minor legal role compared to civil registration. On points involving inter-religious marriage, adoption, inheritance, marriageable age, polygamy, and remarriage the bill was quickly attacked as contrary to Islamic law and an encouragement to sexual licence outside marriage. Seen as an assault on the fundamentals of Islam, the issue united and aroused the Muslim community. As protests flowed in to the government, young Muslims began picketing the DPR building, on one occasion forcing their way into the chamber before being evicted by troops.

Muslim leaders blamed Catholics and mystics in the army–Golkar camp for the attack. They also attacked the growth in 'sinful' activities under the New Order, as shown in the spread of massage parlours, casinos and poker-machines in the cities, and the 'immodest' Western styles of dress and behaviour infecting the young. The Muslim community felt it was ignored and distrusted in favour of the Chinese and the foreigners.

As the protest threatened to get out of hand, the two generals most closely concerned with security stepped in. General Sumitro, the head of the armed forces internal security command, Kopkamtib, and General Sutopo Yuwono, head of Bakin, the Intelligence agency, initiated behind-the-scenes discussions with the Muslim parties in October, and reached a compromise after some weeks. This understanding was the basis for redrafting by a committee drawn from all groups in the DPR, and in December the amended bill passed without a vote. Although the Muslims were far from happy with the result (again, the phrase 'and belief' appeared, among other contentious points) the new bill gave continued emphasis to religious courts and the individual marital laws of each religion.

The intervention of Sumitro and Sutopo signalled another struggle that had broken out, this time within the armed forces leadership itself. Sumitro, born in East Java in 1923, was one of the most professionally skilled and politically astute officers in the Indonesian Army. A graduate of the West German military staff college, immediately after the 1965 coup attempt he had been given the delicate task of establishing full control in East Java, the strongest bastion of Sukarnoism. Then, as Chief of Staff to the Defence Minister (who was at that time held by

Suharto himself), he supervised the reorganization of the armed forces that took effect in 1969. When Suharto delegated some power by appointing the trusted Maraden Panggabean, a Protestant Batak from a political base (North Sumatra) safely outside Java, as Deputy Commander-in-Chief, Sumitro became Deputy Commander of Kopkamtib, responsible directly to Panggabean. In Suharto's reshuffle of Cabinet in March 1973, Panggabean took over as Defence Minister and Commander-in-Chief, while Sumitro became concurrently his deputy and full commander of Kopkamtib. Sutopo Yuwono had a reputation as a reformist, which increased as a result of his association with the 1970 Commission of Four on corruption. Through 1973 both men were generally believed to have grown opposed to the political activities of Ali Murtopo and Sujono Humardani. They were said to be dismayed at the degree of military strong-arming necessary to achieve a Golkar victory in the 1971 elections, and disappointed both at the calibre of representation in the Golkar faction and its public reception. Since the election, the two security officials felt their task made unnecessarily heavy and the risks made too great by the high-handed political changes initiated by the two *aspri*, as finally shown in the Marriage Bill affair. Throughout 1973 political speculation in Jakarta centred on the rising influence of the two security officials *vis-à-vis* the two presidential assistants.[15]

While the Muslim protest mounted the government also came under sharper criticism from a renewed movement among university students, the press and modernist intellectuals. With the economy beset by mounting inflation sparked by the 1972 rice crisis, evidence had also accumulated of a growing inequality in wealth. The Bandung riot of August 1973 was followed by new protest activity in the universities, which queried the achievements of the regime's economic programme. The movement crystallized at a discussion convened by the Students' Council at the University of Indonesia on 24 October 1973 at which several speakers questioned the continuance of the military's Dual Function and the 'theoretical' approach of the Technocrats. Afterwards, a group of students went to the Heroes' Cemetery on the outskirts of Jakarta, where they issued a 'Petition of 24 October' calling on the 'Military Government, Intellectuals, Technocrats and Politicians' to review their development strategy in order to remove inequalities, free the people from corruption and abuses, and strengthen representative institutions. General Sumitro, who the month before had annoyed students with a campaign against long hair, took a surprisingly conciliatory approach to this. He toured the campuses, received student delegations, and held debates with intellectuals. At the end of November 1973 he declared that a 'new style of leadership' was needed. He promised it would begin the following April when the second five-year plan began.

Protests which had initially concentrated on the development strategy based on large amounts of foreign aid and investment and thus made the Technocrats the butt of criticism, turned by the end of 1973 to the misdirection of this funding. The target now became the presidential advisers, the *cukong*, and the chronies and relatives of those in power. Ali Murtopo, Sujono Humardani, Liem Siu Liong, Liem Bian Kie, and Mrs Tien Suharto came under direct attack. The students issued a list of 'Three Demands' (Tritura 1974) calling for dissolution of the *aspri*, lowering of prices, and eradication of corruption.

While Sumitro held to his responsive approach, Ali Murtopo issued demands for the campaign to cease. The rumour spread, probably encouraged deliberately, that Sumitro was using the criticism to further his own ambitions, and that his 'new style of leadership' statement implied a change of leaders. On 2 January 1974, Suharto summoned Sumitro, Ali and Sutopo Yuwono. Sumitro emerged from the meeting to denounce 'wicked, cruel and dirty ideas' that he and Ali Murtopo were contenders for Suharto's position. Protests rose in intensity towards the visit of the Japanese Prime Minister, Kakuei Tanaka, on 15 January. Students demonstrated outside Ali Murtopo's offices calling him a 'political pimp' and Sujono Humardani was burnt in effigy. The outcry was joined by several prominent voices from off campus, among them the lawyer, Adnan Buyung Nasution, who pressed for the abolition of such 'extra-constitutional' bodies as the *aspri* and Kopkamtib and the annulment of the Supersemar declaration and the Dual Function doctrine which justified them. On 11 January Suharto received representatives of thirty-five student councils in an awkward, formal meeting during which the students raised the *aspri* issue, the business activities of senior government figures and their wives, and the government's connections with the Chinese business community. Suharto's smiling, non-committal response and his pointing out of the formal truth that the *aspri* held no executive powers, exasperated the students.

Tanaka arrived in Jakarta on the evening of 14 January to be met by several hundred student demonstrators with posters attacking Japan for an 'economic animal' approach to Indonesia. As Tanaka went to meetings the next day the streets of central Jakarta filled with demonstrators and onlookers. Over 11 000 troops were on standby around the city, but the Kopkamtib commander continued desperately to talk down the protest, at one point addressing the crowds blocking the main boulevard, Jalan Thamrin, from the top of an army vehicle. After midday, as students converged on the Merdeka Palace to press their demands to Tanaka, violence broke out in two nearby chinese commercial areas. Crowds swelled by school students and young bystanders attacked the headquarters of Astra, the Chinese-run Toyota agency linked by repute with Mrs Suharto, and then began burning Japanese cars or manhandling them into drainage canals. Late that afternoon mobs ransacked and burned the huge new Senen market building across the city. Shortly afterwards the military declared a dusk curfew and began cracking down on mob violence, firing shots and making hundreds of arrests as incidents continued through the night. By the next day the Defence Minister, Panggabean, appeared on the streets supervising operations. By the time Tanaka left the palace in a helicopter on 17 January the city was tense but firmly under army control. In the two days eleven people had been shot dead, some 470 arrested, and some 800 cars and 150 buildings destroyed, according to official figures. Figures given by Kopkamtib a month later revealed that of those arrested only fourteen were university students and eighty-three schoolchildren, while over half were labourers.

A decisive change of power occurred on the night of 15 January. The next morning Sumitro appeared before Jakarta editors, flanked by senior officers who pointedly included Ali Murtopo and Sujono Humardani, to declare the situation had 'forced' stern action against those who directly or indirectly added to tensions. What this meant soon became clear. First, the critical newspaper *Nusantara* was banned. Then followed the weekly *Mahasiswa Indonesia*, run by the disillusioned '66 Generation leader, Rachman Tolleng. On 21 January licences were withdrawn from six more publications, including *Harian Kami*, *Indonesia Raya*, *Abadi*, and the *Jakarta Times*. Finally, on 23 January the socialist-leaning *Pedoman* was banned, along with the weekly magazine *Ekspres*.

While police chased looters (arresting a further 300) the security forces carried out discriminating raids on individuals singled out as the intellectual driving force of the protest movement. Some forty-five people were arrested. By the end of February this group contributed all of the forty-two people still held over the Malari affair, as the riots had come to be known (the word derives from the Indonesian for '15 January Incident'). They included several student leaders and noted long-time critics of the New Order's political and development strategy. Generally their arguments were based on the reformist ideals typical of the Bandung–Siliwangi group who had lost so heavily in 1967–71; Western legal–constitutional concepts of individual rights and government responsibility; opposition to Suharto's heavy reliance on foreign aid and investment. Rachman Tolleng, Adnan Buyung Nasution, and Professor Sarbini, who were among these Malari detainees, epitomized these basic tenets. Those detained were not the only ones to suffer: a former Ambassador to the USA, Sudjatmoko, was among several forbidden to travel abroad, while some journalists marked as critical were black-listed by the Information Ministry, and were barred from the Indonesian press.

The government also blamed figures in its own ranks. On 28 January Suharto abolished the council of *aspri*; removed Sutopo Yuwono from Bakin and dispatched him as Ambassador to the Netherlands; and assumed personal command of Kopkamtib, leaving Sumitro as Deputy Armed Forces commander. Suharto then placed two trusted comrades from his old campaigns into the day-to-day security positions. General Yoga Sugama became head of Bakin and Admiral Sudomo Chief of Staff in Kopkamtib. Sumitro refused an offer of the ambassadorship to Washington. Early in March 1975 he offered his resignation, and abruptly left the political scene to 'play golf' and tend his private business interests. He was replaced as deputy head by another Diponegoro veteran, General Surono. Suharto, meanwhile, had announced several shrewd policy changes aimed at cooling the political situation. Changes to investment laws emerged, speeding up the process of local share divestment for foreign companies and stipulating higher levels of *pribumi* (indigenous) equity in domestic investments within set periods. Suharto also sought to restrain the more excessive displays of luxury by officials through a code for the 'simple life'. Officials were no longer to organize lavish parties or to frequent such places as nightclubs and steam-baths. The import of built-up cars was banned, as was the availability of 'luxury' cars, defined as the Mercedes 300 and above or those of more than four-litres engine capacity. Finally, Suharto moved to curtail the independence of Kopkamtib, and to improve the conditions of the rank and file of the armed forces whose friendliness towards student demonstrators had caused concern.

In one sense the victors were the *aspri* who retained important positions: General Ali Murtopo as a deputy head of Bakin, General Sujono Humardani as an inspector-general of Development, General Tjokropranolo as Suharto's Military secretary, and General Suryo as head of the Hotel Indonesia empire. Ali Murtopo retained his Opsus and Golkar network, while his recent opponents, Sumitro and Sutopo, had been vanquished. His role in their downfall is apparent, although indefinable until more information about the Malari affair emerges. Many of those who suffered in the aftermath believe Opsus played a key role in exacerbating the anti-Tanaka protests to bring down Ali Murtopo's enemies. Reports are cited of mysterious figures urging or initiating the most destructive episodes such as the burning of Senen Market or the Blora Street massage parlours. Ali is accused of twisting the intentions of Sumitro who merely sought to win the trust of the government's critics.

The question of personal ambition for presidential power may be a smokescreen. The truth of the Malari affair may lie in the answer to such questions as the role, if any, of Sumitro and Sutopo Yuwono in diverting the students' anger away from the Technocrats, the IGGI and the World Bank towards the *aspri* and the 'corruptors'. That this may have been the secret *causus belli* behind Malari was indicated by the magazine *Ekspres* on 18 January, a week before it was banned. The magazine, long known for its closeness to Ali Murtopo, carried an anonymously written article attributing the unrest to the work of 'traitors' aligned with the banned socialist Party (PSI) and Masyumi, part of a constellation involving the US capitalist establishment and its local agents. None too delicately the article alluded to the government's planners, well known as the former students of the PSI's Sumitro Djojohadikusomo and American schools. *Ekspres* saw two trends emerging from the student movement:

> One leads via the Bappenas technocrats to a free-fight and *laissez faire* pattern of development in the Western and American fashion. Another trend takes the form of co-operation with Japan on the basis of one's own strength without loans from the IGGI, the IMF and the World Bank with Pertamina as guarantee.[16]

An alliance had formed between Ali Murtopo and Sujono Humardani on one hand, and Ibnu Sutowo, head of the oil empire Pertamina, on the other. Far more strongly connected than the Technocrats to Japan, and deeply involved in the spread of bureaucratic capitalism, they tended to see the answer to Indonesian development problems in the growth of the private sector, but with the lines between government and business blurred to ensure effective intervention to raise *pribumi* participation. they sought the same aggressive partnership achieved by the Japanese Government and big business, with the success of Pertamina as a pointer.

But Suharto did not move against the Technocrats. Nor was Ali Murtopo's scenario of a PSI–Masjumi plot taken up by the mainstream generals in the armed forces. It became clear that Suharto had decided not to let any of his advisers gain a pre-eminent position. Ali Murtopo worked hard to produce successful 'projects' that might restore him, among them the ill-fated *Pop* affair, in which a magazine of this name owned by a senior Opsus man published a spurious family-tree showing Suharto to be 'descended' from the Jogjakarta royal house. this earned a public rebuke for Ali Murtopo. The arguments against the Technocrats, in favour of Pertamina-style entrepreneurship, were promoted relentlessly.[17] But a year later Ali Murtopo was thrown on the defensive by the dramatic collapse of Ibnu Sutowo's oil empire.

NOTES

1. Benedict Anderson, 'The Idea of Power in Javanese Culture' in Claire Holt (ed.), *Culture and Politics in Indonesia*, Cornell University Press, 1972, p. 12.
2. Polomka, *Indonesia Since Sukarno*, Penguin, Harmondsworth, 1971, p. 201.
3. See R. A. Robison, 'Toward a Class Analysis of the Indonesian Military Bureaucratic State', *Indonesia*, Cornell University Press, no. 25, April 1978, and H. Crouch, *Army and Politics in Indonesia*, Cornell University Press, 1978.
4. 'Survey of Recent Developments', *Bulletin of Indonesian Economic Studies*, no. 9, March 1968, p. 9.
5. See Parsudi Suparlan, 'Democracy in Rural Java', *Prisma* (Jakarta), no. 5, March 1977.
6. *Tempo* (Jakarta), 6 October 1976.
7. Ian Verchere, 'Liem Siu Liong, Indonesia's Imperial Cukong', *Insight*, Hong Kong, May 1978.
8. See Robison, op. cit.
9. *Kedaulatan Rakyat* (Jogjakarta), 16 August 1958.
10. J. A. C. Mackie, 'The Report of the Commission of Four on Corruption', *BIES*, vol. VI, no. 3, November 1970.
11. Roger M. Smith (ed.), *Southeast Asia: Documents of Political Development and Change*, Cornell University Press, 1974, p. 228.
12. Crouch, op. cit., p. 292.
13. Smith, op. cit., p. 237–9.
14. D. Reeve, *An Alternative to the Party System in Indonesia: An Historical Evaluation of the Functional Group Concept*, PhD thesis, University of Sydney, 1977; and Donald K. Emmerson, *Indonesia's Elite: Political Culture and Cultural Politics*, Cornell University Press, 1976, p. 237–8.
15. For a discussion of the Marriage Bill crisis and the pre-Malari politics, see Emmerson, op. cit., p. 223–58.
16. *Far Eastern Economic Review*, 4 February 1974.
17. *Far Eastern Economic Review*, 20 May 1974.

7. The Rise and Fall of Ibnu Sutowo

The career of Ibnu Sutowo owed nothing to the footnoted scholarship of the Ivy League, the Sorbonne or Leiden. He was a man who fixed things. He sucked out the dregs of abandoned oil wells, he repaired wheezing oil refineries with scrap-iron, then bartered the output for new oil-rigs and new distilleries. He bought, hired and borrowed ships to carry the oil, planes and cars to ferry round the oilmen, hotels for them to sleep in, golf courses for them to play on, soldiers to guard them, and churches and mosques for their neighbours to pray in. As long as the oil and money flowed in a thicker and wider cycle the levitation of Ibnu Sutowo continued. It became a moot point whether he or Suharto was the less dispensable in the New Order.

As head of Pertamina, the state oil corporation, Ibnu Sutowo had an electric brilliance about him. If he short-circuited conventional systems of government and finance, he made sure he was shielded from the heat. He moved in a world of sheik-like luxury and credit-card extravagance, a fulfilment of the air-conditioned, Mercedes-driven fantasy of Asian escapism. A slim, rakishly handsome man whose dark face often relaxed into a wide, dazzling smile, always immaculately tailored, he seemed living proof to many Indonesians that the tables could be turned on the foreign mortgagers, and that boldness could achieve short-cuts in the laborious task of developing this impoverished country. He seemed to have created a new, indigenous entrepreneurship. If this did not fit the rules then the rules were wrong.

To the foreigners he was the 'Black Diamond'. He was a man whose word was his bond, who could cut through Jakarta's bureaucratic maze, get their money in, and get the profits out. But to his critics he was the epitome of all that was wrong in Suharto's Indonesia. Ibnu was beyond reach of constitutional authority, answerable only to Suharto and, even then, through private channels. He ran a massive, expanding section of the economy with little reference to agreed goals and priorities. He set an example of personal extravagance and financial irregularity which was repeated in smaller fiefdoms down the massive pyramid of corruption. He was a sultan in collar and tie presiding over a new bureaucratic feudalism.

The Technocrats and the international banking agencies had a more specific worry. They were concerned at Pertamina's potential to get Indonesia into a new foreign payments problem through its largely unregulated borrowing programme which was encouraged by a scramble among Western private banks to lend it money. But despite the intervention of the US Government and the IMF, the Technocrats remained impotent until their worst predictions were realized in the Pertamina crisis of early 1975. Even then, supporters of Ibnu Sutowo claimed it was precisely because of their attempt to hobble him that the disaster occurred.

Born in the shadow of the kraton in Jogjakarta on 23 September 1914, Ibnu Sutowo came from a vastly more privileged background than Suharto and most other New Order leaders. His father had been a regency head near Semarang in Central Java. Ibnu was thus able to attend a superior Dutch school and go on to medical college in Surabaya. After graduating in 1940 he was assigned to a new colony of Javanese transmigrants at Belitang in South Sumatra. The first recorded instance of his unorthodox approach occurred here: because of a high incidence of malaria he instituted regular house-to-house calls to force the colonists to take quinine tablets in his presence. During the Japanese occupation Ibnu assumed many local administrative powers. By the end of the Pacific War he was leading irregular forces backing the Indonesian Republic.

In 1945 Ibnu Sutowo moved to Palembang, the main city of South Sumatra, where he became a combined staff and medical officer of the republican army which was fighting the Dutch for the region's oil-fields and plantations. After the transfer of sovereignty in 1949 Ibnu worked in the region's civilian medical service, but remained on active duty in the army. In 1955 he was appointed commander of South Sumatra's Sriwijaya Division, named after the ancient empire whose capital may have been near present-day Palembang. The Sriwijaya Division established a reputation as an income-earner for the Indonesian Army, occupying as it does one of the richest export-producing areas in Asia. During the war of independence vast quantities of rubber, tea, pepper and coffee that had accumulated during the Japanese occupation were taken over by the army and smuggled to Singapore to buy weapons and supplies.[1] The trade continued after its war-time justification ended. Ibnu Sutowo himself benefited from the province's wealth through his wife, Zaleha, who was the daughter of a prominent South Sumatra family with interests in tin, rubber and tobacco, and who later became a successful businesswoman in her own right.

Ibnu Sutowo's administrative talents were recognized by the army commander, General Nasution, who brought him to Jakarta in 1956 as chief of Logistics, and then concurrently as chief of Operations. In 1958 Ibnu Sutowo returned briefly to Palembang to talk his former troops out of joining the anti-Sukarno revolt in Sumatra and North Sulawesi. However, the spectacular Tanjung Priok smuggling scandal later that year (see chapter 2), in which he was the main and unabashed culprit, seems to have ended any purely military ambitions Ibnu might have had (Nasution announced that Ibnu had wanted to retire from active service a year previously, and had only stayed on because of the PRRI–Permesta rebellion). Ibnu Sutowo continued with a more recently found interest: the oil industry, which Indonesia desperately needed to rescue from neglect.

The archipelago had long been noted as an important oil supplier. The story of its oil began in 1883 when a Dutch planter, Zijlker, was forced by heavy rains to shelter overnight in one of his North Sumatra tobacco sheds. His local foreman lit a torch which burned brightly despite the soaked conditions. Zijlker found the torch had been dipped in a black liquid seeping into a nearby pond. Subsequent drilling by Zijlker proved the existence of exploitable oil, and within a few years the basis of what was to become the Royal Dutch-Shell petroleum empire was established in the area. Other finds were made further south in Sumatra, in Java and in Borneo. The Royal Dutch-Shell oil-fields, refinery and shipping terminal in North Sumatra were extensively bombed in the Second World War and contested during the war of independence. Local insurgencies and warlordism had made rehabilitation impossible until 1957 when the fields were turned over to the army, and Ibnu Sutowo given charge.

The army sent in reinforcements to secure the oil-fields from local rebels and to quell unruly workers, while Ibnu directed makeshift repairs and arranged marketing through a small independent US oil firm. Early in 1958 the new army company, Permina (an abbreviation of National Oil Company Ltd), made its first shipment of 1727 tonne of crude oil aboard a tiny coastal tanker. It fetched $30 000.[2]

Within a month Ibnu Sutowo was expanding operations. For six years Japanese officials and industrialists had been negotiating with Jakarta over war reparations. The final agreement resulted in the opening of full diplomatic relations in 1958. A tooth-and-nail scramble resulted among Japanese business interests to win supply contracts financed by reparations, intriguing dealings which reached into the heart of the ruling Liberal Democratic Party. Former militarists and underworld societies took part. One businessman owed his success to the good fortune of introducing a nineteen-year-old nightclub hostess, Nemoto Naoko, to Sukarno. She later became the president's third wife, changing her name to Ratna Dewi Sari.

The Japanese link with Indonesian oil shows an important foreign contact with the Indonesian Army, and gives an intriguing glimpse of the Japanese business style. An approach to Ibnu Sutowo was made through Nishijima Shigetada, a private consultant, on behalf of industrial interests who had become interested in Indonesian petroleum during the war reparations talks. In the guise of a shop assistant in a Japanese store, Nishijima had been an intelligence agent in Bandung from 1937 to 1941. Later he had met Indonesian nationalists as a staff member with Admiral Maeda Tadashi, the war-time commander of eastern Indonesia, who encouraged the 17 August 1945 declaration of the Indonesian Republic. Through old contacts Nishijima met Ibnu Sutowo in June 1958. Because several competing Japanese interests soon became involved, Prime Minister Kishi invited a prominent businessman, Kobayashi Ataru, to negotiate with Permina on behalf of a cartel virtually representing 'Japan Incorporated'. A survey team from Tokyo recommended an investment of $50 million in Permina, and a provisional agreement was signed by Kishi and Sukarno in 1959. But because Kobayashi failed to convince the Keidanren, Japan's business federation, to subscribe funds the Japanese Export–Import Bank was called in.

This sparked the first row involving one of Ibnu Sutowo's ventures and the international banks. At the time Japan was borrowing $200 million from the World Bank, which objected to an amount equal to one quarter of it being lent externally. Permina set a deadline on the deal. Shortly before this expired Kishi authorized the finance, defying the World Bank. Ibnu Sutowo's bravado had succeeded. The agreement was a step towards the 'production-sharing' contract pioneered by Ibnu, in that a $53 million credit over ten years was to be repaid by fixed percentages of Permina's crude oil output over the same period. To carry out the deal Japanese business and government combined in a new company, North Sumatra Oil Development Company (Nosodeco) with Nishijima, the former Bandung spy, as its Jakarta representative.[3]

Permina and Ibnu Sutowo were still small in the Indonesian oil industry. By tacit agreement during the revolution and with the backing of property guarantees in the 1949 accord, the three big companies who had dominated the Dutch Indies petroleum industry returned to their old concessions, with the exception of Shell's North Sumatra area and some of its Central Java plant. While the Indonesian government debated an oil policy, Caltex (a joint venture of Standard Oil of California and Texaco), Stanvac (founded by Standard Oil of New Jersey and Standard Oil of New York, now Mobil), and Shell, operated under short-term agreements, raising national production from 152 000 barrels a day in 1951 to 373 000 barrels a day in 1959, with nearly all the increase coming from the new Caltex 'Minas' field near Pekanbaru, Central Sumatra.

As the army's company Permina was given charge of the deserted North Sumatra oil-fields, national control was consolidated over two smaller ventures. Former Shell oil-fields in Central Java went to a small company, Nglobo Oil Mining, which was controlled by the Diponegoro Division, while a long-standing joint venture between Shell and the government was separated from the Shell management structure and named Permindo. In 1960 a new law, number 44, was issued to cover the management of the national oil industry, including foreign companies. The law reserved oil and gas exploitation for state enterprises, but added that contractors could be employed if the state was incapable of meeting the task. Relations between the contractors and the state enterprises (which were unspecified) would be governed by a 'contract of work' to be ratified by law. Soon after the law was enacted in 1961 the three existing state oil companies became designated enterprises under it:

Permina, the former Nglogo Oil Mining (renamed Permigan) and the government–Shell joint venture, Permindo (which became Pertamin).

The problem then became to bring the 'Big Three' foreign companies within the ambit of the law and to define their operating terms. The negotiations took over two years against a background of turmoil and change in the world oil business. The Organization of Petroleum Exporting Countries (OPEC) had been formed in 1960 and host countries were generally extracting greater benefits from the 'Seven sisters' who dominated the oil production of the non-communist world. Indonesia joined OPEC in 1962 when Jakarta officials (including Ibnu Sutowo) had become well acquainted with the ideas of its founding members. A decree by Sukarno in August 1961 unilaterally settled two main issues. Earnings were to be split 60:40 in favour of the government, instead of the previous 50:50 arrangement. The Indonesian Government would take part in setting prices of crude oil and refined products.

It took a further ultimatum from Sukarno in mid-1963 to reach final agreement. The companies were given seven weeks to reach accord with Jakarta or get out. This move brought in the US State Department which, anxious to retain American influence in Indonesia, chaired a meeting of the parties in Tokyo. A single all-night session saw major concessions given to the Indonesians. The companies relinquished existing arrangements and became contractors to the state firms: Caltex to Pertamin, Stanvac to Permina and Shell to Permigan. They were given twenty-year contracts on the former concessions and thirty-year contracts for new areas. The 60:40 profit split was accepted, and Indonesia allowed to check on pricing. The government gained the right to take a certain proportion of its share in oil, while domestic supplies were to be contributed at cost plus fixed fees. The companies retained management and control of their production facilities, but had to sell off their refining and domestic supply operations.

This settlement was bitterly contested by the Indonesian Communist Party and its affiliated unions. The three companies experienced continual labour unrest and official harassment. Caltex was the best protected by virtue of its remote location in the swamps of Riau, and Shell was the most vulnerable because of its Dutch and British ownership. By 1965 both Shell and Stanvac, experiencing declining production and little chance of getting on with new exploration, had decided to sell out. Negotiations were nearly finished at the time of the coup. Stanvac withdrew from the sale, but Shell proceeded. Early in 1966 it sold out to the government for $110 million, payable over five years. Ibnu Sutowo, as chief negotiator, saw that the assets went to his own firm, Permina. When he purged PKI unionists from Permigan it was decided to break up this small state enterprise. Its main bureaucratic domain, supervision of oil and gas throughout Java and Eastern Indonesia, also went to Permina. The formation in 1965 of a new joint venture with Permina's Japanese friends, Far East Oil Trading Co. Ltd, to sell exclusively Indonesia's oil to Japan, likewise extended Ibnu Sutowo's dominance of the Indonesian oil industry, as well as opening up what became Indonesia's biggest oil market for the next decade.

How Ibnu Sutowo's relationship with Suharto began has never been revealed. That it was close from 1966 onwards is an undisputed fact in Indonesia. The involvement of Palembang interests, linked by repute to Ibno Sutowo's business group, with the Diponegoro Division's fund-raising activities during Suharto's tenure as Central Java commander, and the Diponegoro interest in Permigan would indicate an earlier connection. According to some Western intelligence sources, Ibnu Sutowo's encouragement and his agreement to finance Suharto was crucial to Suharto's decision to move against Sukarno early in 1966. Some of these sources claim the initiative in fact came from Ibnu Sutowo.

Ibnu Sutowo and Suharto quickly developed a working friendship that Suharto defined as *tepo seliru*, a Javanese term usually translated as 'mutual understanding' and signifying a deep, intuitive accord. When Suharto lost his simple soldier image and assumed the remote dignity of a well-entrenched ruler, Ibnu Sutowo was one of the very few inner courtiers who continued to talk to him in familiar Javanese instead of the elaborate high Javanese appropriate to a superior. Suharto needed Ibnu Sutowo to get things done. He needed Permina to provide funds for a threadbare army, to wean troops away from regional commanders, and to carry out essential political patronage. Ibnu Sutowo provided access to a vast, invisible system of taxation and expenditure that would be difficult to justify to the public if added to the official budget. He also needed Ibnu Sutowo to maintain the self-esteem of Indonesians: Ibnu's Permina was an outstanding example of local enterprise keeping up with the big foreign corporations and even bending them to its will. Moreover, it was run by indigenous Indonesians, not Chinese.

In return he gave protection. The first important demonstration of this came in 1966 when Ibnu clashed with the Minister of Mines, Slamet Bratanata. Ibnu Sutowo, as head of Permina and Director-General for Oil and Gas, was officially answerable to Bratanata. Ibnu Sutowo had at last gained firm interest in his production-sharing contracts. Several foreign 'independent' oil companies (i.e. those not tied to the seven oil 'majors') had accepted contracts conceding Permina management control and splitting takings out of production rather than profit. The company agreed to carry all pre-production risks and to be recouped by a maximum 40 per cent deduction from eventual production. The remaining output would be split 65:35 towards the government via the state enterprise. All equipment would become Permina property immediately it entered Indonesian territory.

Mines Minister Bratanata flatly opposed the concept, believing such Indonesian management control would be illusory and that the existing 'contracts of work' were necessary to ensure rapid foreign investment. Disregarding explicit, written directives from his minister in favour of work contracts, and despite the fact that under Law 44 of 1960 his signature was by no means sufficient endorsement, Ibnu blithely continued to sign up American and Japanese firms throughout 1966. The dispute reached a head in November 1966 when Suharto bluntly told the minister to let Ibnu Sutowo have his way. Bratanata persisted. In January 1967 he offered offshore leases in areas already covered in Ibnu's contracts. Two days later Suharto excised Ibnu Sutowo's domains from the Mining Ministry, making them part of his own presidential responsibility.

The arrangements continued until Bratanata was dropped from the Cabinet in October 1967 and replaced by a rather more sympathetic minister, Dr Sumantri Brodjonegoro, an academic engineer. In 1968 the second state oil firm, Pertamina, was merged into Permina to create a single state company, Pertamina (Pertambangan Minyak dan Gas Bumi Nasional, or National Oil and Gas Mining). Doubts over the legality of production-sharing contracts were not cleared up until new legislation was passed in 1971. It was conceded that no contract was valid until ratified by legislative procedure under Law 44. But Ibnu Sutowo found his reputation enough to sweep aside such irritating strictures. In the four years from 1966 over thirty foreign oil companies entered production-sharing contracts. At first they were the small independents, often in *ad hoc* alliance. Then, when it became clear that the choice exploration areas were being snapped up, the oil majors joined in.

The production-sharing contract was often cited as a tighter squeeze on the oil companies, an assertion of Indonesian control. But as one analyst, Robert Fabrikant, noted: 'The legal differences between production-sharing contracts and concession contracts are often void of operational significance'.[4] He saw the advantage for the Indonesian Government more in 'short-term political benefits' and a long-term promise of real control. On the financial side the payment in production avoided the arduous, often impossible task of checking profit across international frontiers. The contracts helped Indonesia to get in on the fringe benefits of oil exploration, the contracting work and supply. For the company the arrangement entailed less haggling over financial returns, and provided a strong local agent to deal with the bureaucracy, since Pertamina took over many of the ordinarily time-consuming administrative tasks such as arranging visas and work permits. It was also a generous deal. The 40 per cent cost deduction was usually allowed in full, no matter how little money had been invested. Together with the profit cut, contractors gained a percentage of the price fetched by each barrel of oil vastly higher than that fetched by firms in the Middle East. This was justified, they claimed, by the more costly nature of Indonesia's offshore or jungle-swamp discoveries.

As time went by Pertamina tightened the terms. Production thresholds were introduced to set higher government takes above set output levels. 'Signature bonuses', usually $5 million, were demanded. Companies were obliged to contribute certain percentages of total output for domestic consumption at cost plus 20 cents a barrel to Pertamina. Thus, and in apparent violation of laws against state enterprises doing so, an enormous amount of cash flowed through Pertamina: share of profits from Caltex and Stanvac, various bonuses, eventually a share of the new offshore finds, the proceeds of its own production, and profits from a range of marketing, shipping and insurance subsidiaries established in Tokyo, Los Angeles, Hong Kong and Singapore. The flow increased as Indonesia's production climbed from 510 000 barrels a day in 1967 to 1 080 000 by 1972.

Ibnu Sutowo's free-wheeling personal style of life blossomed. He himself saw no need, and a positive disadvantage, in wearing sackcloth and ashes while developing the oil industry. 'It is simply not psychologically possible for men who wear threadbare clothing and who ride in old cars or *becaks* to negotiate satisfactorily with men who earn $50 000 a year and fly by company jet aircraft', he argued.[5] Pertamina's star and seahorse emblem became emblazoned on status symbols throughout Indonesia, attracting the anger of students and intellectuals who had once supported Suharto for his stand against Sukarno's corrupt Old Order. Sutowo's monstrously extravagant wedding party for his daughter in 1969 put him in the firing-line of protesters later in the year. This criticism was supported by a hard-hitting series of exposés of dubious Pertamina deals by the journalist, Mochtar Lubis, in his newspaper *Indonesia Raya*.

As we have seen in chapter 6, Suharto was forced by public pressure to appoint, in January 1970, a 'Commission of four' to investigate charges against Pertamina and other instances of alleged corruption. The commission produced hard-hitting reports which were leaked in July 1970 to the Jakarta newspaper *Sinar Harapan*. Pertamina was found to have badly neglected its duty to pass on to the Treasury much of the revenue it collected on the government's behalf. The commission pointed out several instances of illegality, relating to Pertamina's foreign subsidiaries and bank accounts, and brought to light the skimpy nature of the company's internal auditing. The inquiry did result in a new law instituting more formal controls through a Board of Commissioners (chaired by the Minister of Mines) responsible to the president. But the substance of the highly embarrassing report of the Commission of Four was ignored. In practice Ibnu Sutowo's lines of responsibility went over the head of ministers and directly into the presidential palace. Suharto was soon quoted as telling Pertamina employees, at the opening of a new offshore field, to forget the critics and get on with the job.[6]

The seeds of the later disaster were sown in 1972. In December 1971 Indonesia had been promised an unprecedented $670 million in IGGI assistance for the year ahead. In March 1972 it concluded a standby agreement with the IMF which required a ceiling on medium-term loans, defined as loans repayable between one and fifteen years. In October that year the government issued a decree requiring state corporations and other bodies to seek Finance Ministry approval for any such medium-term borrowings. But by the end of 1972 the IMF and the US Government found that during 1972 Pertamina had borrowed over $350 million, much of it medium and short-term, without officially informing the government. This was estimated to have doubled the corporation's total foreign debt. The IMF and the US State Department began applying pressure on Jakarta. American aid was temporarily suspended, and Ibnu Sutowo warned that finance he was relying on from the US Export–Import Bank was in jeopardy. US authorities canvassed American banks to stop them plying Pertamina with loan offers. In February 1973 Vice-President Spiro Agnew raised the problem with Suharto during a visit to Jakarta. But Suharto delivered a vigorous defence of Ibnu Sutowo, saying he had personally charged him with important national projects and trusted the oil chief to find his own finance. Shortly afterwards US aid resumed. Pertamina quietly left the medium-term loan field, but IMF and IGGI recommendations that Pertamina's ministerial-level Board of Commissioners be given more effective control went unheeded.

This compromise turned out to be more dangerous than the original problem. Ibnu Sutowo had been stopped taking loans of one- to fifteen-year terms, and the foreign banks virtually barred from extending them. Instead Ibnu Sutowo began taking loans of less than twelve-months duration, relying on his ability to roll them over on expiration, or else took long-term loans that had repayments heavily weighted to the early period of their terms. The years 1973 and 1974 saw vigorous growth and competition in foreign lending by Western banks, especially among many smaller institutions eager to expand their loan portfolios. Short-term lending was highly profitable, and the risks seemed lessened by Pertamina's position within Indonesia and the strength of the oil industry generally. Normally sober-minded American and European bankers lent huge sums to Pertamina without sighting a single balance sheet that could have given a realistic summary of the company's financial position. Perhaps such a statement existed nowhere outside Ibnu Sutowo's head, since six separate accounting systems were used by Pertamina. According to an American journalist, Seth Lipsky, who has closely followed Pertamina, the first stirrings of anxiety came for one US banker when he noticed at Pertamina headquarters an open filing-cabinet drawer with loan agreements casually tossed inside.[7]

It was a royal time for Ibnu Sutowo. A massive investment by Caltex saw its production reach 1 million barrels a day, while from the early 1970s the offshore platforms of the production-sharing contractors were contributing to bring total national output to nearly 1.5 million barrels a day by 1975. Ibnu Sutowo confidently predicted that Indonesia would produce 3 million barrels a day by 1980. Not only that; Indonesia also multiplied its oil income because of the price rises set by OPEC in 1973–4. The price of Indonesian crude rose from $1.70 a barrel in October 1970 to $4.75 in mid-1973, then after the Middle East War and boycotts (in which Indonesia took no part) climbed steeply to $12.60 a barrel by mid-1974. From being a country with a chronic balance of payments problem, Indonesia's position seemed reversed. Gross foreign exchange earnings from oil rose from $965 million in 1972–3 to $5200 million in 1974–5 (and a lesser commodities boom more than doubled non-oil exports over the same period, although oil's proportion of total exports rose from 50 per cent to 72 per cent). The annual total of investment by foreign companies in Indonesian oil rose also by a factor of five to nearly $1000 million in 1975. The funds flowed through Pertamina into the central bank (Bank Indonesia) and a certain amount stuck to the pipe along the way.

Pertamina needed all the funds it could get. Not only was it initiating a vast diversification programme itself, but

Ibnu Sutowo was the willing recipient of new tasks entrusted to him by Suharto, many of them only distantly related to petroleum. Two huge liquified natural gas projects were begun in East Kalimantan and Aceh with American partners at a cost of a billion dollars each. Fertilizer, petrochemical and refinery plants added hundreds of millions of dollars more to the programme. The Pertamina oil tanker fleet was rapidly built up on hire-purchase to total more than 3 million tonnes. The Pertamina airline, Pelita, purchased South-East Asia's biggest fleet of helicopters and branched out into jet passenger aircraft, even though this was officially reserved for the national carrier, Garuda. Work began to turn the island of Batam in the Malacca Straits into a new industrial entrepôt to rival Singapore. The untried concept of a floating fertilizer plant, to be anchored over offshore gasfields, was adopted and European machinery manufacturers set to work. The heaviest task lay in the Krakatau Steel project at Cilegon in West Java, where an earlier Soviet-built steel mill had been rusting since 1965. The economics of the Krakatau plant were dubious from the start: the site had no nearby sources of ore, energy, or trained manpower, and basic infrastructure was entirely missing. But Ibnu Sutowo took on the task, raised the planned output target four times, and engaged a West German–Dutch consortium to build an innovatory steel mill using gas which had to be piped from 220 kilometres away. The cost of Krakatau Steel alone was estimated at about $2500 million.

Pertamina donated roads, schools, mosques, and a massive new hospital in Jakarta. Its network of hotels, guest houses and offices stretched from North Sumatra into the remote Baliem Valley of Irian Jaya. Its senior executives basked in luxury that rivalled that of their oil industry counterparts in Houston and the Gulf. One celebrated his birthday with a party in Geneva. Another group amused themselves with a safari in East Africa. Those so inclined took their pick of models at lunchtime 'fashion parades' in Jakarta's new hotels. Among equipment on order in 1974 was a Boeing 727 jet fitted out for executive travel. Ibnu Sutowo found himself courted as local partner for a variety of non-oil ventures – all in his spare time of course – that included car importing, metal-working and cattle ranching.

It was a heady time and, as the economist Peter McCawley has pointed out in his study of the Indonesian economy under Suharto,[8] not only Pertamina became careless. That much of the new foreign wealth was spent as though it were domestic revenue contributed greatly to inflationary pressures that had broken out with the rice crisis of 1972–3, forcing inflation to over 30 per cent by 1974. This was exacerbated by a boom mentality that spread among officials from the president down. One of Suharto's projects was a domestic satellite and communications investment that was to total $1400 million. In contrast to preceding years when budgets were actually underspent, expenditure went over budget by 35 per cent in 1973–4 and by 25 per cent in 1974–5. The Technocrats had lost control, but at the time it no longer seemed to matter.

Towards the end of 1974, Ibnu Sutowo was also beginning to lose control of the Pertamina conglomerate. The recession in the Western industrialized countries, ironically a result of the oil price surge, had its effects on the supply of short-term funds, as had the crash of two Western banks during the year. It was increasingly hard to roll over Pertamina's bundle of short-term loans, now amounting to some $1500 million owing to foreign creditors. A curious parallel to events a year later in Australia occurred.[9] Ibnu insisted he was offered by a London-based financier, acting on behalf of Middle East interests, a long-term, moderate-interest loan of $1700 million; the Australian Labor Party Minister for Minerals and Energy, Rex Connor, believed he could raise up to $4000 million in cheap loans from a similar broker in London. According to sources close to Ibnu Sutowo,

President Suharto himself had signed documents to help raise the loan. But it fell through. The big difference with the Connor–Khemlani loan affair in Australia was that Ibnu Sutowo, by signing contracts to quadruple production at Krakatau Steel, had already committed the money.

In February and March 1975 Pertamina fell behind in repayments to the Republic National Bank of Dallas and the Toronto Dominion Bank. As US banking regulators began pressuring banks to get clear of Pertamina, Indonesia's allies became aware that the country's entire financial structure hung in the balance, not least because US banks had placed 'cross-default' clauses in their loan agreements, whereby if a default occurred in one loan, all other lending could be called in. If such an economic crisis was to occur, the future of the Suharto Government would also be on the line.

The fact that Pertamina was heading for trouble had been a talking-point for some months in the cocktail circuits and other rumour mills where Jakarta's Indonesian and foreign decision-makers traditionally flesh out the skimpy information available on public record. The true dimensions of the Pertamina debt burden were not to be revealed for over a year, perhaps even to the handful of officials who worked frantically to avoid a crash. Perhaps this was just as well. As the US State Department persuaded American banks not to call in their loans, the head of the Indonesian central bank, the Rachmat Saleh, sent out a tersely worded statement to Pertamina's creditors. Bank Indonesia had taken over responsibility for meeting outstanding obligations, and Pertamina would not roll over any of its short-term loans nor 'borrow directly from the international market for the foreseeable future'.

Rachmat Saleh's central bank began paying out $207 million in March 1975 alone, and $1021 million over the next six months. Suharto, having responded slowly to the warning signs of late 1974, at last acted decisively, chopping the large non-oil projects out of the Pertamina empire and handing them over to the Technocrats. The Krakatau Steel project was given to Dr Sumarlin, the deputy of Dr Widjojo Nitisastro in the state planning body. When the Krakatau's director proved unco-operative, and was found to have awarded himself substantial benefits including a million-dollar house and personal helicopter from company funds, he was immediately sacked. Sumarlin then moved to discuss contracts with Krakatau's West German and Dutch builders. Perhaps because it was pointed out that the project was costing three times the price of a similar steel plant in Taiwan, the contractors proved willing to cut Krakatau back towards its original size, saving $750 million in future payments. Some projects were dropped altogether, and others trimmed down. Sumarlin haggled successfully with contractors and suppliers, since Pertamina had partly to get things done quickly, and partly for less creditable motives, been noted for its over-generosity in prices. American accountants were engaged to begin sorting out Pertamina's books, and a group of European and North American merchant banks was engaged to put together large medium-term commercial loans to cover the pay-out on short-term debts. Although the ripples were still spreading throughout the business communities of North America, Europe, Asia and Australia, by mid-year the immediate cash problems were overcome.

In June 1975, Economics Minister Widjojo Nitisastro gave the first comprehensive statement on the situation to DPR (Parliament), putting a tentative estimate of $2300 million on Pertamina's overseas debt ($1500 million of this was short-term) and $120 million on local moneys owing. But as Suharto continued with the reorganization of Pertamina, ironically following the broad lines recommended so fruitlessly by the Commission of Four five years earlier, rumours spread of a much larger debt burden. Suharto spoke in ominous terms of the Pertamina crisis in his budget speech to the DPR in January 1976. Then, early in March 1976 Ibnu Sutowo was suddenly 'dismissed with honour' from his post as Pertamina chief. In April the Minister of Mines, Mohammad Sadli, went before Parliament. He confirmed the worst rumours.

Pertamina's total commitments had been $10 500 million at the beginning of 1975. But cancellations and renegotiations had cut this to about $7600 million, of which $1400 million was no longer within Pertamina's responsibility. The most startling revelation was that Ibnu Sutowo had plunged heavily into the international supertanker trade, committing Pertamina to the purchase or charter of some thirty-four tankers, totalling approximately 3 million tonnes, at a total cost of about $3300 million, payable at the rate of nearly $300 million a year. However, with the industrial countries in recession, the tanker market was in the doldrums. Pertamina's tankers were laid up from the fiords of Norway to the backwaters of East Asian ports, earning nothing.

At what point Suharto decided to sack Ibnu Sutowo has not been reliably determined. Certainly in the early stages of the rescue Ibnu Sutowo displayed every sign that he still enjoyed much of the president's confidence, indeed that Suharto felt himself as partly to blame for having heaped development tasks on Ibnu. According to one contemporary rumour, Suharto's attitude changed abruptly around December 1975 when the tanker debt became clear. By that time the budget for 1976–7 would have been framed, and Suharto would have realized how greatly Indonesia's economic future would be affected by the Pertamina affair. A final, galling factor might have been Ibnu Sutowo's unwillingness to put on even a show of repentance. It was noted that Ibnu Sutowo had virtually gate-crashed the Association of South-East Asian Nations (ASEAN) summit conference in Bali in February 1976, shortly before his dismissal. Ibnu Sutowo's successor, the former military administrator, Major-General Piet Haryono, who had worked for many years with the Technocrats as the Finance Ministry's Director of Budgeting, quickly carried out a purge of Ibnu's senior management, at one stage carpeting the more conspicuously corrupt officials for a group tongue-lashing in which he called them 'cannibals'.

The tanker deals provided the hardest fought episodes in the Pertamina rescue. As well as being white elephants in the over-supplied world tanker market that developed in 1974, the ships were soon found to be grossly over-priced. According to the Indonesian Government, just two of the ships entailed contingent liabilities of $900 million. Indonesia refused to pay, and braced itself for law suits. The network of ownership of the tankers ran through several hands in half a dozen countries. But the central figures in the deals with Ibnu Sutowo turned out to be three brokers, based in London, Geneva and New York respectively, whose interests overlapped. For eighteen months battles raged in the courts of London and New York, while accessory actions in several other capitals saw Pertamina ships and property 'attached', i.e. seized, against the outcome of the principal litigation. Finally, in August 1977, the two ministers in charge of the tanker affair, Sumarlin and Radius Prawiro, were able to announce that liabilities on twenty-seven ships had been reduced, from $2280 million down to $256 million, while it was hoped to cut the remaining debt, at that stage $470 million on seven ships, by further negotiation.

The Indonesian Government's most damaging evidence against the most heavily involved broker, Bruce Rappaport of the Geneva-based Intermaritime group, had been a sworn statement by Ibnu Sutowo. In it he admitted signing some 1600 promissory notes, which had a face value of $1266 million, in order to provide collateral to Rappaport. Ibnu Sutowo said he had not even read these notes as he signed. In addition Ibnu said he had asked for a $2.5 million loan from Rappaport, banked it in his own account, and never repaid it. He had failed to seek proper government approval for the tanker deals, and violated Indonesian law by sitting on the advisory board of Rappaport's Swiss bank. Rappaport replied by calling this affidavit 'an extracted banana republic confession'. However, the testimony served both Indonesia and Ibnu Sutowo. Soon after the settlement with Rappaport, the Indonesian Attorney-General announced that an 'investigation' of the tanker deals had cleared Ibnu Sutowo of any suspicion of corruption or conspiracy in the Rappaport contracts. Although other matters were left hanging over his head and he was instructed to stay out of the public eye, Ibnu Sutowo was left in comfortable retirement tending his private empire of thirty-seven companies.

What was the impact of the Pertamina affair? The most obvious result has been to increase greatly Indonesia's indebtedness. By how much is a matter of definition. By 1978 some of the very large projects such as Krakatau Steel and the liquified natural gas plants were coming on stream, thereby recovering outlays. Over half of the $10 500 million contingent liabilities outlined by Mohammad Sadli in April 1976 had, by the end of 1977, been expunged by project cancellation or renegotiation. Many of the projects that continued were based on dubious economics; others were more expensive than they might have been if rigorous feasibility work and tendering had been applied. But Indonesia was at least getting an impressive array of new industry and infrastructure whose cost would be lightened by inflation. On the other hand, the Pertamina 'state within a state' had initiated many of these schemes, mostly capital-intensive, with little regard for the priorities officially espoused by the government. Pertamina had pre-empted a large part of the government's resources for years to come.

The crisis coincided with marked changes in Indonesia's markets. Industrial nations experienced an economic recession. China began exporting oil to Japan at lower prices. Demand for Indonesian oil and other commodities weakened. This recession and the Pertamina crisis knocked the hopes of Indonesian planners and some foreign advisers that the oil boom heralded an era of rapid economic growth, backed by both strong exports and foreign aid and loans rising to some $4000 million a year in 1980. Instead of a billion dollar rise in reserves in 1975, Jakarta saw its foreign exchange holdings dwindle to almost nothing for an uncomfortable period around September that year. The central bank stopped publishing its statistics to cover the embarrassing position. Moreover, after the first round of borrowing to cover Pertamina's immediate commitments, foreign borrowing had to be reined in to just over half the originally planned level for the rest of the decade. Even then the net resource transfer (disbursement of new loans minus servicing of the old) was predicted to drop to a mere $130 million in 1979, when loan servicing would come within half a percentage point of the 20 per cent of exports generally regarded as the limit of comfortable borrowing.

One result of the squeeze was Suharto's decision to take more in taxes from the foreign oil companies. After the companies refused to concede a higher proportion of profit to the government, Suharto replied by issuing ultimatums just as Sukarno had effectively done in 1963. First Caltex and Stanvac, still working under the old contracts of work, then the production-sharing contractors reluctantly agreed to a rewriting of their operating agreements. Thus an additional $600 million was gathered; about half of which was reported to come from the $756 million repatriated profit level reached by Caltex in 1975. Many other factors were at work, but the government's decision was followed by the almost complete withdrawal of foreign oil exploration rigs from Indonesia. It was not for over two years that drillers returned, too late to prevent national oil production levelling off and declining by the end of the 1970s. Before this occurred revived exports, particularly to the USA which took over from Japan as Indonesia's biggest oil customer in 1977, and earlier discoveries took oil production up to 1.7 million barrels a day in 1977. Together with improvements in other exports, Indonesia's debt position eased from the gloomy days of 1975–6, and the tight ceilings on borrowing were allowed to rise in 1978.

After a heady few years oil and its glittering technology had come to be seen as helpful, but a distraction from Indonesia's basic problems. The boom was over.

NOTES

1 Anthony J. S. Reid, *Indonesian National Revolution 1945–50*, Longman, Melbourne, 1974, p. 125–6.
2 Anderson G. Bartlett *et al.*, *Pertamina, Indonesian National Oil*, Amerasian, Jakarta, Singapore and Tulsa, 1972, p. 206. This semi-official company history proved a valuable source on Pertamina's antecedents and history, as have contemporary articles in the *Bulletin of Indonesian Economic Studies*, through to the present.
3 Masashi Nishihara, *The Japanese and Sukarno's Indonesia: Tokyo–Jakarta Relations 1951–1966*, monograph of the Center for South-East Asian Studies, University of Kyoto, published as an East-West Center Book, University Press of Hawaii, pp. 117–21.
4 Robert Fabrikant, *Legal Aspects of the Production-Sharing Contracts in the Indonesian Petroleum Industry*, Field Report Series no. 3, Institute of South-East Asian Studies, Singapore, 1973, p. 128.
5 Bartlett *et al.*, op. cit., p. 13.
6 Ibid., p. 322–3.
7 Seth Lipsky, 'The Billion Dollar Bubble', in Seth Lipsky (ed.), *The Billion Dollar Bubble*, Dow Jones, Hong Kong, 1978.
8 Peter McCawley, 'The Indonesian Economy under Suharto: A Survey', working paper, Research School of Pacific Studies, Australian National University, 1978, p. 74.
9 Peter McCawley, 'Some Consequences of the Pertamina Crisis in Indonesia', *Journal of Southeast Asian Studies*, vol. IX, no. 1, March 1978, pp. 13–16.

8. Village and Kampung

Across the road from the gleaming Bappenas building in Jakarta in which Indonesia's economic planners set their growth targets, a different kind of dream is marketed. Along the iron railings of a neat park small traders have set up an informal art gallery to sell gaudily coloured visions of agrarian Java: towering volcanoes, sunlight glistening on paddy fields, red-flowering flamboyant trees set against deep-green jungle, mysterious forest pools; a land populated by full-breasted women in *sarong-kebaya,* and hard-working men ploughing rich, damp soil.

More or less refined versions of the same paintings are often found in the formal front rooms of the more prosperous homes throughout Indonesia. The beauty of the land and its people can exceed the image, no more so than on the inner islands of Java and Bali. Despite the growth of towns and industries under later colonial rule and independence, Indonesia remains a predominantly agrarian country with some 85 per cent of its people living in rural areas and about 70 per cent drawing directly on agriculture for a substantial part of their livelihood.

The realities of life in the villages are far from the harmonious ideal. These inner islands remain caught in an ecological trap, placing a question mark over the achievements of both the Technocratic planning apparatus and entrepreneurs like Ibnu Sutowo. Under the Suharto Government, a large proportion of village people seem to have gained little of the overall rise in prosperity, and some may have seen their welfare actually decline. Even the beauty and fertility of Java is threatened because the desperate efforts of this poorer class to scratch a living are turning large parts of the island into what some scientists warn could soon become arid savannah.

For perhaps 150 years population has been moving further and further out of balance with the land. During the brief British rule over Java in the Napoleonic wars, Stamford Raffles estimated that the island's population stood in 1815 at 4.5 million. By the end of the century it was close to 30 million, and by 1930, when the first reliable census was made, it had reached nearly 41 million. It was a period of tragically misused opportunities, attributable to the Dutch colonial system and to the nature of Javanese society. The Dutch built up a booming plantation sector, the surplus from which financed the industrialization of the Netherlands rather than being employed in Java to absorb the expanding population. The Javanese turned inwards, applying more and more hands to work the paddy fields while intricate social arrangements helped divide the yield. Where the paddies could not be enlarged, dry-farming was extended up onto previously forested slopes, exposing the soil to erosion. Food production increased, but per capita yields remained static. The Javanese shared their poverty, while immigrant groups such as the Chinese, preferred by the Dutch on political grounds, tended to dominate the secondary and tertiary spin-off from Dutch investment.

The Great Depression (which severely hit the export industries of the Dutch Indies), the disruption incurred by the Japanese occupation and the struggle for independence, and the economic stagnation of the Sukarno era did little to change the structure, except for replacing the Dutch with a new Indonesian elite in the commercial sector. The essential 'dualism' of the economy remained. The population of Indonesia, however, had grown to 97 million by 1961 (when the republic's first census was taken), of whom 63 million were in Java (which here includes the island of Madura, part of East Java Province). After quick results from rehabilitation during the first three years of independence, food production in Indonesia barely kept pace with population increase and in the last years of the Old Order was marked by a shift away from rice to corn and other dry crops, possibly because irrigation and services were neglected.

The situation that the Suharto Government faced when it took power was that welfare levels had been declining in rural Java throughout this century, as measured in falling real earnings, falling nutritional standards, and even falling average body sizes. The average intake of calories and protein among Javanese was already well below internationally recommended standards in 1960, and was still lower by 1967. Whereas in 1905 nearly 70 per cent of rural landowners in rural Java held an average of 1.27 hectares, the average landholding was by 1966 less than half a hectare, and the landless engaged in agriculture had risen from a small fraction to over 30 per cent. Small farmers and labourers were often deeply in debt to wealthier patrons, working off their credit at punitive rates of return. In the more arid areas famine was a frequent occurrence between harvests. For years Indonesia had been the world's biggest rice importer. Population growth rates had reached 2.3 per cent per annum for all of Indonesia and 1.9 per cent for Java. Yet in 1964 Sukarno was still saying 'the more the better', arguing that Indonesia was capable of supporting two and a half times the 103 million it held that year.[1]

As we have seen in chapter 4, creation of a firm rural base which steadily increased output was an integral part of the Suharto Government's development plans. It was hoped that a new attack on agriculture in line with the 'Green Revolution' then under way through Asia would quickly produce dramatic increases in rice yields, bringing new prosperity to peasant farmers at all levels. New fast growing strains of 'miracle rice', artificial fertilizers, extension services, improved irrigation, and special credit facilities were introduced. Despite scepticism about the self-sufficiency target contained in the first five-year plan, rice production, aided by favourable seasons, got off to a good start.

In 1972, after several good years, it suddenly became apparent that the agricultural programme was deeply in trouble. A long dry season caused a drought in many parts of Java, resulting in a sharp drop in rice output of about half a million tonnes. The shortfall caught the national commodities distribution agency, Bulog, unprepared. It was forced to resort to the international market during world grain shortage, incurring a heavy import bill and failing to meet needs. As we have seen in chapter 4, resulting sharp increases in domestic rice prices triggered off a sharp increase in inflation that proved difficult to control in the oil and commodities boom of the next two years. The authorities also attempted to make up the shortfall in Bulog stocks by increased local purchasing early in 1973. A series of targets were transmitted down to local level, requiring district administrations to acquire set amounts of rice at government-determined prices which were substantially below prevailing market levels. Farmers were understandably reluctant to sell. In some areas officials under pressure from above resorted to force to buy rice. Others accepted cash from farmers who had sold off family possessions, but then had to scour markets for rice to deliver to central stocks. Before the purchasing programme was called off, after a highly critical Defence Department report on the disruption being caused by 'target fever', enormous damage had been done to the already fragile relationship between government and farmer, particularly since many newly established village co-operatives had been charged with executing the programme.

Some disturbing data had begun to emerge also about the trend of agricultural development in Java, even without drought-induced crisis. While rice output had been increasing under the New Order, production of important crops such as maize, cassava, peanuts and soya beans had dwindled or stagnated, causing a serious loss in available protein as well as subtracting from total food output. It appeared that much of the early gain in rice had come from substitution for other crops or from rehabilitation of run-down infrastructure, rather than improved yields.

The new rice technology itself had not provided uniformly beneficial results in Java, partly because of inherent biological factors and partly because of the social and political context in which it had been applied. The new wet rice varieties have a shortened growth period, and are not as sensitive to seasonal changes as the old varieties. This permits five crops to be grown in two years as against two or three crops. Yet they are more susceptible to drought, insect attack, flooding, and careless weeding than the old types. The multiple cropping means that pests nearly always have a host plant nearby so that their cycle of existence is not broken. Moreover, the taste of the new rice strains is rated by Javanese as inferior to that of the old grains, so that the new rice tends to attract lower prices. The need for greater inputs such as fertilizer and irrigation makes them more costly to grow. As an American economist, William Collier, reports from work with Indonesian Government agricultural surveys:

> In our studies in Java we only rarely found that the high yielding varieties (HYVs) had significantly higher yields than the local varieties when averages were compared... Since the HYVs require more purchased inputs, these relatively small gross rice yield differences by varieties mean that average farmers' net returns are not significantly different between traditional and modern varieties.[2]

The political and bureaucratic framework also mitigated against the careful management needed to handle the more complex rice technology. New approaches to agriculture began around 1960 when artificial fertilizers were first used, although success was limited by foreign exchange problems. Then in 1963 students from the country's leading agricultural college in Bogor worked in three West Java villages to lend advice, and to intercede with often disinterested or corrupt officials to ensure the peasants received seeds, fertilizer and insecticides. They achieved an immediate 50 per cent increase in output on the 105 hectares covered. When the idea, called Bimas (mass guidance), was taken over by the government the next year it was applied to 11 000 hectares and then to 462 000 hectares by late 1966. The results were in inverse ratio to the area, because skilled and dedicated extension workers were not available. However, Bimas programmes were pushed ahead to cover more than 2 million hectares or 27 per cent of the area under rice by 1969.

The Bimas schemes came to be regarded in many areas as another government imposition on farmers, and frequently they were just that. Very soon widespread defaults in Bimas credit became a huge budget problem for the government. The employment of large European chemical corporations in 1969 to provide a package of Bimas services also caused resentment, especially when use of new insecticides had the side-effect of killing fish in village ponds. Moreover, this particular experiment soon became notorious for corruption. One particularly gross example was that of an unknown Liechtenstein-based company which, after being awarded a contract, failed to make any contribution for the $400 000 paid to it, and was exposed in the Jakarta press as being owned by a group of army officers on Suharto's personal staff. Suharto refused to let the case go to court.

A rather more deeply embedded and pervasive shortcoming derived from the village political system as it developed after 1965. In Java, village rule has traditionally been invested in a *lurah* (headman), usually elected for life. A substantial amount of patronage and voter-bribery, usually from the wealthier sections of the village community, is often involved in the election. Once installed, the headman receives, instead of a salary, a parcel of village land which generates income. Other village officials are similarly imbursed. A natural alignment of interest between village leadership and local wealth often follows. As the killings and arrests on Java in 1965–6 virtually wiped out bodies which articulated the interests of less privileged groups, and added a fear of organizations in general to an age-old fear of government, this village leadership grew even more free of control or countervailing pressure from below. Yet it was this leadership that was charged with setting up farmer co-operatives to administer the Bimas programmes, and to direct public works projects aimed at servicing agricultural producers. Predictably, complaints have been constant that village authorities have manipulated Bimas inputs to benefit their own circle. One Western irrigation expert working in Java describes the effects:

> The benefits from expenditure, if you look at them, are pretty God-awful. The pay-offs don't yet begin to approach the kinds of returns they should. One project near Jogjakarta was designed to irrigate 100 hectares, but reached only 10 to 12 hectares. The ownership of the land you can guess: village land used by the *lurah* and his colleagues. I get the impression this is pretty typical of the labour-intensive projects.[3]

Along with the new rice varieties have come drastic changes in the organization and technology of working rice in Java, changes that have sharply reduced work opportunities for rural labour. A 1973 government agro-economic survey found that some 30 per cent of those employed in agriculture were landless. Of these with land, almost 60 per cent owned an average of 0.25 hectares (equivalent to a 50-metre square) and were therefore dependent on outside work to supplement what they could grow themselves. Thus about two-thirds of the rural workforce stood to lose rather than gain from the direct effects of the new rice-growing methods. Only partly due to the new rice technology itself, these changes have been ascribed to population pressure breaking down old institutions as well as the greater inability of the poor to voice their interests in the post-1965 political system.

Traditionally landowners opened their harvest to anyone who wanted to join in, rewarding them with a percentage of rice they cut. As labour increased, large numbers of workers roamed further afield looking for harvest work until pressure of numbers reduced the harvesters' share of the rice. Often the landowners abandoned the old harvest arrangement and began selling their standing crop to contractors who selected their own harvest labour in limited numbers because they felt less obliged to provide work. This change alone was estimated by researchers from the Bogor Agricultural Institute to reduce employment in harvesting by at least 18 per cent. It came with a change from the use of a hand-knife, known as the *ani-ani*, to the sickle in cutting rice. The new rice strains seem to have enabled this change since they produce a more easily shattered stalk of even length. Moreover, where superstition allowed the traditional strains to be cut only with the *ani-ani* to avoid offending the Rice Goddess, this could now be dispensed with, since the new breeds were 'foreign'. According to some estimates, if both harvest contractors and the sickle were used employment was cut by 60 per cent. In Bali the transfer from knife to sickle was almost completed in the five or six years to 1978, with farmers placating their supernatural worries by leaving small patches to be cut by the knife and to be offered to the goddess.

Up to 1971 it was estimated that 80 per cent of Java's rice was hand-pounded to remove the husks, but within two years the proportion was put below 50 per cent. The women who pounded rice in a wooden trough were replaced by hundreds of mechanical mills. It was a loss of drudgery, but a relief only for the relatively few families who found work in the new mills. A permissive attitude by the authorities also enabled larger landowners to introduce mechanized tools. One study found that a paddy tractor in Java displaced 2210 man-days of human labour a year. In Java and Bali use of these tractors has diverted money away from labourers and small farmers (in Bali they often pooled resources to form buffalo-ploughing teams for general hire) towards larger landowners who could afford the tractors, and ultimately back to factories in industrial countries.

This change in technology struck hardest at women in the rural workforce. Pounding rice and harvesting with the *ani-ani* is mostly the preserve of women. Men work in the rice mill and wield the sickle (which is regarded as a 'male' instrument). If the family as a whole were compensated for the loss then abandonment of these traditional, dreary tasks might be welcomed, but this does not appear to be the case.[4]

Indonesian rice production recovered quickly from the 1972 crisis, and the various intensification programmes like Bimas were extended to cover nearly 50 per cent of the total area under rice. But after 1974 rice output has hovered above stagnation point. Growth in production has been disappointing at about 2.3 per cent a year, while the area under intensification has increased only marginally. The three years 1975–7 were beset with natural calamities in the rice-growing areas of Java and some other islands. Wet season floods were followed by droughts. Plagues of rats attacked crops, and a new insect pest, a tiny rice-hopper which transmitted plant disease, devastated huge tracts of riceland. Government spraying services proved to lack the organizational ability to respond to the insect swarms in time. The rice-hopper was able to develop into new biotypes as fast as scientists could get new rice variants in the fields. Severe hunger, often resulting in hunger oedema (the swollen belly of starvation), has been a regular dry season occurrence in the arid mountains of southern Java. At the end of 1977 a severe crop failure, caused by pests and drought, threatened the same precarious condition, where life can be measured in weeks, among an estimated 50 000 villagers only an hour's drive from Jakarta in a district known as the city's 'rice-bowl'. After newspaper reports of destitute peasants selling off their possessions down to the tiles from their roofs, and surviving on swamp-weed, the government mounted a relief operation. Circumstances were different from 1972. World rice stocks were high and prices low, while the state logistics agency, Bulog, had greatly improved its stockpiling capacity and market-watching. The agency mounted a quick, skilful buying operation in Asian markets to increase rice purchases from the planned 1.75 million tonnes to 2.6 million tonnes, roughly one-third of the world's export surplus, which was recognized as a dangerous level of external dependence.

The outcry that followed in the Jakarta press and political circles enormously heightened the tension around Suharto's re-election in March 1978, as we shall see in chapter 11. It also lent a new sense of urgency to the debate on development strategy that had surfaced, occasionally in violent form, from early in the 1970s. Many of the criticisms were reinforced when the results of a survey of social and economic welfare, taken by the Central Statistic Board in 1976, began to filter out through academic writings. Although Suharto had claimed in his 1977 Independence Day address that Indonesia had moved out of the United Nations category of extremely poor nations (those with per capita annual incomes less than $200), this was shown to be based more on monetary movements than real progress. Moreover, while it was agreed that overall real average income had increased steadily, the benefits were far from equally spread. The number of the extremely poor had increased absolutely and, some even argued, proportionally.

Most of this was attributable to the stubborn poverty of rural Java. Nationally, income levels had been increasing at about 4 per cent in real terms prior to 1976, as measured by gross domestic product per capita. This was not a spectacular gain, but one which, when compounded, raised income by about 50 per cent over ten years. In terms of prevailing prices this had taken income from $US131 a head in 1973 to $279 a head in 1976, while at constant 1973 prices the level had risen from $131 to $147.[5] One saddening estimate of how this has been distributed has come from the Bogor Agricultural Institute's leading researcher into village economics, Professor Sajogyo, who developed a measurement of basic income levels by equating all sources to their rice-purchasing equivalent.

Sajogyo put his rural poverty line at 240 kilograms of rice per person a year. At this level the individual would be spending about 80 per cent of income on food to maintain a calorie level of about 2000 a day, plus some protein such as groundnuts and dried fish. A 50 per cent higher income is needed in the cities to maintain the same level of welfare. Clearly this is the level at which destitution and dangerous deprivation becomes mere poverty, rather than being a poverty line in the Western sense.

Sajagyo found that over a six-year period to early 1976, the proportion of 'very poor', people below this line in Indonesia fell from 36.4 per cent to 33.4 per cent, although their numbers increased by about 2.4 million to 45.1 million. However, within this group those on an 'extremely poor' income level of only 180 kilograms rice equivalent a year rose from 19.7 per cent of the total population to 20.2 per cent, their numbers rising from 23.1 million to 27.3 million. Thus, while the 'very poor' declined as a proportion within the population (and the percentage of 'moderately poor', with rice equivalent incomes between 240 and 320 kilograms in the villages also declined) Sajagyo found that the poor became poorer.

In cities and towns, both on Java and on other islands, the number of poor in all categories dropped proportionally and absolutely, while in rural areas outside Java there were significant proportionate declines with a small increase in absolute numbers. On Java, the proportion of poor in all categories dropped from 61 per cent to 58.6 per cent in rural areas. But those below Sayogyo's 240 kilogram poverty line increased slightly from 39.5 per cent of population to 39.8 per cent, and those below the extreme poverty level of 180 kilograms rice equivalent a year rose from 20.9 per cent to 25 per cent. What this meant was that out of Indonesia's 68 million poor (all categories) in 1976, just over 40 million were in rural Java, an island only slightly larger than half the size of the Australian state of Victoria. Of the 45 million in Indonesia below the poverty line needed to maintain basic welfare,

27.5 million were in rural Java. And of the 27.3 million below the grossly inadequate level of 180 kilograms rice equivalent (or in the cities 270 kilograms), 17.2 million were in the Javanese villages. According to this disturbing research the benefits of development had not yet trickled down to the bottom 40 per cent in the Javanese countryside (where some 66 million of Indonesia's 135 million people live) and for many of them the position had worsened.[6]

How the process has worked is illustrated by a village, Srihardjo, near Jogjakarta, which was the subject of a case-study, over roughly the same period, by the Population Institute of that city's Gadjah Mada University. Srihardjo's population density had risen from 740 people a square kilometre in 1940 to 1290 persons per square kilometre thirty years later. The average amount of land per family was down to less than a quarter of a hectare, and two-thirds of its people could not afford to eat rice all year round. To make ends meet, they worked at a diversity of tasks including palm sugar tapping and production, firewood collecting, and labouring when it was available. It was difficult to afford meat, eggs, visits to the doctor or even the 16-kilometre bus trip into Jogjakarta. Five years later at the end of 1975 the Director of the Population Institute, Dr Masri Singarimbun, found many visible signs of improvement: new school buildings, a new concrete-lined irrigation channel, a repaired bridge and a market financed out of government funds and built with *gotong royong* (co-operative) labour. Of the 195 hectares of rice paddies, 145 were under the Bimas scheme and yields had been raised 30 to 50 per cent. Three new mechanical rice mills had also increased the farmers' profits. Family planning and migration to the Outer Islands had begun. The number of motor-bikes, bicycles, and transistor radios had multiplied.

Srihardjo's landless labourers did not appear to have shared in this prosperity. Wages had not kept up with prices and job opportunities were becoming scarce. Contractors on the new projects imported their own labour, and outsiders were competing for agricultural labouring jobs. The three rice mills had removed a principal source of work for the women, and farmers were introducing contract harvesting. A typical Srihardjo couple, *Pak* Tarno and his wife, worked at several tasks: tapping sugar, labouring in other people's fields, weaving bamboo mats and cultivating a swimming pool-sized paddy field under a share-cropping arrangement. For this the Tarnos gained $180 a year to support themselves and their three children. Perhaps the most telling detail Dr Singarimbun noted was that despite a population increase and the new investment in primary schools the number of pupils had dropped. Their parents could not afford the fee of 12 cents a month which was introduced in 1972.[7]

Such poverty levels are reflected in the appalling nutritional standard prevailing throughout Java, with perhaps three-quarters of the population on inadequate diets. Dull eyes, distended bellies, and russet-coloured hair are common signs of malnutrition. Dr Jon Rohde, one public health specialist working with the Rockefeller Foundation in Jogjakarta, estimated in 1978 that about 25 per cent of the child population is so severely undernourished that life is threatened. Those that survive from this group could expect to suffer life-long mental and physical defects. Another 25 per cent were moderately undernourished and would reach an adult physical size less than their genetic potentials; their brain would not be physiologically affected but their school performances would not be good. Another 25 per cent would have minor malnutrition that would cause some diminution of body size. The more severe levels of malnutrition lay people wide open to infections and disease, particularly young children. It has been estimated that about one in five children born in Java never live to the age of five. A Javanese has a life expectancy at birth of about fifty years. If he gets past his fifth birthday he can expect on average to reach sixty-three. Malnutrition tends to strike the young in two ways: through low body-weight at birth due to malnutrition of the mother, or by weakening their ability to withstand simple illnesses such as diarrhoea and pneumonia.[8]

The combination of population pressure and extreme poverty has also accelerated the ecological decline of Java to the point where the whole community is affected. The poor have extended their cultivation further up mountain slopes, and have moved into forest reserves in their search for firewood, building materials and edible plants. Indonesia's foremost ecologist, Professor Otto Soemarwoto, of Bandung's Padjadjaran University states bluntly: 'Floods and drought have their source in the same principal factor, that is the destruction of our forests'.[9] Despite attempts to promote use of alternative fuels, principally by subsidization of kerosene, firewood has remained Indonesia's principal source of energy for household use and cottage energy, and perhaps the major fuel overall. One estimate given to a conference in Jakarta in 1975 suggested that the biggest province, East Java, was consuming by itself 14 million cubic metres of firewood a year, equivalent to two-thirds of the peak lumber export of Kalimantan and Sumatra. The people of Java are still too poor to buy the world's cheapest kerosene, as it has been in Indonesia for some years. The deforestation of Java, proceeding rapidly as measured by satellite monitoring, is causing a dramatic deterioration in soil and water qualities. Irrigation channels and dams are silting up far more rapidly than predicted. Dr Sumitro Djojohadikusumo, Minister for Research until 1978, now puts the effective life-span of the huge Jatiluhur dam in West Java, opened in 1967 to supply power and water to Jakarta and the north coast nearby, at about half the originally planned 120 years. With the personal interest of Suharto behind it the government has been spending over $30 million a year on 'regreening' of denuded hills, but the impact has been disappointing, since local people have no incentive to care for plantings. In areas of intense population pressure armed guards have been unable to prevent local people entering state forests to cut firewood. In one incident, in the

Kuningan area of West Java in 1976, a forestry policeman was hacked to death by an angry mob after fatally shooting a local boy found illegally cutting timber.[10]

Set against this desperate and growing surplus of labour in Java, the creation of new jobs under the Suharto Government has been modest and has come to be recognized as perhps the major weakness of its economic policy. The displacement of agricultural labourers by new tools and techniques has been followed in other areas: traditional fishermen by diesel-driven trawlers, small handicraft and processing industries by modern enterprises, human-powered transport and carrying by motor vehicles. Jobs created by the modern enterprises coming under Investment Board approval have covered perhaps 10 per cent of the annual increase in the workforce, while the less formal manufacturing sector has probably absorbed a small proportion also.

Some government policies have attempted to redress the employment balance directly. A substantial amount of employment has been created by Inpres (Presidential Instruction) grants to regional governments for labour-intensive public works. In 1975 this scheme was officially estimated to have provided over 100 million man days of work in a year. However, since the levelling off in oil revenues in 1977, these grants have been among the victims of budget restraint and have shown little real growth. Moreover, wages paid under the scheme have been criticized as inadequate to support families, and allegations that funds have frequently been diverted for cars and offices for officials, or unproductive prestige use such as town monuments, appear to have some truth. Official protection of labour-intensive techniques has been the exception, the notable case being the *kretek* (clove-scented cigarette) industry whose biggest producer, the Gudang Garam company in Kediri, East Java, employs over 22 000 people in one plant, mostly young girls engaged in hand-rolling cigarettes on simple wooden forms made by the firm's own carpenters.

Economic policy has often tended to promote, sometimes unconsciously, use of capital-intensive methods. Administrative and banking services are geared towards larger-scale enterprises (although these have not always proven to be responsibly managed) and are generally weak in dealings with small firms, particularly outside the major cities. An experiment was begun in 1975 to provide credit to small traders, in a field where as little as $25 can start a business, but not enough information has appeared to evaluate its success. Smaller enterprises, with less worldly management and fewer resources for setting up, are also more likely to be deterred by bureaucracy and corruption. They are also more likely to favour a high degree of state intervention in the economy, the individual enterpreneur not being able to offer any compelling national reasons as to why he should be allowed to prosper. Labour-intensive enterprises were discouraged by such policies and the exchange rate from 1971 to 1978 was fixed at a level which eroded the comparative advantage of Indonesian firms in the export market. This, together with the level of domestic inflation, enhanced the security of imported capital.

How then have Indonesians who do not own land or hold jobs with the government and established enterprise managed to get by? In many cases, it appears, by extension of the rural Javanese poverty-sharing approach to service jobs. The economist, Peter McCawley, notes: 'To the casual visitor, Indonesia seems to almost float on a sea of services provided by millions of underemployed people doing petty, low-paid jobs.' The big cities have provided a venue for this splitting down of functions. The capital, Jakarta, grew from 3 million people in 1961 to an estimated 6 million in about fifteen years, and may keep growing to reach more than twice that population level by the end of the century. Declared a 'closed city' in 1971, Jakarta saw migration from the countryside slow from 130 000 a year, but only down to 80 000 a year. Many of the newcomers have crowded into squalid *kampung liar* (literally 'wild settlements'), constructed of flimsy materials and receiving no utility services, except perhaps where electricity can be illegally tapped. The city is harshly sited: hot in the dry season and subject to flood when the rains come. People without residents' cards can be harassed by the authorities. Occasionally the less presentable have been loaded into trucks and taken out of the city.

Yet somehow Jakarta provides a living. The complicated machinery of the bureaucracy creates a parasitic need for legions of middlemen and brokers. Matching buyer and seller fetches a commission. Even picking up cigarette butts (to be boiled up and the essence used for proofing batik) supports scores of people. The competition for the most demanding, menial employment can be seen from the *becak* (pedicab) business in Jakarta. Introduced by the Japanese, the *becak*s multiplied to about 400 000 in Jakarta in 1964, making them the biggest source of employment in the city. Until the early 1970s the *becak*s roamed freely through the city. In 1974 a five-year plan to make Jakarta '*becak*-free' was announced by the police. The pedicabs were to be replaced by about 10 000 scooter-cabs, which have increasingly pushed the *becak*s back to the more inaccessible *kampung*s, aided by tighter traffic zoning. But whole fleets of *becak*s have been shipped to country towns, to be manned by unemployed agricultural labourers. The drivers who stayed in the city have created a new class of transport – the *ojek* – which is simply a bicycle with a pillion seat. These 'informal' sector jobs are available only in Jakarta, and to some extent in Surabaya, but not in the majority of towns. Most people still have to seek jobs in rural areas.[11]

The problem is to provide the rural poor of Java with better paying work and to change patterns of consumption from those with adverse economic or environmental implications. More fundamentally, it is to curb population growth, though by international standards it is not high, and, since Java is already overburdened, to shift the population balance towards the Outer Islands where better livelihoods can be provided more easily. The problem is hard to overstate, with perhaps 3 million people being added to Indonesia's population a year and about 1.4 million each year to the workforce, the majority in Java. Even with a moderate decline in fertility the population could reach 250 million by the turn of the century.

It is in the area that might have been considered the most difficult, population control, that the Suharto Government has turned out to be the most successful. After taking power Suharto quickly reversed Sukarno's policy of population expansion, signing the United Nations Declaration on Population in 1967 and setting up in 1970 a National Family Planning Co-ordinating Board reporting directly to himself. The board quickly gained a reputation as the most creative, least bureaucratic of all Indonesian Government agencies. Its propaganda included imprinting the family planning symbol, a couple with two children, on the smallest coin in circulation and even a condom advertisement on the approach road to Sukarno's phallic National Monument in Jakarta. Concentrating for the first few years on Java and Bali, by 1976 the board expanded the existing 116 private clinics providing free contraceptive services to a network of 2700 government-sponsored clinics and 20 000 village distribution centres. Some 7000 field-workers were recruited.

Again, it was a non-bureaucratic approach that worked: the best field-workers tended to be people similar to those they were trying to motivate, older married women with little formal education for whom rewards came more in community approval than money. By 1977 it was estimated that about 24 per cent of couples of child-bearing age in Java and Bali were using modern contraception supplied by the government. In the five years to April 1976 the child-bearing rate had dropped by 34.5 per cent in Bali, from 5.8 to 3.8 children, on average, to each woman. In East Java, Central Java and Jakarta, the fertility rate dropped by more than 15 per cent, while in the more strongly Muslim province of West Java the fall was about 12 per cent. In the highly traditional Jogjakarta Special Region the drop was only 6.4 per cent. The success was achieved without the coercion that followed family planning in India, apart from some early instances involving some local military and civilian officials in East Java in which pills were almost thrust down the throats of women in an effort to meet recruitment targets. One of the most encouraging results was that over 80 per cent of people who have taken part in the scheme have been wives of peasants, fishermen and labourers. Surprisingly, the middle-class urban wife has shown a tendency to have more children.

While a factor in the achievement was certainly relentless government propaganda at all levels in favour of family planning and a small family size, the example of Bali seems to have shown that greater success comes with a higher level of community control. Bali's relatively permissive attitude to sex and reluctance to use abstinence and abortion as forms of contraception were offset by cultural and economic factors predisposing the Balinese to accept modern family planning: fewer religious scruples from the island's Hinduism; participation of Balinese women in heavy manual work outside the home; and greater communal projects, ceremonies and mutual aid. The government family-planning effort was conducted almost factor was the form of local government contained in the 3500 *banjar* (hamlets) throughout the island. The *banjar* is renowned as a cohesive administrative and social unit, in which household heads meet at least monthly to discuss communal projects, ceremonies and mutual aid. The government family-planning effort was conducted almost entirely through the *banjar,* a household map of the village in each *banjar* hall plotted in different-coloured inks according to the kind of contraceptive each family is using. As one report noted: 'The contraceptive situation is discussed at each monthly meeting of household heads. If an apparently fertile couple are not trying for a pregnancy and are also not contracepting, the husband will be questioned.'[12]

Despite this success, women on Java and Bali are still having an average of four babies. Even if the progress continues, the most optimistic projections which aim at an average of 2.39 children per woman (which because of the higher incidence of male children means women give birth on average to only one female) still put Indonesia's population at 209 to 215 million in the year 2001, and suggest it would continue to grow until levelling off at 330 or 335 million. Slower progress puts the zero population growth point at anything up to several hundred million people more, while the turn-of-the-century figure could be up to 277 million. The government's target is the most optimistic rate of growth outlined above, although the former Minister for Research, Dr Sumitro Djojohadikusumo, in 1975 thought it 'realistic' to assume only 25 per cent attainment of that planned fertility decline by the year 2000, giving a total population of around 250 million in that year, of whom 146 million would live in Java (including Madura).[13] Taking the assumption of 209–215 million Indonesians by 2001, it has been estimated that the labour force would increase by up to 139 per cent over 1971 to 96 million. The population of Java and Bali would increase to between 100 million and 124 million, depending on the degree of urbanization and, more importantly, emigration to the Outer Islands.[14]

The prospects for a heavy shift in the population by migration from Java and Bali are not good in the short to medium term. 'Transmigration' in Indonesia has a long history, starting with Dutch efforts to ameliorate what was seen as overpopulation on Java in 1905. Yet in the following seventy years only about 810 000 people were moved under official programmes. The Suharto Government's first five-year plan target of 38 000 families, about 190 000 people, was almost met with some 182 000 persons leaving Java, Bali and Lombok (the island east of Bali). The second plan's target was for 250 000 families, over 1 million people, to move in the five years from 1974, but by the end of 1976 this was reduced by more than half to 108 000 families. Even then the practicality of this was considered doubtful. Strong misgivings have been voiced about the practicality of the Repelita III (1979–84) target of 500 000 families announced in 1977. The target is seen as hopelessly over-ambitious and likely to result in coercion on the part of local officials to meet quotas.

While the official programme has probably been exceeded by self-supported migration, especially to the southern part of Sumatra, transmigration has so far had a very small effect on the population burden of Java. It would now take an annual migration of about 1 million for the rest of the century, assuming the government's family planning target is achieved and the cities grow at their present rate, to hold the rural population of Java and Bali to about 74 million during the 1980s and then effect a reduction to 70 million by the year 2000. Transmigration settlements to date have had a generally poor reputation due to neglect, exploitation by administration, and poor planning. An underlying fault has been the tendency to attempt wet-rice cultivation in unsuitable areas. Settlers have frequently ended up subsistence farmers no better off than they were back in Java, if not because of poor soil and water then because of inadequate support services and isolation from markets. To expand the programme to have a significant impact on Java's population, radically different approaches would need to include dry-land and swamp farming, public works and processing among migrant employment opportunities, and would require substantial investment in transport, communications and administrative services.[15]

Such a sweeping mass migration must be judged unlikely to eventuate within the near future. Indonesia's planners, by the time they formulated a new five-year plan in 1978, had therefore to prepare for great increases in the population and workforce on Java. To many Indonesians and outside observers it appeared that an inevitable part of the cure to Java's problems would require a redressing of imbalances in political and economic power imposed since the island's nightmare of 1965–6.

NOTES

1 See Clifford Geertz, *Agricultural Involution*, University of California Press, Los Angeles, 1963, and G. J. Missen, *Viewpoint on Indonesia, A Geographical Study*, Nelson, Melbourne, 1972, for an introduction to the Indonesian agro-economy.
2 William A. Collier, 'Food Problems, Unemployment and the Green Revolution in Rural Java', *Prisma* (Jakarta), no. 9, March 1978.
3 Interview by the author, Jogjakarta, May 1978.
4 For evaluation of new rice technology see Richard W. Franke, 'Miracle Seeds and Shattered Dreams in Java', *National History Magazine*, January 1974; William A. Collier, Gunawan Wiradi and Soentoro, 'Recent Changes in Rice-Harvesting Methods', *Bulletin of Indonesian Economic Studies*, vol. IX, no. 2, July 1973; Ketut Sudhana Astika, 'Social and Economic Effects of the New Rice Technology: the Case of Abiansemal, Bali', *Prisma* (Jakarta), no. 10, September 1978.
5 Sumitro Djojohadikusumo, quoted in *Kompas* (Jakarta), 17 March 1978.
6 Sajogyo, 'Garis Kemiskinan dan Kebutuhan Minimum Pangan' ('Poverty lines and Minimum Food Needs'), *Kompas* (Jakarta), 11 November 1977.
7 D. H. Penny and Masri Singarimbun, *Population and Poverty in Rural Java: Some Economic Arithmetic from Srihardjo*, Department of Agricultural Economics, Cornell University, 1973; and Masri Singarimbun, 'Srihardjo Revisited', *BIES*, vol. XII, no. 2, July 1976.
8 Jon E. Rohde, Terence E. Hull and Lukas Hendrata, 'Who Dies of What and Why', *Prisma* (Jakarta), no. 9, March 1978; and interview with Dr Rohde by author, Jogjakarta, May 1978.
9 Otto Soemarwoto, quoted in *Kompas* (Jakarta), 9 July 1977.
10 See Sumitro Djojohadikusumo, 'Indonesia Towards the Year 2000' in his *Science, Resources and Development*, Lembaga Penelitian, Pendidikan dan Penerangan Ekonomi dan Sosial, Jakarta, 1977. Also information given during interview with author, Jakarta, 1978.

188 Suharto's Indonesia

11 For a discussion of employment, see Peter McCawley, 'The Indonesian Economy under Suharto: A Survey', working paper, Research School of Pacific Studies, Australian National University, 1978. A fascinating study of the informal sector in Jakarta is Lea Jellinek, 'The Pondok of Jakarta', *BIES*, vol. XIII, no. 3, November 1977.
12 Terence H. Hull, Valerie J. Hull and Masri Singarimbun, 'Indonesia's Family Planning Story: Success and Challenge', *Population Bulletin*, vol. 23, no. 6, Population Reference Bureau Inc., Washington DC, 1977, p. 28.
13 Sumitro Djojohadikusumo, op. cit.
14 Hull, Hull, Masri, op. cit. This *Population Bulletin* contains a comprehensive survey of population and family-planning issues in Indonesia, from which data in the foregoing section is drawn.
15 Suratman and Patrick Guinness, 'The Changing Face of Transmigration', *BIES*, vol. XIII, no. 2, July 1977; H. W. Arndt and R. M. Sundrum, 'Transmigration: Land Settlement or Regional Development', *BIES*, vol. XIII, no. 3, November 1977; Alden Speare Jr, 'Alternative Population Distribution Policies', *BIES*, vol. XIV, no. 1, March 1978.

9. War and Diplomacy: The Timor Case

No more clear illustration of Suharto's approach to war and diplomacy can be found than in the curious and costly campaign to capture the tiny former Portuguese colony of East Timor. The Indonesian invasion of December 1975 came at the end of Suharto's patience in an attenuated political and military war of entrapment. It was the start of perhaps the most severe test of arms for the Indonesian military since Independence. It exposed the web of alliances and hostilities surrounding Indonesia. For some outsiders the Timor Affair was conclusive proof of Indonesia's aggressive, expansionist tendencies and the cynicism of its Western friends. Most Indonesians saw it as the painful redrawing of artificial colonial boundaries, the rescue of an endemically poor region from repressive white rulers, and the pre-emption of hostile foreign involvement.

The campaign brought Suharto close to the kind of adventurism he had forsworn on taking power. The methods he chose further emphasized the continuities in Indonesia. These evolved perhaps from a cultural propensity for intricacy and dissimulation, combined with the internal complexities of power in the Suharto Government. Perhaps unconsciously, key figures drew on their past experience under Suharto in the West Irian and Konfrontasi commands to shape the Timor campaign.

East Timor was no great prize in itself. It is a narrow island in the Lesser Sunda chain, a rugged place of savannah and mountain where heavy monsoonal wet seasons alternate with long, parched dry seasons during which food runs short. The 650 000 to 670 000 East Timorese (estimated at the beginning of 1975) are a mixture of Malay and Melanesian racial types. They tend to have darker skin, a more wiry build and more crinkly hair than the majority of Indonesians, but are similar to the peoples of the nearby Indonesian provinces. The most common of some fifteen languages on Timor is Tetum, with currency in the central part of the island on both sides of the border. Earliest known contact came around 1000 AD from Malay and Chinese traders who brought the horse, the buffalo and several crops in return for the perfumed sandalwood which grew in Timor. The Portuguese began calling between 1512 and 1520 and established their first settlements at the end of the sixteenth century. Three centuries of rivalry with the Dutch saw the reduction of Portuguese control to the eastern half of Timor and a small enclave, Oecusse, on the north coast. The history of Portuguese rule is largely one of ecological plunder and social neglect. In his novel *Victory,* Joseph Conrad described the capital Dili of the late nineteenth century as 'that highly pestilential place'.

Unrest grew with tightening Portuguese control around that period, ending in a major uprising under a traditional ruler, Dom Boaventura, in 1910–12. It was crushed by Portuguese gunboat diplomacy with the loss of 3000 Timorese lives. In normal times the Portuguese kept few officials there: in 1928, only 200 civilians and 300 soldiers. They ruled indirectly through the local chiefs, known as *liurai*, who awarded themselves such titles as 'Son of God'. Punitive raids followed any disobedience. A mixed-race community and several thousand Chinese migrants formed a bridge to the local population, controlling much of the modern agricultural and commercial sectors. The Portuguese population was augmented under the Salazar regime in Lisbon by political *deportados*. Constitutionally it came to be regarded as an overseas province of Portugal.

The Japanese and Allies pushed aside Portugal's neutrality in the Second World War. The Timorese suffered greatly under Japanese occupation, losing unknown hundreds in executions and reprisals. Perhaps 40 000 died in a famine caused by ruthless food collection. Unlike the Dutch East Indies, no independence movement waited the returning power, and Australia felt obliged, under war-time treaties covering the Atlantic, not to interfere. By the end of Portuguese rule per capita gross national product was about $40 a year, with most Timorese living by subsistence agriculture. About one third were Roman Catholic, the rest animist. A belated development programme in the 1960s had created some infrastructure, and reduced illiteracy from near total to about 90 per cent. The territory had a handful of university graduates and about forty young people still studying in Lisbon. Exports, mostly high-grade coffee, amounted in 1973 to $3.5 million, with local revenue contributing about half the colony's budget of $5.5 million. The principal hope for ending this deficit lay in petroleum. A sporadic search had been carried out since 1903, with many indications of oil. However, no commercial discoveries had been announced by the time political crisis forced exploration rigs to withdraw.

Indonesian interest in Portuguese Timor was desultory. The 1945 constitutional committee sympathized with arguments advanced by Mohammad Yamin which included East Timor (and West New Guinea, North Borneo and Malaya) as part of a Pan-Indonesian nation both on ethnic grounds and on claims of an earlier unity under the Majapahit dynasty. More out of simple anti-imperialism, Sukarno endorsed the Yamin's idea, and it was adopted over the objections of moderates like Hatta and Sutan Sjahrir by thirty-nine votes out of sixty-six. But the idea sunk out of sight during the independence struggle, and Portuguese Timor received only passing attention thereafter. During the West Irian crisis Subandrio based his claims solely on the former boundaries of the Dutch East Indies. The Portuguese themselves regarded Indonesia with disdain and suspicion, discouraging contact until the late 1960s. A small group of refugees from the North Sulawesi rebellion of 1958 were granted asylum in Portuguese Timor, but a year later mounted an anti-Portuguese uprising at Viqueque, that was put down with the reported loss of between 150 and 600 lives. Little barrier could have been put to informal border contacts, since the boundary intersected linguistic and traditional political entities. Raiding cattle or going to market, the Timorese ignored the border.

The situation changed immediately after middle-ranking officers overthrew the Caetano Government in Lisbon on 25 April 1974, and installed General António de Spínola, who was conservative but convinced of the futility of the empire. Although it possessed no liberation movement in being like the Portuguese African colonies, Timor was included in immediate decolonization plans. The new Armed Forces Movement sent representatives to Timor to supervise the disbandment of the fascist corporate state party, the secret police (PIDE) and the censorship commission. A vague programme for village elections the following year and a plebescite on the territory's future was announced.

Three main political parties emerged within a month, reflecting the choices open to the territory. Established elements of the Portugal-oriented elite, possessing some education (numbering perhaps 25 000), the coffee planters, the Chinese, and some traditional chieftains gravitated to the Timor Democratic Union (UDT) which initially favoured continuing links with Lisbon but later shifted towards independence after several years of preparation. A small group of civil servants and younger high school and seminary graduates formed the Timor Social Democratic Association which later in 1974 took a more radical stance and named itself the Revolutionary Front for an Independent East Timor (Fretilin). Leaders, such as José Ramos Horta and Lieutenant Roque Rodrigues, who had spent some time in Mozambique contributed an African-style socialist ideology to its demand for immediate independence, much to Indonesia's alarm. Rated as weakest was the Association for the Integration of Timor with Indonesia, which quickly changed its unpopular name to Timorese Democratic Peoples Association (Apodeti), and used arguments similar to those used by Mohammad Yamin thirty years earlier.[1]

Indonesian reaction was equally prompt. In response to news reports from East Timor carried in Jakarta papers, the Muslim party (PPP) Vice-Chairman of Parliament, John Naro, who, as we have seen in chapter 5, was close to General Ali Murtopo, expressed the hope that 'the Indonesian Government takes preliminary steps and finds a special policy on Portuguese Timor so that finally that area will once again return to Indonesian control'. Within two months of the Lisbon coup, Indonesia's intentions had become a major preoccupation for Timor's parties and neighbouring states. From 1974 the Australian Department of Foreign Affairs began privately warning journalists that Indonesia had considerable strategic anxieties about Portuguese Timor. Indonesia was concerned that an independent Portuguese Timor might not be able to resist external influences inimical to Indonesia as a result of its inevitable economic and military weakness. Such developments could disturb national unity among Indonesia's ethnic groups and Timor could become a base for incursions into Indonesia.

For Indonesia the problem was that the whole drift of the Portuguese decolonization process encouraged independence. It would need time to build any campaign for integration but this would also allow UDT and Fretilin to arouse nationalist feeling.

Indonesia spent the first few months after 25 April 1974 quietly sounding out the internal politics of East Timor and the attitudes of foreign leaders. Fretilin's foreign spokesman, Ramos Horta, paid early attention to Indonesia by visiting Jakarta where he obtained a letter from Adam Malik stating that independence was the right of every country 'with no exception for the people of

Timor'. Indonesia had no ambitions in East Timor, Malik said, and sought good relations with 'whoever will govern in Timor in the future after independence'.

In Apodeti Indonesia saw strengths that were largely missed by other observers. The party's leader was a self-willed, uncommunicative school teacher, Arnaldo dos Reis Araújo, then sixty-one, who by his own account had spent the post-war years under restricted liberty for his assistance to the Japanese, a record that bore fewer nationalist credentials in Timor than in Indonesia. Apodeti's following in the towns was soon revealed as considerably weaker than that of the other parties. But it had some support among the *liurai*, notably with the *Raja* (King) of Atsabe, Guilherme Maria Gonçalves, whose domain lay close to the Indonesian border. Another source of support lay among certain Roman Catholic priests, who were close to the well-established church in East Nusatenggara. The Indonesians took comfort from the shallow penetration of all the parties, and pinned their hopes on regional and clan politics proving more influential. Nor did the presence of some 3000 Timorese soldiers armed with modern NATO-pattern weapons escape observation.

By the end of August 1974 the Indonesian agencies handling Timor were beginning to show their hand. An editorial in the Ali Murtopo group's newspaper, *Berita Yudha*, warned that rights of self-determination could not be separated from 'general world strategies'. It said Indonesia did not want Timor to become 'a possession or an instrument in the interests of big powers which, without us being aware enough to avoid it, could disturb our neighbourhood at a moment's notice'. Two days later the Indonesian Journalists' Association, itself the subject of a recent Ali Martopo intervention, introduced the Apodeti leadership to the Jakarta press. *Berita Yudha* claimed that Timor's weakness would invite foreign intervention; it had received reports that Fretilin had communist backing from Portugal.

On 6 September 1974, Suharto gained a new advantage when the Australian Prime Minister, Gough Whitlam, met him for informal talks at Wonosobo, Central Java. Whitlam told Suharto he thought the best solution would be for East Timor to join Indonesia, adding with somewhat less emphasis that the wishes of the Timorese should be respected and that public reaction in Australia would be hostile if Indonesia used force. An important factor in reassuring Suharto was not so much what Whitlam said, but the degree of *tepo seliru* (mutual understanding) Suharto believed the two had reached (see page 1). Suharto went immediately to talks with the Malaysian Prime Minister, Tun Abdul Razak; it would be surprising if Timor was not also discussed there in similar vein. Within a few days of the meetings the Indonesian Government, through Adam Malik and the Interior Minister, General Amir Machmud issued its first major statement on Timor. While Malik stressed that Indonesia would accept the decision of the Timorese, Amir Machmud said integration would be accepted although Indonesia itself had 'no territorial ambitions'. The reaction from Fretilin to this was a large demonstration against 'Expansionism' a few days later outside the Indonesian Consulate in Dili. But two UDT leaders visiting Jakarta (Augusto Mousinho and Domingos Oliveira) were reported on 25 September 1974, as saying that their party would not oppose integration if the people wished it, that UDT was anti-communist like the Suharto Government, and that Fretilin's choice of name showed its communist identity.

By October 1974 Ali Murtopo had firmly taken control of the Timor 'project' for the Indonesian Government, issuing press commentary and sending personal emissaries abroad to inform governments about Indonesia's concerns. The job suited him well. Ali Murtopo was still under a cloud from the Malari affair and fighting to regain his former closeness with Suharto. Timor was his kind of assignment, like the 1969 'Act of Free Choice' in West Irian and the 1971 Golkar victory. A purely military solution had been ruled out, for diplomatic reasons if not for the fact that Portugal still kept enough well-armed and Africa-hardened troops in Timor to deter the Indonesian Army, whose elite units had only just begun to receive comparable modern weaponry under the US military aid programme. The trend of Timor's politics, left to itself, would have been against integration. The answer was a special operation, which would immensely enhance Ali Murtopo's problem-fixing image in the process.

On 5 October 1974, Suharto authorized Ali Murtopo to take over negotiations with Portugal. His letter of introduction described Ali as 'my trusted personal representative [who has been] specially sent to you in order to obtain first-hand information concerning your Government's policies with regard to the process of decolonization of the territories under Portuguese administration', and to convey Suharto's own views. By then Ali Murtopo had begun his approach to Lisbon. The Indonesian Ambassador in Brussels, Frans Seda, had contacted an old university friend, Dr Jorge Campignos, now a senior Portuguese diplomat, to organize Ali Murtopo's visit. When Ali Murtopo arrived on 14 October the sudden removal of General Spinola from the Portuguese presidency and his replacement by the leftist General da Costa Gomez on 30 September had raised fears of lessened sympathy. But as Ali Murtopo put Indonesia's position to the president, to Prime Minister Vasco Gonçalves, to Foreign Minister Mário Soares, to the Minister for Decolonization, Almeida Santos, and to Dr Campignos, his fears were allayed.

According to an account published by members of Ali Murtopo's special Operation unit (Opsus)[2], Dr Campignos (accompanied by Major Matello, the Portuguese military chief in Timor who was regarded as sympathetic to Indonesia) said his personal view was that Indonesia had an 'historic right' over East Timor. But Portugal had to carry out an act of self-determination and Campignos hoped Indonesia would assist. The socialist Soares gave Ali a reception described as 'rather stiff' but which became 'more fluid' after Ali Murtopo gave his pitch. Soares told Ali Murtopo what he had told Malik at the United Nations General Assembly shortly before: Portugal had a 'moral obligation' to heed the wishes of the Timorese. It would take account of the concerns of neighbouring states, among them Indonesia and Australia, but Soares hoped events would not be forced and would be given enough time. The immediate thing was to gain closer co-operation between Lisbon and Jakarta, with full diplomatic relations to be a first step. With da Costa Gomez, Ali Murtopo claimed a warmer reception. When Ali Murtopo began his list of the alternatives facing Timor, the Portuguese President, da Costa Gomez, cut him short. There were not three options, but two: joining Indonesia or self-government under the Portuguese umbrella. Full independence was 'unrealistic', he is quoted as saying. Even Timor remaining with Portugal did not accord with Lisbon's new politics. But in the ultimate report East Timor's future was up to the forthcoming referendum. Prime Minister Gonçalves was said to have exclaimed that independence was 'nonsense', and that the Timorese should be directed towards integration. He hoped for closer and steady co-operation with Indonesia to this end. The last meeting was with Decolonization Minister, Almeida Santos, and Major Matello, and was also a friendly occasion. The Portuguese Foreign Ministry asked that the meetings be kept secret, to avoid any impression that the pro-Indonesian cause was gaining an unfair advantage. Finally, Ali Murtopo briefed the Australian Ambassador, F. W. Cooper, who offered assistance, especially in opening an Indonesian mission in Lisbon. While the Indonesians were later to realize that not all Portugal's elements were willing to work to those formulae, at the time they took their reception as a green light to begin 'directing' opinion within Timor, with the tacit connivance of Portugal and Australia.

Dr Almeida Santos was one Portuguese leader soon swayed in another direction. Within a few days of Ali

Murtopo's Lisbon visit Santos visited Canberra, Jakarta and Timor. In Dili and Maubisse he spelled out three options as open to the Timorese and said: 'Timor will be what the majority of its people want it to be.' Santos was moved by the sight of centuries-old Portuguese flags brought out of sacred houses by mountain people who flocked to see him. Back in Lisbon he said this was 'a phenomenon of which I was unaware, a mythology of love of Portugal'. Australia was concerned about threats to regional instability, he said, and Indonesia feared only premature independence. On 3 December 1974, Santos told the United Nations General Assembly that immediate independence was an 'impossible dream'. Portugal had rejected the original idea of a referendum as impracticable, and proposed a choice by a Timorese constituent assembly in 1976.[3]

Ali Murtopo, meanwhile, was proceeding on the basis of his understanding in Lisbon. During his visit to Portugal, the Chief of Staff of Opsus, Colonel Aloysius Sugianto, had travelled to Australia and East Timor. Sugianto, an elegant moustachioed former Special Forces (RPKAD Regiment) officer who held side-interests in publishing and film-making, is one of the best-known Opsus members. After the January 1974 riots he was rumoured to be facing arrest, and immediately after his return from Timor about 23 October 1974, he was in hot water again over the printing of a spurious Suharto family tree in *Pop* magazine, which he owned.

Indonesia's campaign now took more definite shape as 'Operasi Komodo' (Operation Dragon). Opsus took the leading role, with other agencies contributing where necessary. Ali Murtopo's network ran from Jakarta across to and over the border. Advising on diplomatic strategy were his political backroom team in the Jakarta academic-style institution, the Centre for Strategic and International Studies (CSIS), which had become an important point of contact for foreign diplomats, academics and journalists. Two key figures in the CSIS on

Timor were its Director, Harry Tjan Silalahi, the self-effacing former Catholic Party figure, who became respectfully dubbed 'The Foreign Minister' by his military counterparts for his effective secret diplomacy with Portugal and Australia, and Yusuf Wanandi (Liem Bian Kie), the sometimes volatile West Sumatran-born political strategist who paid particular attention to the USA. On the operational side, the operation worked out of the closely guarded AKA Building, Ali Murtopo's business headquarters in a quiet Jakarta suburb. The newspaper *Berita Yudha*, which listed Colonel Sugianto as a publisher, took on another senior intelligence officer, Colonel Yusack, under journalistic cover. The paper's cartoonist, Lieutenant-Colonel Alex Dinuth, who was by chance from a Timorese family, was sent to Kupang in Indonesian Timor to direct a base for infiltration and psychological warfare under the cover of a fictitious trading company, PT Arjuna. Dinuth's job was to monitor radio transmissions, direct vernacular language broadcasts into East Timor, instruct visiting Indonesian pressmen on what to write, and to provide accommodation and good times for important visitors. Assisting the operation was another Timorese, Louis Taolin, the son of a West Timor *raja* with relatives across the border. Taolin had been prominent in the 1966 student movement before drifting into Bakin, writing a thesis on propaganda and psychological warfare for a higher degree in communications at the University of Indonesia. From 1973 he had been involved in trading with Dili. Now his studies were to get practical application.

By January 1975 Operasi Komodo was functioning. Menacing propaganda was being beamed into East Timor from Kupang, claiming that the 'communist' Fretilin and its Portuguese supporters were victimizing the pro-Indonesian 'majority'. Refugees started appearing across the border, and this was played up in the Indonesian press. The Indonesian consulate in Dili became blatant in its support of Apodeti. Towards the end of February, propaganda reached a crescendo, with the national newsagency Antara carrying lurid reports from its 'special correspondent' in the border area, most likely Colonel Dinuth. Then the Australian press quoted Canberra intelligence sources as warning that Indonesia might be preparing an invasion on the lines of India's seizure of the Portuguese colony of Goa in 1961.

The outcry following these reports killed whatever plans there might have been. In retrospect, the Indonesian press campaign seems aimed at the new Governor of Timor, Colonel Mário Lemos Pires, who had arrived in November 1974 with a group of young officers from the Armed Forces Movement. These more radical officers were accused of encouraging Fretilin and of organizing a revolutionary committee among Timorese non-commissioned officers. Two of them, the Chief of Political Affairs, Major Francisco Mota, and the Chief of Social Affairs, Major Costa Jonatas, were indeed described later by Fretilin-inclined observers as in touch with 'radical thinking' in Lisbon, and one detailed study does point to their covert support for Fretilin.[4] Their conduct of decolonization was seen by one visiting diplomat as 'scrupulously fair', although 'deep down their feeling was for independence and each move was aimed at producing a viable state'.[5] If so, this was far from the understanding Ali Murtopo claimed to have reached in Lisbon four months earlier. Another factor in the propaganda offensive may have been the start of village elections on 26 February and continuing to July (the few results eventually published showed little party politicization). But perhaps most importantly, the Indonesians must have been alarmed at the formation of a coalition by Fretilin and UDT on 22 January 1975, which supported independence, repudiated Apodeti and the idea of integration, and sought a transitional government by negotiation with Lisbon. This united front immensely strengthened the case for independence. Indonesia was undoubtedly tempted to work on reservations among conservative UDT members about their new coalition mates. Overall the propaganda campaign resembled the confrontation technique employed against West Irian and Malaysia, described by J. A. C. Mackie as

> a combination of threats, brinkmanship and play-acting which could be modulated at will to a pitch of fierce hostility at one extreme or, at the other, of patient acquiescence while waiting for favourable opportunities to resume the long-term struggle.[6]

At Lisbon's request Ali Murtopo went in secrecy to a second meeting with the Portuguese, in London on 9 March 1975. The Portuguese side was led by Major Vitor Alves, a member of the Armed Forces Movement's Supreme Revolutionary Council, who was regarded as sympathetic by Indonesia. Other members were the Minister for Decolonization, Almeida Santos, Dr Campignos, and Major Mota, the political chief from Timor. Signs of Portuguese concern can be read clearly in the Opsus account. In the three-hour morning session the Portuguese said they were not willing to simply transfer sovereignty to Indonesia, but wished to form a provisional government in Timor comprising the Portuguese Government and representatives of the three parties. This would be recognized *de jure,* and would operate for between three and eight years awaiting East Timor's political maturity and economic self-sufficiency. Alternatively, Lisbon could remain in full power with the assistance of a consultative body drawn from the three parties. Portugal hoped that Indonesia would accept such a scheme and encourage Apodeti to participate. It still believed integration to be the most rational and convenient solution, as long as the majority of Timorese wanted it. Indonesia's image could be improved since a section of the population, especially in the Fretilin–UDT coalition, regarded their neighbour as 'unfriendly and hostile'. Finally, the Portuguese warned that they could not accept open politicking by the Indonesian consulate even though they still wanted consultation with Indonesia. Ali Murtopo must have been appalled.

When the meeting resumed after a four-hour break Ali Murtopo said he agreed the Timorese were still not ready for a decision. But the proposed provisional government would impede integration, which both sides agreed would be the best outcome. He suggested, instead, an advisory body in Timor drawn from the Portuguese and Indonesian governments to advise the governor 'in the context of preparing the local people in deciding their own wish which would be guided towards integration with Indonesia'. Indonesia would accept suggestions about its consulate officials, but hoped Portugal would similarly control its own personnel (Major Mota's reaction is not recorded). According to the Opsus account the London meeting decided against Ali Murtopo's advisory body and against the first Portuguese proposal of a provisional government, in favour of a consultative body from the three parties. Portugal would not hinder moves towards integration, as long as they were constitutional and did not invite international involvement. To this end Portugal 'gave the Indonesian Government liberty to increase its support for Apodeti covertly and inconspicuously' and suggested its image be improved by aid and tourism. Portugal hoped Apodeti would co-operate in the consultative body, to be formed at a planned meeting in Macao, and that a high-level Indonesian delegation would be at hand in Hong Kong for emergency consultation.[7]

As a result of the London agreements Colonel Sugianto, Taolin and two others arrived soon after in Dili, meeting administration and party officials. Apodeti, they reported later, sought help against victimization and demanded an immediate referendum. With three leaders of UDT (Lopes da Cruz, Mousinho and Oliveira) the Indonesians played on the dangers of communism. Fretilin said they sought co-operation with Indonesia after independence, listed the possible sources of aid for an independent Timor (mainly Portugal and its former African colonies and Australia), and complained about the broadcasts from Kupang. Both UDT and Fretilin accepted invitations to send missions to

Jakarta at Sugianto's expense. Governor Pires asked of Sugianto that the Kupang broadcasts be toned down and that the position of the Indonesian Consul, Elias Tomodok, be reconsidered since he was acting like an Apodeti leader. Questioned about 'communist teachings' by armed forces members, Pires is reported as saying it would not be surprising to find communists in the garrison as the Communist Party was legal in Portugal. The Opsus men say they concluded from their visit that Major Mota was very influential, and that Fretilin was 'the only party that possessed any capability whether in its organization and tactics of struggle'. While Fretilin always derided the notion, its behaviour clearly indicated it was 'communist or at least supported by communists'. But Apodeti was resolute and prepared to use force if other roads failed. UDT was 'beginning to show understanding and appreciation' of Indonesia's concerns, particularly about regional stability and communism.[8]

Operasi Komodo's main aim now was to split the UDT–Fretilin coalition by working on the conservative UDT leaders. At some stage towards the middle of 1975 Sugianto won over Lopes da Cruz of UDT and guided him towards favouring integration, a vital alliance. Sugianto also cultivated the *liurai* (chiefs) and was later to claim that as a result of this unprecedented attention about ten of the thirteen districts were leaning towards Apodeti.[9] Visitors to the border were shown 300 well-drilled young East Timorese in simple uniform who were said to be undergoing 'agricultural training'. These were Apodeti recruits, working for the *Raja* of Atsabe and his son Tomás Gonçalves, and being trained by Indonesian soldiers. On 27 May 1975 UDT finally did withdraw from the coalition, accusing Fretilin of 'outrageous' behaviour. On 26 June the Macao talks convened, but Fretilin refused to attend because of the presence of Apodeti. Its leaders travelled instead to the Frelimo movement's independence celebrations in Mozambique, perhaps an indication of the road they hoped to follow. As agreed in London, the

Portuguese delegation stopped in Hong Kong to consult the Indonesian Consul-General who was representing Ali Murtopo and assisted by several Opsus men. Again the idea of transitional or provisional government met strong Indonesian objections. Another meeting took place at the close of the Macao conference on 29 June.

The result of the Macao talks was promulgation of Constitutional Law number 7/75 in Lisbon on 17 July 1975. While this law made no mention of a provisional government, it cannot have pleased Jakarta. It set October 1976 as the time for general elections for a popular assembly which would determine the future of the territory. Within 100 days of 17 July 1975 'transitory organs of representation and of the government of the territory of Timor' would be formed, comprising a high commissioner and five deputy secretaries in charge of portfolios, with a consultative council comprising two members from each region and four from each party. Portuguese sovereignty would end in October 1978, although Lisbon's role could be shortened or lengthened by agreement. Portugal would promote the 'economic independence' of Timor and seek international assistance for it. It would defend the 'political balance of the strategic area in which Timor is included, and on the other hand, with total precautions against any risk of neo-colonialist ambitions'. Ali Murtopo's secret diplomacy with Lisbon had failed.

But other Indonesian contacts abroad had not. The Australian Government remained sympathetic, if nervous, despite growing pressure from an articulate opinion group based principally in the parliamentary backbench, the universities and the trade unions. A quiet visit by the Bakin chief, Lieutenant-General Yoga Sugama, in May 1975 had sounded out, among others, Opposition Leader Malcolm Fraser, and found no reason for alarm. Suharto himself was confident enough on his return from Washington on 8 July 1975 to make his first public statement ruling out the feasibility of independence for East Timor.

In Timor the tensions had grown, with violent clashes occurring in Dili between UDT and Fretilin groups at the time of the Macao talks. Governor Pires requested additional troops from Lisbon soon after, his garrison by then having run down to 300 Portuguese soldiers. At the end of July 1975 three UDT leaders (Lopes da Cruz, Oliveira and João Carrascalão) went quietly to Jakarta to query Suharto's 8 July statement. Some UDT figures say they were also becoming suspicious of Lopes da Cruz and his mysterious access to huge funds. They wanted to observe him in contact with the Indonesians. The Opsus account says they sought 'concrete help' should they be forced to attack the 'communists' in East Timor and asked Indonesia's likely reaction to such a move. 'Indonesia would just close its eyes', Ali is reported as saying.[10] UDT sources say their leaders were pressed by Sugianto to stay in Jakarta. When they refused they were approached again by Sugianto, who introduced a man as a Malaysian Government minister. The Malaysian told the UDT leaders regional countries would never allow a leftist movement in Timor. The Malaysian and Sugianto both repeated something that Ali Murtopo had said in Jakarta: Fretilin planned a coup on 15 August. But still there was no support offered to UDT.

When they returned to Dili on 6 August they found a new level of hostility. Fretilin had taken over the small township of Remexio not far from Dili. Foreign travellers going by road from Baucau to Dili on 8 August said their bus was stopped and searched for weapons by youths described as 'communists' by Timorese passengers. That night UDT decided to move. Well-attended demonstrations were held in Dili on 9 and 10 August, and a strike closed most shops. At midnight on Sunday 10 August several hundred UDT members led by João Carrascalão seized arms from the police headquarters and took control of most of Dili, without much opposition from anyone, least of all the Portuguese garrison.

The ensuing civil war unfolded rapidly. Pires sent the

two alleged 'red majors', Mota and Jonatas, back to
Portugal on 12 August at UDT's insistence and confined
Timorese soldiers to barracks. On 15 August Fretilin
retaliated by proclaiming a 'general armed insurrection'
against all 'traitors of the fatherland'. The first refugees
began arriving in Darwin, in northern Australia, aboard
small freighters. On 18 August Fretilin forces occupied a
military training centre in the mountain town of Aileu.
Timorese soldiers there and in nearby Maubisse declared
themselves for Fretilin, as did most of the troops in Dili at
the urging of the most senior Timorese army man, Lieutenant Rogério Lobato, whose brother Nicolau was a senior
Fretilin leader. Fighting started in Dili on 20 August.

At this stage Governor Pires and his small but tough
force of Portuguese paratroopers could have easily quelled
the fighting in Dili by a determined use of authority.
Instead he and the remaining Portuguese retreated to a
small defensive area around the port, where they were soon
flooded with refugees and came under sporadic fire. On 22
August Pires loaded his establishment onto landing barges
and moved his 'seat of government' to Ataúro, a small
Portuguese island on the horizon from Dili. Fretilin walked
into the Portuguese arsenal, which contained some 15 000
NATO-pattern self-loading rifles, and pushed UDT out of
Dili within four days. By mid-September some UDT
forces were driven back to the east where they capitulated;
the main body fled to the west. By the end of the first week
in September, UDT held only the deserted village of
Batugade and its ancient fortress, about 2 kilometres from
the Indonesian border. UDT had about 200 fighting men,
rifles with about fifty rounds of ammunition a man, no
mortar shells, and no radio sets. Fretilin had *de facto*
control of nearly all of East Timor. In Africa, similar
situations had been an excuse for Lisbon to hand over
sovereignty and its responsibilities cheaply. Remarks made
by influential Portuguese officials in September 1975
indicated the same solution was being considered for
Timor. Perhaps this was the reason for the passivity of

Governor Pires all along. But would Indonesia accept such an outcome? And if not was not Indonesian intervention an equally cheap result for Portugal?

Indonesia had maintained a naval squadron on patrol close to Dili since 28 August, but had turned down the opportunity presented by street-fighting in Dili to move in with the convincing mission of restoring order, bolstered by the desperate radio messages for help sent out by Governor Pires. Intervention did not lack supporters in Jakarta. On 14 August Bakin chief, Yoga Sugama, quietly sounded out the Australian and other concerned governments about their likely reaction. (Australia's reply was non-committal.) At successive meetings of the Cabinet political and security group on 15 and 18 August the Defence Department leadership (Defence Minister Panggabean, Deputy Armed Forces Commander Surono and Intelligence chief, Benny Murdani) strongly urged Suharto to authorize occupation of Dili. They were supported by Yoga Sugama and Foreign Minister Adam Malik, who is said to have feared being blamed if a more diplomatic path led into a quagmire. The proposal at that stage was for a limited operation, involving one battalion or about 500 men, to seize only the township of Dili. Portugal would then be invited to return and resume decolonization, but with a dominating Indonesian presence it could not easily dislodge.

Yet Suharto held back. His only supporter was Ali Murtopo, more closely attuned to the president's thinking and with a vested interest in events running along the elaborate course Operasi Komodo was manipulating. Suharto was undoubtedly mindful of the warnings he had received from Australian Prime Minister Whitlam about a hostile public reaction, even though a statement by Whitlam on 26 August said that 'Indonesia may be the only power capable of being turned to restore order'. Whitlam also sent Suharto a private message saying that nothing he said earlier should be interpreted as a veto on Indonesian action in the changed circumstances. Suharto needed to retain the confidence of Western Countries. The Pertamina crisis had broken just six months before and Indonesia still needed massive new overseas financing. Intervention would upset the confidence of foreign bankers. It would draw a protest, however dutiful, from the Portuguese. Even though circumstances had changed, Suharto's undertakings on the use of force were still fresh. Finally there was the factor of Suharto's own personality. Suharto's favoured approach to war and politics ('make war without an army, win without defeating anyone', see chapter 1) led him to lecture his generals at this crucial stage of the Timor fighting on the lessons of the Javanese classics. His faith that events would throw up a less costly way to control Timor derived in part, according to sources close to the palace, from the advice of his *guru* and political counsellor Lieutenant-General Sujono Humardani, that East Timor would inevitably 'fall' into Indonesia's hands.

While selected units of the armed forces were put on alert, Indonesia began a complicated diplomatic campaign. On the formal level it attempted to win an invitation from Portugal to restore order. An offer was made to Lisbon early in the civil war and pushed to the reluctant Minister for Decolonization, Almeida Santos, who spent the last week of August and the first week of September 1975 in fruitless efforts to gain either a more international peace force or negotiations with the warring parties. The obverse side of Jakarta's diplomacy was directed towards confounding all such Portuguese efforts. The countries likely to be called on to join such a peace-keeping force (Australia and Malaysia) were reluctant to risk becoming either an open acccomplice to Indonesian trickery or having to faithfully monitor and perhaps chide Indonesia. While Fretilin made little effort to co-operate with Santos and, after his return to Lisbon, refused to enter talks that involved the other parties, Indonesia used its powers to obstruct contact between anti-Fretilin groups and Lisbon. A Portuguese emissary, sent by President da Costa Gomez in August 1975 immediately after the UDT coup to bring the Timorese parties together, was so obstructed on his way through Indonesia that he abandoned his task. Later, when the Minister for Decolonization waited on Atauro Island, he sent an aircraft to West Timor to bring UDT leaders back for unconditional talks. The aircraft was detained by Indonesian authorities until Santos had given up his mission and departed for home.

This gave Colonel Sugianto total control over the UDT group clustered on the border. In August while the UDT still controlled Dili he had flown in with Taolin and others to meet Lopes da Cruz. João Carrascalão, already deeply suspicious of the Indonesian contacts of Lopes da Cruz, met him, saying that Lopes could not come to the airport. Sugianto flew back to Kupang. Soon afterwards Lopes volunteered to lead a force to attack Fretilin at Aileu. Lopes used this opportunity to break away from the main UDT group and travel to the Indonesian border. When the remnants of UDT fell back to the border under Carrascalão, they found Lopes had already signed a petition on their behalf calling for Timor's integration with Indonesia. Carrascalão and other UDT leaders were now completely dependent on Indonesian goodwill, and in no position to countermand Lopes. Infiltrated by Sugianto's spies they sat sullenly in their border camp, while Indonesia made the most of a new 'Anti-Communist Movement' of Apodeti, UDT and two tiny parties included for effect, the former monarchist KOTA and Trabalista (Labour). Five Portuguese soldiers who crossed the border and were initially brought to Kupang were taken back and handed to UDT, where they joined eighteen other Portuguese hostages.

For several weeks a group of seasoned Sandi Yudha (formerly RPKAD) Indonesian commandos under Colonel Dading Kalbuardi had been training Apodeti forces. In September 1975 border incursions were made in the southern part of the border to keep some pressure on Fretilin. Thousands of refugees had been pushed westwards across the border, and were shown to foreign observers as evidence of Fretilin's unpopularity. On 24 September Fretilin pushed UDT even out of the border fort of Batugade. On 6 October, as Ali Murtopo, beaming in a new cream-coloured safari suit, held open-house in Jakarta to celebrate the end of the Muslim fasting month, Colonel Dading's commando force and Carrascalão's UDT remnants counter-attacked with naval gunfire support and strafing by two ancient aircraft, a B-26 and a DC-3 gunship. A new phase of the Timor war had opened. When Fretilin was dislodged Colonel Dading set up headquarters at Batugade. Carrascalào's force was ordered to the rear, and within days several hundred Indonesian troops had come across the border, all identifying badges removed. Sugianto's political operations were reinforced by three other senior officers, Colonel J. F. Sinaga, a tough Sumatran from army Intelligence with long Opsus connections; Colonel Agus Hernoto, a communications specialist, and Colonel Rudolf Kasenda from the navy, who liaised with the navy over supplies and support. On 16 October Dading's forces made a quick strike across the border, taking the villages of Maliana and Balibo.

By this stage the 'covert' war was straining the ability of Indonesia's friends to avert their eyes and causing protest from its ideological opponents. It is important to note that this was largely a 'duty' protest by the communist powers, the only likely source of Fretilin support. The Australian envoy in Peking, Stephen Fitzgerald, likened the Chinese comments to the firing of 'empty cannon'. The Soviet Ambassador in Jakarta, when asked about the USSR's Timor policy would turn vaguely to the regional map in his office and say: 'Where is Timor?' In Australia the Whitlam Labor Government was under strong internal pressure, particularly after the killing by Indonesian forces at Balibo on 16 October of five newsmen working for Australian television stations. In this souring atmosphere Indonesia slackened its military pressure and accepted a Portuguese invitation for talks. Malik and the new Portuguese Foreign Minister, Major Melo Antunes, agreed in Rome on 1 and 2 November that Portugal should seek simultaneous talks with all Timorese parties, and that it should still safeguard Indonesia's interests. Predictably such a meeting proved impossible to organize. Jakarta, meanwhile, was reassured that Lisbon would not transfer sovereignty to Fretilin, an idea Major Mota and other radical officers had floated. Perhaps out of desperation, perhaps influenced by the success of the MPLA nationalist movement in Angola (which unilaterally declared independence on 11 November), and perhaps reading too much into the reception of Fretilin envoys abroad, Fretilin proclaimed the 'Democratic Republic of East Timor' on 28 November 1975.

Indonesia's reaction was prompt. On 29 November Sugianto assembled the UDT-Apodeti alliance at Balibo for a counter-declaration that East Timor was 'integrated' with Indonesia. On 1 December Adam Malik flew to the border where he told a Timorese crowd that the time for diplomacy was over; what was now called for was the 'spirit of the fighting cock'. An attack on Dili was to have been made on 5 December, the day US President Gerald Ford and his Secretary of State, Henry Kissinger, were due to arrive in Jakarta from China. American intelligence learnt of this highly compromising timetable, and successfully demanded that the operation be postponed until after Ford left on 6 December. In Jakarta Kissinger raised no objection to the intervention, stipulating only that the Indonesians did it 'quickly, efficiently and don't use our equipment'. (He was to be disappointed on all three counts.) On 4 December Jakarta declared that Indonesia had to protect the Timorese by ensuring that decolonization followed the majority wish. Foreign governments were quietly warned to evacuate their nationals from Dili. To add to the 'constitutional' trappings, Parliament was convened on 6 December to urge 'more resolute and positive' action on the Suharto Government.

On 7 December Indonesia moved. At dawn Indonesian

troops landed in Dili and fighting broke out. Operasi Komodo was now dead, replaced by Operasi Seroja (Lotus). It turned out a clumsy exercise which caused great civilian suffering and vastly worsened already large diplomatic problems for Jakarta. The first operational test of the new integrated armed forces command structure, it was marked by poor co-ordination and showed up serious deficiencies in the discipline, training and equipment of some of Indonesia's best units. Kostrad Eighteenth Brigade paratroops were dropped on top of Fretilin forces withdrawing from the town, instead of behind to block off their retreat. After taking heavy casualties from Fretilin, the paratroops then came under fire from an Indonesian marine force driving inland. The remnants of the paratroops then rampaged through the town, killing and looting at random. An Australian freelance reporter, Roger East, who had refused evacuation was shot dead in a shop along with a group of Chinese. The confusion allowed Fretilin to carry out a planned withdrawal to the mountains, broadcasting details of the Indonesian attack as they went. Follow-up Indonesian attacks captured Baucau, with its jet airstrip, and the south coast.

In the following weeks successive United Nations resolutions (which sought further efforts by Portugal towards a peaceful solution, participation of all Timorese factions in such a solution, withdrawal of Indonesian forces and United Nations action to assure self-determination) achieved little. Portugal, having introduced censures of Indonesia, was not prepared to take any active steps. Fretilin was successfully isolated from all but radio contact. Indonesia controlled all the other Timorese groups, and maintained the fiction that it had no troops in Timor, only 'volunteers'. In January 1976 a United Nations emissary was blocked by Indonesia mounting lightning raids to head off any meetings with Fretilin. He could note only a 'slender common assumption' that the Timorese should be consulted on their future. Jakarta formed a 'provisional government' under Apodeti's Araujo and UDT's Lopes da

Cruz on 17 December 1975. District councils were reformed, said to be based on 'principles of consensus and consent and with consideration of the traditional and cultural values prevailing and developing in the area'. On 31 May 1976 a 'Popular Assembly' in Dili obligingly endorsed a petition for integration, and after some ritual to-ing and fro-ing on 17 July 1976 Suharto issued a decree making East Timor the twenty-seventh province of Indonesia.

The pacification of East Timor severely tested the Indonesian Armed Forces over the next three years. While with the co-operation of Australia the territory could be cut off from the outside world, the local terrain favoured guerilla warfare. Even with troop strength up to 30 000 the Indonesian Army favoured a strategy of wearing down Fretilin, of destroying food resources in the mountains to deny the guerillas an easy environment. Ambushes, raids and sniping were the Fretilin tactic. Even Dili remained a dangerous place for Indonesians for months after the invasion. Fretilin, as late as September 1977, was managing to engage the Indonesians at company strength. Lack of training and equipment failures caused morale to drop in the Indonesian forces. Casualties were high: over 1800 killed and probably four times that many seriously wounded over four years. While logistics for the troops were poor, several senior officers made small fortunes from plunder, with air-conditioners and stocks of Portuguese wine the prize items. A stockpile of 3000 tonnes of high grade arabica coffee was sold secretly in Singapore to buy war supplies. The poor logistics had produced a throw-back to the 'barter' trade of the Sukarno years.

But in late 1977 a split occurred in Fretilin. Its President, Xavier do Amaral, sought negotiations with Indonesia and was placed under arrest by Nicolau Lobato, who assumed the leadership and vowed to fight on. Even so, Fretilin's fortune had changed for the worse. The first of two Timorese battalions joined the Indonesian Army regular structure early in 1978. The appointment of

General A. M. Yusuf as Defence Minister in Jakarta in April 1978 signalled a change of strategy. Yusuf, the 'boy general' who had crushed the Kahar Muzzakar insurrection in his native South Sulawesi in the early 1960s, directed the Timor effort more closely, visiting the territory at three-week intervals. His application of the Indonesian Army's territorial warfare doctrine in a more active fashion produced results against the elusive Fretilin. The main Fretilin radio was captured, along with 'Information Minister' Alrico Fernandes who was then induced to make broadcasts calling for Fretilin to surrender. The capture of Xavier do Amaral soon followed. In December 1978 Indonesian Intelligence agents heard of contact between Nicolau Lobato and a relative in the mountains south of Dili. A patrol found an abandoned machine-gun and a rolled-up field mattress, correctly interpreted as the baggage of an important man in Fretilin. The army's newly acquired helicopter strength ferried 2500 soldiers from point to point in a three-week chase. On 31 December 1978, Nicolau Lobato was shot dead by a Timorese sergeant of the Indonesian Army.

Meanwhile, attempts to build a competent civil administration had a slow start. A substantial annual budget above $20 million has been allocated since April 1976, but in the first year or two proved impossible to disburse. Timorese leaders remained very much figureheads, with real control held by (now) Brigadier-General Dading and Colonel Sinaga. A number of large development projects were announced late in 1978, as the territory was opened to the first detailed inspection by foreign diplomats. It was then, in the crowds of emaciated Timorese mountain people who had gathered around Indonesian food relief centres in the towns, that the outside world could first judge the terrible cost of East Timor's integration with Indonesia.

A year later the position had not improved. A Red Cross official was quoted as saying in October 1979 that East Timor's situation was 'as bad as Biafra and potentially as serious as Kampuchea'. Some 300 000 people required basic food relief. Foreign-aid workers and Indonesian officials estimated that some 100 000 East Timorese had died since the start of civil war in August 1975. Many were the direct victims of hostilities between Timorese factions, and then between the Indonesian Army and Fretilin. The majority died from starvation and disease, never far away in East Timor, brought on by disruption and permitted by Jakarta's neglect.[11] A massive international-aid programme began, forcing open the territory to intermittent outside inspection. News of the suffering was suppressed in Indonesian newspapers, and there seemed to be few second thoughts on the wisdom of annexing East Timor. But in Jakarta, not a few of the officials involved in the Timor campaign had reflected on the price of Suharto's Javanese circuitousness – in Timorese suffering, Indonesian casualties and damage to their country's international standing – and concluded that even the direct option presented in August 1975 would have been far less costly.

NOTES

1. For accounts of Portuguese Timor's history see Peter Hastings, 'The Timor Problem – I', *Australian Outlook*, vol. 29, no. 1, April 1975; and Jill Jolliffe, *East Timor: Nationalism and Colonialism*, University of Queensland Press, Brisbane, 1978.
2. Soekanto (ed.), *Integrasi*, Yayasan Parikesit, Jakarta, 1976.
3. Hastings, op. cit., p. 30.
4. See Jolliffe, op. cit., ch. 4, and Bill Nicol, *Timor: The Stillborn Nation*, Visa, Melbourne and Norwalk, 1978.
5. Confidential interview with author, Jakarta, December 1976.
6. J. A. C. Mackie, *Konfrontasi: The Indonesian–Malaysia Dispute 1963–1966*, Oxford University Press, Kuala Lumpur, 1974, p. 126.
7. Soekanto, op. cit., p. 116–39.
8. Ibid., p. 140–46.
9. According to confidential interviews by the author with Indonesian officials, Jakarta, June 1978.
10. Soekanto, op. cit., p. 198.
11. Peter Rodgers, *Sydney Morning Herald*, 1 November 1979, pp. 1, 7.

10. The Prisoners

For a significant number of Indonesians, the years under the Suharto Government have held a special dimension of hardship and fear. In addition to the unknown hundreds of thousands killed in the great bloodletting of 1965–6, many more Indonesians lost their normal freedoms because of connections, real or suspected, with the 30 September Movement and/or with the Indonesian Communist Party (PKI). Estimates given by the Suharto Government's spokesmen have varied between 750 000 and 600 000 for the total arrested since 1965. Many were released quickly, although this did not always mean the end of their troubles. Until 1979 there remained a huge population of political prisoners, including some of the most prominent national figures under the old regime. Their fate troubled the world's conscience, and has probably constituted the biggest single obstacle to Suharto's acceptance abroad. Inside Indonesia the prisoners were a subject rarely discussed in public.

Mass political detentions were not a new event to Indonesia in 1965. Following the 1926 communist uprising and the rise of the nationalist movement in the late 1920s the Dutch had resorted increasingly to detention and exile as weapons of suppression. Sukarno himself was detained in Bandung, and exiled for many years to remote Bengkulu and Flores. The Dutch established a penal colony, Boven Digul, in the south-east corner of their New Guinea Territory. After the first years of the Indonesian Republic Sukarno, too, resorted to jailing his critics, among them figures such as the journalist, Mochtar Lubis. During the PRRI–Permesta rebellion in 1958 many thousands were arrested, but most were released in the early 1960s under an amnesty.

Following the 30 September 1965 attempted coup people simply disappeared from their homes and workplaces as Kopkamtib's sweep caught up with them. The net was cast as widely as possible to gather in not only those who might have been involved in the coup attempt but also anyone considered likely to have welcomed it. It was a time when simple absence from work on 30 September was enough to invite suspicion. The country's prisons, particularly in Java, became packed with detainees. Also new prison camps were quickly constructed. Between 1966 and 1972 over half a million people passed in and out of this prison system. Isolated from their families and any resort to legal protection, the prisoners were in many cases not even interrogated but simply thrown into gaol and forgotten. Miserably provided for, they were at the mercy of guards often nearly as deprived as themselves. Parcels sent in by relatives were plundered, bribes were exacted to allow authorized family contact, and in some cases the families of prisoners were harassed and blackmailed.

Kopkamtib adopted a rough classification to process these detainees. Those identified as directly involved in the coup attempt were classified as category 'A', to be brought to trial. Among them were the PKI leaders not summarily executed, military personnel clearly linked with the Untung movement, and senior members of the Sukarno Government who had appeared to sympathize with the PKI. The PKI leaders, Njono and Sudisman, were tried, sentenced to death, and executed in 1966 and 1967 respectively. Brigadier-General Supardjo was likewise sentenced in 1973 and it is believed the penalty was carried out although no official announcement of the execution was made. Colonel Latief eventually stood trial in 1978, and was sentenced to life imprisonment. The former foreign minister, Subandrio, was sentenced to death in 1966, but remains indefinitely in prison with no move on the government's part either to carry out or commute the penalty. In 1971 the 'A' category was said to include about 5000 prisoners. Five years later it was reduced to about 1800 untried people, the rest having been reclassified. Of these only about 800 had been tried. Such was the laborious pace of prosecutions in a grossly inadequate legal system.

Those reclassified joined the majority of prisoners who would never see a courtroom. The 'B' category were detainees who were deemed to have supported the coup, but who could not be brought to trial for lack of clear evidence. By early 1976 Kopkamtib gave a total of nearly 29 500 for this group, after having released some 1300 others in the preceding few months. These faced indefinite detention, along with another 3270 new detainees in an 'X' group awaiting firmer classification. By that time the remainder of the original detainees, some 550 000 people classed as 'C' category, had been released according to government pronouncements, although implementation lagged badly behind in some areas. The 'C' group remain marked men, however, even after their release. Those most clearly identified as former communist sympathizers are barred from holding jobs in the government or in 'strategic' industries. The rest may hold such employment very much at the discretion of local security authorities. Since a certificate of non-involvement in the 30 September Movement is required generally for many normal activities, the 'C' category people remain vulnerable to intimidation from officials.

By the end of 1975, then, the Suharto Government admitted a total of 36 000 untried prisoners held for involvement in the coup attempt.[1] This figure was vehemently disputed by the organization, Amnesty International, which said the total was 55 000 at the very least, and probably closer to 100 000. The government figure, it said,

> takes into account only 'A' and 'B' category prisoners held in

established detention centres in large cities. There are a great
number of other political prisoners – those held in the prisons
of small towns, those used as servants in military camps, those
serving as conscripted labour in government projects.[2]

Some three years of debate have not narrowed the difference. Over that period Kopkamtib statements have shown a rough consistency, and have been supported in testimony to the US Congress by the US State Department, among other foreign ministries who accept the Indonesian figures.

A tentative decision to begin releasing the 'B' category prisoners appears to have been taken in 1975. The financial crisis of Pertamina and the sudden collapse of noncommunist regimes in South Vietnam and Cambodia abruptly ended a brief period of greater than usual self-assertiveness by Jakarta towards American, European and Japanese allies. Needing to borrow large amounts of money from the Western banking system and hasten its arms acquisition programme, the Indonesian leaders were also aware, over the next year, of the looming victory of Governor Jimmy Carter in the 1976 US presidential elections. In December 1976, after some eighteen months of internal government debate, the Kopkamtib Chief of Staff, Admiral Sudomo, announced the immediate release of 2500 'B' group prisoners and the future release of the remainder at the rate of 10 000 a year. This would mean all prisoners in this category would be free by the end of 1979. Meanwhile, all untried 'A' category prisoners were to be brought before courts by the end of 1978 or put into the 'B' group and released. However, Sudomo stated that:

> There must be sufficient employment opportunities for the released detainees, since unemployment would constitute fertile ground for resorting to acts that are contrary to law, and this in itself means a threat to the national stability, particularly security stability. For this reason the government plans to establish resettlement centres in Sumatra, Kalimantan, Sulawesi and other places for those who come from these places, while those who come from Java, due to the density of

the population, will be transmigrated to the island of Buru and other islands.[3]

The misgivings felt by Amnesty International and many other observers over this last 'transmigration' proposals were deepened by a degree of evasiveness among officials in their pronouncements over the degree of choice allowed the 'released' detainees, and by the announced intention of one regional security authority, in South Kalimantan, to transport all but the elderly or infirm among his 'B' group charges to a new settlement deep in the jungle. The nub of the proposal centred on Buru Island, the penal centre in the Moluccas where over 10 000 'B' category prisoners, almost entirely from Java, had been placed since 1969. It was voiced privately that several thousand of the 'hardcore' among the detainees would be persuaded to remain in Buru as 'free' settlers, where their families could join them. This proposition was dealt a devastating blow in December 1977 when a party of Indonesian and foreign journalists (including this author) were taken to Buru for a three-day inspection, the first such visit since 1971. Before a description of Buru through a visitor's eyes, here is the account by one prisoner about his arrival on the island. The man, Pramoedya Ananta Toer, is Buru's best known detainee. A novelist and essayist, Pramoedya is widely regarded as Indonesia's finest living writer. Born in Blora, Central Java, in 1925, Pramoedya spent over two years imprisoned by the Dutch for his part in the independence struggle. His writings begun in jail quickly earned him renown. He fell afoul of authority again in 1960 over a book which defended the Chinese community, and spent several months in detention. Towards the late 1950s Pramoedya turned towards strident polemics through the PKI-sponsored Peoples' Cultural Institute (Lekra), sadly lending his talents to attempts to establish a uniformly 'revolutionary' stamp on Indonesian art and culture. Because of this, Pramoedya was arrested and dispatched with the first group of prisoners to open up the jungles of Buru for a new penal colony.

This is his story:[4]

On 13 October 1965 between ten and eleven at night a crowd of youths arrived. I don't know from what group. They called on my house. At the time I was alone with my younger brother, Kosala Subagyo Toer, who had just come home after graduating from the Lumumba University [Moscow].

They showered my house with rocks, because next door was a house under construction. I don't think the bigger rocks could have been thrown by just one person – perhaps they were launched by two people with a sarong. At that moment I sat down in front of the house and turned out the light on the fence. But I saw people running . . . Because so many rocks were falling I went inside. Shut the door. But one blow from those rocks smashed the door completely. Because I wasn't ready to go out and face them just like that, I fetched a mop-handle to defend myself and took up a samurai sword . . . put them down nearby and went outside. I asked them: 'What do you want? Because this isn't the way to fight. I was once a fighter too. But it's not like this that one fights!' But the reply that came was a hail of rocks! I said: 'Don't smash up this house!' Because at the time I was compiling the literary writings of Sukarno which had been written when he was young in various newspapers under pseudonyms. But they didn't slacken up, and I could see for myself the roof above me was broken in by stones. But my fence was made of iron, so no one could get in. They were jostling in front of my house and I turned on the light. They ran away. When I turned out the light they came back . . . I concluded they didn't want to be seen. Maybe I knew them . . .

After these attacks intensified there came the sound of gunshots. The mob scattered, then stopped. What came then was the military, a team of police and soldiers. They came in and asked for the door to be opened. They entered and said I was going to be 'secured'. At that time 'being secured' meant, according to my understanding, being given support. As it turned out I was taken away to a certain place while the people who had been making the attacks tagged along and followed from behind. I was still carrying my samurai sword when I went but I left my stick, my mop-handle, behind! I was taken to a jeep waiting at the back of my house. My house, even now, is still occupied. Then I was taken off.

Before setting off I spoke to a policeman in that team. I said this: 'Do you know me? Do you? I request that my library and records be saved. Don't let them be destroyed. The rest can be wrecked. But don't let those be destroyed.' All right. Really they would see to it. Really. Then I was driven off. The jeep moved through the deserted streets. During the trip I was beaten. Even now these ears of mine are still half deaf. With the stocks of their guns. That was the beginning ... And with me was taken a manuscript I was still working on, and press reviews of my work, both local and foreign, that had been collected and translated. About 140 pages.

I was taken to – I don't know the name of the first place – possibly Kostrad [Army Strategic Reserve] ... I realized I was under arrest, not 'secured', but detained. So I asked this lieutenant-colonel to see that my library and records were not destroyed. If the government wanted to take them, then take them ... From there I was taken to the Kodam [Jakarta Military Command], and to the Kodam were brought all these possessions. I had with me a typewriter. I don't know where that typewriter is now. The manuscript – all that – I don't know about either. There were already many people there who had also been arrested. And two hours later vehicles brought my books, including my records and pictures of people from the period of the nationalist movement that were in negative. Also my typewritten index cards were shown to me. And there was a corporal who said to me: 'Those are your Party cards' and so on. Maybe all that has been destroyed, my records – I don't know. But I think by now there's not one page at home. [Amnesty International reported that Pramoedya's family were forced out of their home and all the book collection pillaged or destroyed.]

From there my interrogation began, and surprisingly, among other things, in one question session was an accusation taken from the Nahdatul Ulama (Muslim Scholars' League) newspaper *Duta Masyarakat*. Those people in *Duta Masyarakat* reported I had stolen many museum books and that these had been 'discovered' in my house. Among other things I was interrogated on the basis of this! And I replied that if it were investigated at the museum, maybe they would find ten times more books that I had donated to the museum than there were museum books at my house. And there weren't any charges whatsoever.

After that: taken to Guntur [a military prison in Jakarta]. From Guntur to Salemba [a civil prison in Jakarta]. In December, taken to Tanggerang [another large civil jail, on the western outskirts of the city]. In May, due to the efforts of my wife, I was moved to Salemba because she had been too far away to arrange my food. Then in Salemba until August 1969; then moved to Nusakambangan [a large island close to Cilacap in South Central Java used almost exclusively as a prison and military training ground]. In Tanggerang, for example, I was in the position of witnessing in a single day sometimes two or three men die because their food was extremely bad, and they were stricken by dysentery. And many people because of hunger: if they received a parcel from their family, say, some cassava if it was a poor person or peasant, because of their hunger they couldn't restrain themselves and eat it properly. They just wolfed it all down. A few minutes later – dead!

I once went into the hospital there. No medicine. Blood everywhere. One man who rendered great service to his fellows was Hasyim Rachman [former editor of the leftist newspaper *Bintang Timur* also imprisoned on Buru Island]. He had a great deal of medicine brought into that prison . . . At Tanggerang there were very many deaths. When I was taken to Karang Tengah, Nusakembangan . . . there was a sign. It read: 'Total of Prisoners: 400 (or so). Died: 200 (or so).' Thus 50 per cent. I read that myself.

From there we were brought here to Buru in a ship, the *Atri 15*, which later sank, so I heard. I don't know if that's true or not. This ship of 3000 tons, if I'm not wrong, deadweight, was very old, so old. I myself, as we left from Java, got a place furthest at the front in the bow, up there. At the peak was the toilet. We were accustomed, as political prisoners, to clean out. We tried to clean it, that toilet. But the water we poured down wouldn't go in. So it just stopped there, the water that was flushed down with human waste. If the ship pitched the water ran all over the ship – water and human filth. I was amazed! How was this ship run? Everything was jammed. And this ship sounded as though it was about to break up: creak, creak, creak! Its passage – a bicycle would have been faster! And we were not allowed outside from below, from below deck. Everything was locked. Several times that ship stopped in mid-course because it broke down.

Reaching Namlea [the main township on Buru] a few of my

friends were made to disembark first to set up a kitchen. About fifteen or twenty-five men. They landed. That was the first time. I was amazed. Because on the ship, on 16 August 1969, they wished us: 'Safe journey, towards a new life.' And when about twenty-five men landed at Namlea, they were greeted with blows from rifle-butts . . .

After that, we got off, it didn't matter. And we were placed at Jiku Kecil for a few days. Then my group was split up, forming the first group who went into Buru, into the interior of Wai Apu, that is Unit III. A journey of 5 kilometres at that time took six hours, because of the difficulty of moving, because the path had to skirt around fallen trees, to go under them, and with rattan thorns everywhere. When I looked at the jungle it appeared very infertile.

After arriving at Unit III we woke up early in the morning, still tired. The men were woken up and ordered to engage in exercises led by a sergeant who couldn't be seen because of the dark. After waking up we were organized for working. Because we didn't have tools the first order was to open up roads. Because we didn't have any tools we had to pull up the sword-grass with our hands. It's sharp, sword-grass. Everyone's hands were bleeding. And we knew that our ration of food was 600 grams [a day]. We got so much dried fish, so much salt – that was the regulation. But it turned out the 600 grams lasted only a week. Then 500 grams. Then the 500 grams disappeared altogether after three months and was switched to bulgur wheat. This bulgur was very dirty, contaminated with rust from the ship. So if you ate it, your stomach hurt or you had to rush to the latrine with diarrhoea. If you didn't eat it, you went hungry. Hungry and hungry again. But the work was very heavy. We were under guard. When we came here there were men who were already broken in health, some of them with body weights of only 29 kilograms. So anything at all had to be eaten. Lizards. Lizard's eggs! Cats. We also had to eat cats! Dogs, snakes, birds! All that was caught was eaten so we could survive. And beatings kept coming beyond reason . . .

No prisoner ever escaped from Buru. About 1500 kilometres east of Java, the island is slightly larger than Bali. But unlike that fertile island which supports nearly 3 million people, the local population of Buru is only about 40 000. A few thousand live around the Chinese-dominated township of Namlea. The rest are native Buru people who remain close to their primitive hunting and foraging culture in the island's rugged interior, or later arrivals who live in impoverished fishing villages around the coast. Three times this century the island has been investigated as a transmigration site. Each time the idea lapsed, probably due to the paucity of the land and harsh climate.

Nowadays the prison settlements can be reached in a day's long travel from Jakarta. An Indonesian Air Force DC-3 waits at Ambon's airport for passengers arriving by Garuda jet. It climbs over a blue, limitless sea, and dodges around cumulus clouds for half an hour before putting down on a coral airstrip still surrounded by bomb craters from the Indonesian attack on the 'Republic of the South Moluccas' in 1950. The airstrip is close to Namlea where Javanese prisoners serve at the officers' mess, nervously obeying orders at the double under the occasional mockery of local children. As the afternoon fades a workboat carries the visitors across a wide bay towards a low, forested shoreline. It enters a fishing village built on stilts and a narrow corridor opens inland: swift brown water between walls of sago palms, reeds, and vine-shrouded trees. The boat chugs on for four hours into the darkness, until the forest and swamp give way to open land and the prison settlements visible under the starlight.

Pramoedya's cautious account of the early days in Buru (he would say no more) was extended in further, necessarily anonymous, interviews by visiting journalists with dozens of other prisoners. They confirmed that these years had seen intense privation and harsh treatment, worsened and made even more pointless by the failure of the land on Buru to respond to the wet-rice agriculture the government insisted on introducing. The staging camp of Jiku Kecil became a special punishment centre. The hardship appears to have reached a peak in the years 1972 and 1973, particularly towards the end of this period when the usual Moluccan guard battalion was replaced for a year by a unit from South Sulawesi, a strongly Muslim region. Late in 1972 a month-long security disturbance led to tightened control of the prisoners. Those suspected of organizing disturbances were taken to Jiku Kecil. With great consistency, numerous prisoners alleged that guards carried out vicious beatings and torture. Often they were deprived of water and fed salted food, so that they drank their own urine in desperate thirst. One man, Prawoto, who died of this treatment was officially reported as having hanged himself. In 1973 a group of prisoners from Jiku Kecil collecting timber angered their guard. He shot one man dead, then lined up the remaining five and shot them one by one in the chest with a pistol. Only one survived.

By the end of 1977, however, the barbed-wire fences and guard towers described by earlier visitors had been removed or had fallen down. According to the prisoners conditions began improving after a visit by the former Kopkamtib commander, Sumitro, late in 1973, and took a marked change for the better in 1976, about the time the government decided on its release programme. The punishment centre, which had been moved to a camp cynically named 'Ancol' after a seaside resort in Jakarta, was converted to a normal camp. Beatings became occasional. Pramoedya was one of a few with recognized special talents who were freed from manual labour in 1974, and provided with necessary equipment and materials for their work, in his case an old typewriter and supply of paper. His fellow prisoners partitioned off a tiny study in a small corner of the barrack he shared with them, and positioned a bare light bulb over his small desk. Here he has turned out a huge volume of writings in which he examines, through historical fiction, the cultural background to the Indonesian nation.

The overall impression of the Buru camps was of nature distorted. The land has not become any more fertile, and the prisoners did not retain enough surplus to invest and bring output to a comfortable level. Oppression has been replaced by a routine form of venality among the guards.

Commanders of the various camps, or 'units' were supported by regular monthly payments of about 50 000 rupiah (then about $125) his charges had to accumulate from sales of poultry, eggs and handicrafts. Detainees claimed that more lavish 'gifts' were extracted (usually over $1000) each time the commander went on leave. A depressing example of how traditional cultural values can be abused to justify such occurrences came when the Buru commandant was questioned by foreign journalists about the payments. Reaching exasperation point this lieutenant-colonel summoned a young prisoner and, before the astonished correspondents, made him enact *sembah sungkem*, the traditional homage of the Javanese son in which the boy crouches to kiss the knee of his father. This, said the colonel, was the relationship of guard and prisoner: the payments, voluntary of course, were the equivalent of the *sembah sungkem*. Likewise, in explaining the 'rehabilitation' of the prisoners, the commandant referred to an enormous wall-chart showing the various steps in the prisoner's thinking between 'Marxism' and 'Pancasilaism'. When words failed him in explaining this process, the commandant simply rapped on the diagram with his swagger-stick as if to conjure out a clarification.

Perhaps the biggest distortion of all was the unnatural isolation of 10 000 men, and the attempt to turn them, regardless of background, into happy farmers who would not seek to return to their families or their beloved Java.

Despite the occasional boasts that the prisoners were being 'brainwashed', the visit did not give confidence that great ideological victories had been won. Administrative capabilities had been insufficient even to detect the case of one young man, Mulyadi, who had been twelve years old in 1965 and who had never actually been arrested, just caught up in the system when taking food to his father in jail in Pekalongan, Central Java. Or the illiterate Javanese peasant, Mitro, who was put under a 'psycho-test' in 1975. Mitro was asked to make a series of choices. Which did he prefer: nationalism or internationalism, foreign investment or standing on our own feet, reading a newspaper full of crime reports or sightseeing in the mountains, kissing a woman or eating in a restaurant? 'I just didn't understand it at all. The only thing I understood was kissing a woman and climbing a mountain. For the rest, well, I just let it go, and followed the official as to what he thought was a good answer,' Mitro told an Indonesian reporter.[5] The more sophisticated prisoners showed an alert, cynical attitude to their confinement but no sign of rebelliousness: they did what they believed to be expected, not daring to hope that the promise of release would be fulfilled.

Only 175 prisoners had been joined by their families on Buru. They lived in a separate settlement, Savanajaya, in individual houses, but their circumstances were not greatly happier than those of the others. With few exceptions the families wanted to leave with their menfolk once they were released. On Buru, despite their status as free Indonesians, they were kept virtual prisoners by the difficulty in gaining travel permits, even to move around the island itself. Many complained of coercion and deception in getting them to Buru in the first place. By 1978 officials had given up the pretence that most inmates of Buru would elect to stay as 'free settlers'. By the end of 1979 the Indonesian Government claimed to have released all 'B' category prisoners except for a few hundred it said were still undergoing investigation to see whether they could be put on trial. In many cases implementation of the releases lagged several months behind the official timetable. Pramoedya, who steadfastly refused to sign a statement conceding the Suharto Government the right to have detained him, was among the last group to be released.

The home-coming of the prisoners has been easier in some ways than many predicted. The prisoners certainly face enormous difficulties gaining employment. Getting on in years, often in broken health, the prisoners also have a stigma that causes apprehension among potential associates. Many have found their wives estranged or divorced, living a new life. However, the returning men do not meet the anger and hostility that had been feared, particularly from the Muslim community. Nor have they become destitute, since Indonesians are used to sharing what they have with their unfortunate fellows.

With the final releases in December 1979, Kopkamtib acknowledged that only two dozen prisoners were still being held without trial in connection with the coup attempt. It promised to bring these A category detainees to court within a year. Even apart from this and the question of possible harassment of those released, Indonesia is unlikely to remove itself soon from the list of countries whose record on the upholding of human rights is seriously questioned. In both theory and practice Indonesia quite deliberately holds to its own definition of human rights. During the 1945 constitutional debates the inclusion of a bill of rights was explicitly rejected, by a majority which thought it would place the individual above the corporate good. In the words of Sukarno, a guarantee of rights would create 'a conflict within the soul of the state'. The 1945 Constitution eventually conceded a lesser acknowledgement: certain key freedoms were granted, however, they were 'to be regulated by law'.[6] More recently the Suharto Government argues that it has been unfairly singled out on human rights issues. For example a Foreign Ministry spokesman commented in October 1977 that the preoccupation with political detention ignored other assaults on human rights, including poverty and racial discrimination, which were more serious violations.[7] Certainly political freedoms have remained highly expendable under the New Order, and the usual excuse has indeed been that 'development' must proceed smoothly. Each political crisis brings its crop of detentions without charge or trial (although students and other detainees from the elite are treated comparatively gently), banned meetings and threats against critical newspapers.

Can a desperately poor country like Indonesia do any better even given the will? A major barrier to immediate improvement lies not so much in policy, but in the lack of resources. On the government side the whole legal apparatus is weak, both in number and quality of trained investigators, prosecutors and judges. Effective authority is spread haphazardly through the bureaucracy and administration is lax. The countervailing forces are even weaker. Outside the big cities it is a rarity to find a lawyer in private practice. Even where available such professional services are beyond the pocket of almost all Indonesians. No newspapers are strong enough, either in financial resources or reporting skills, to risk a period of official disapproval.

Yet pressure for change does exist. In Jakarta, the lawyer Adnan Buyung Nasution, and his colleagues have run a Legal Aid Institute since 1971 which has taken up several highly controversial cases, including compensation claims against land development companies owned by powerful military-connected interests. Despite Nasution's own detention for two years the institute has survived, although it has been barred from opening branches in other cities. The non-government press, particularly in Jakarta, has shown a steady expansion, in terms of circulation and profitability. Several journals such as *Kompas, Sinar Harapan* and *Tempo* have developed such professional skills as to make their closures highly embarrassing (as with the temporary banning of *Kompas, Sinar Harapan* and other Jakarta newspapers in January 1978). Further pressure comes from the rising expectations of the urban and better educated classes, even if it is not they who usually suffer under the law. Human rights activitists such as Nasution see part of their task to widen the Indonesian's awareness of the protection that could be afforded under the law.[8]

NOTES

1 Background paper circulated to foreign press, Jakarta, May 1976.
2 Amnesty International USA, *Report on Indonesia,* 18 March 1977, p. 5. See also *Indonesia,* Amnesty International Publications, London, 1977.

3 Press statement by the Chief of Staff, Kopkamtib, Jakarta, December 1976, pp. 3–4.
4 The interview was recorded by the author on Buru Island, December 1977 during a press tour. No restrictions were placed on contact between prisoners and journalists during the three-day visit.
5 *Kompas* (Jakarta), 6 January 1978.
6 David Reeve, 'An Alternative to the Party System in Indonesia: An Historical Evaluation of the Functional Group Concept', PhD thesis, University of Sydney, 1977, p. 121–2.
7 *Indonesia Times* (Jakarta), 21 October 1977.
8 Different viewpoints on 'Human Rights in Indonesia and the Philippines' are expressed in 'Hearings before the Sub-Committee on International Organizations of the Committee on International Relations', House of Representatives, 94th Congress, 18 December 1975 and 3 May 1976, US Government Printing Office, Washington DC, 1976.

11. 'Regeneration'

Harmony has continued to elude Suharto. By early 1974 his subjugation of the political arena appeared total: the critics were in jail, the parties emasculated, a rival dismissed from the army leadership with astonishing ease, the outspoken newspapers closed down. A new timidity pervaded the Indonesian political scene, while the regime could show a new confidence abroad with the backing of multiplying oil revenues. Within three years this had changed. Ibnu Sutowo was sacked, discredited. Indonesia had come to the brink of insolvency. The non-communist governments in Indo-China, with the exception of Thailand, had collapsed. Indonesia was repeatedly censured in the United Nations for aggression in East Timor. Despite these crises an election was due in 1977 and the time had come again to activate the country's moribund official system of politics, if the pattern of 'constitutional' rule was not to be lost. The old criticisms of Suharto were not dead, but reinforced by the new developments. A new generation in the universities was preparing to go through its political rites on the streets. More critically, the message of protest had flowed into the one vessel the government could not break: Islam.

The Suharto Government entered preparations for the 2 May 1977 general election with the public 'minimal' goal of a Golkar vote equal to the 62.8 per cent gained in 1971. With the Political Parties Bill of 1975 enacted to formalize the dragooning of contending parties, election planning began on a finely detailed scale. A budget of approximately

$150 million was set aside, and by a system of 'limited tenders' channelled back towards army-backed groups. As the description of elections in Kediri shows (chapter 5), the civil service was marshalled along the lines set in 1971 to work on behalf of Golkar among the 71 million registered voters.

But disaffection ran deep in many groups. Beneath the bland surface of public political debate, Indonesia was seething with rumour and tension. The revelation of Pertamina's indebtedness, recriminations in the armed forces over the mishandled Timor invasion, and Suharto's temporary incapacitation due to a kidney-stone operation early in 1976, all contributed to speculation in elite circles about army factional politics. In particular, the rumours settled upon alleged petitions signed by the army's most respected retired officers, including General A. H. Nasution, which urged greater discipline against corrupt practices. Despite a new emphasis given by Suharto to a fight against 'commercialization of office' and the purge of Pertamina, it was by no means evident that corruption was in decline. There were even signs that irregularities were growing in the immediate Suharto entourage. The Ali Murtopo group had been hard hit by a drying up of funds from Pertamina after Ibnu Sutowo's removal. They moved successfully, early in August 1976, to place their own man at the head of another lucrative state enterprise, the tin corporation, PN Timah. (The candidate, Intelligence Brigadier-General, Abdulrachman Ramly, cheerfully admitted to reporters at the time that he knew 'zero' about mining.) Suharto himself was the centre of new rumours. The Lockheed scandal in the USA produced testimony in the US Congress that in 1975 Suharto intervened to divert the Lockheed agency for Indonesia away from an Ibnu Sutowo company towards one owned by a family associate, Sularto, and that, further, he had directed the Minister of Communications to award Suharto's company special facilities to build up a new cargo airline. It soon became an open secret that Suharto's eldest son, Sigit, was involved with Suharto in the company Bayu Air. The company built its assets entirely by virtue of a 5 per cent levy on all air cargo movements in and out of Indonesia, enforced by the Air Communications Directorate-General and paid to Bayu Air. Sardonic comment met the Suharto family's construction of an expensive mausoleum upon a hill in Central Java previously preserved for royal graves. Details of semi-official business fiefdoms were widely circulated in underground pamphlets, known as *surat kaleng* (literally 'canned letters').

These issues came into the open with the Sawito affair, the conspiracy case involving the extraordinary Javanese mystic Sawito Kartowibowo. From evidence later given in court, Sawito had been well known in *kebatinan* (mystic) circles, aided by his relationship as son-in-law to *Raden* Said Sukanto Tjokrodiatmodjo, a former national police chief who had become head of the Joint Secretariat of Mystic Beliefs (SKK). Involvement in a yoga-like form of exercise and meditation known as *Orhiba* ('New Life Exercises') had also brought Sawito into contact with Dr Mohammad Hatta, the venerable joint proclaimer of Indonesian independence, and former Vice-President. After nursing his vision of kingly power for four years, Sawito was the go-between for a series of meetings in July 1976 in the West Java mountain resort area, the Puncak.

First, Sawito brought the head of the Roman Catholic Church in Indonesia, Cardinal Justinus Darmojuwono, to see Hatta. According to prosecution evidence the two held a long conversation alone. Another who saw Hatta at Sawito's instigation was Major-General Ishak Djuarsa, one of the original Siliwangi Division 'New Order Hawks' who had been military commander in Aceh and until his arrest for alleged complicity in the Sawito affair, Ambassador to Yugoslavia. General Ishak later gave evidence, and presumably told Hatta, that while in Aceh he had uncovered a large-scale smuggling ring in the free port of Sabang connected to a 'high-ranking officer in Jakarta'. The case had been covered up by the Attorney-General's

Department. Sawito also took the cardinal to meet General Hugeng, the police chief dismissed in 1971 after uncovering a smuggling racket. According to a prosecution witness, Hugeng told Cardinal Darmojuwono he had reported to both the Attorney-General, Sugiharto, and Suharto himself that Mrs Tien Suharto was involved in the smuggling, in alliance with a Chinese businessman. Hugeng had also talked of the Suharto family's growing landholdings in West Java, its mausoleum and other excesses. Moving among these elderly men, Sawito drew up a grandly worded document, entitled 'Towards Salvation', which criticized the conduct of the government in highly general and moralistic terms. Hatta signed this. His signature was followed separately by those of the cardinal, the head of the Indonesian Protestant Church Council, General T. B. Simatupang, who was retired from the army, the author and head of the National Islamic Scholars' Council, Dr Buya Hamka, and Sawito's father-in-law, retired police general, Sukanto.

With this powerful talisman in hand, Sawito moved to give a more practical aspect to the analytical discussions in the mountain bungalows. Ishak Djuarsa and other witnesses alleged that Hatta had agreed to an attempt to persuade Suharto to relinquish political power, along the lines of the Supersemar declaration of 1966. Hatta himself would be given formal power, and would be assisted by a council which included principally the then Deputy Commander of the Armed Forces, General Surono Reksodimejo (who was not approached by the plotters). With two minor documents signed with Hatta, Sawito composed a draft for Suharto's hand-over of power to Hatta.

Sometime in September 1976 Suharto heard of Sawito's strange manoeuvres, possibly through a minister who had been given a copy of 'Towards Salvation'. To the embarrassment of certain advisers, Suharto decided to make an issue of the case with an outburst reminiscent of his angry reactions at the Pertamina Hospital opening, and over the 1974 *Pop* affair. Suharto led with a strong denial that his family was corrupt. The following day Suharto's aide, Lieutenant-General Sudharmono, published an eight-page document linking Sawito's activities with an 'illegal' movement that had misused the names of respected leaders. Included were statements from all the other five signatories that they had signed 'Towards Salvation' 'without reading carefully'. They had signed because of the other signatures and because they did not believe 'Towards Salvation' would be put to any use. Sawito was arrested, along with three former nationalist political figures. A son of the left-wing PNI leader Ali Sastroamidjojo, Karnaradjasa, was detained and quietly released soon afterwards. Ishak Djuarsa's appointment as Ambassador to Yugoslavia was revoked, and without announcement he was placed in military custody.

This strong reaction was received in elite circles with puzzlement and scepticism, which turned to ridicule when, a week later, Suharto's brother, Probosutedjo, held a selected press conference to deny that the presidential family received favours from Suharto. 'Our success is not due to special treatment,' Probosutedjo reasoned through the government newsagency, Antara. 'If government officials sympathize with us because we happen to be a relative of *Pak* Harto [Suharto], it is just good fortune because we haven't asked for it.' In one of the first stirrings of student political activity since the January 1974 riots, three university student councils in Bandung issued a statement supporting Sawito's right to trial by due process of law.

In this unsettled atmosphere another religiously imbued plot was revealed in late 1976. An undergraduate at the University of Indonesia in Jakarta, Fahmi Basya, was arrested for possessing the ingredients of Molotov cocktails with which, it was alleged, he proposed to destroy the Suharto family, centres of prostitution and gambling casinos, out of motives of Islamic fanaticism. The military were aware that Islam had emerged once more as a threat.

It was indeed evident that the greatest threat to the government's carefully laid electoral plans would come from the Muslim Party, the PPP. In July 1976, Interior Minister Amir Machmud and Defence Department officials had failed to dissuade the PPP from use of the *Ka'abah*, the shrine at the heart of Mecca, as the party's election symbol. The PPP affirmed that the *Ka'abah* symbol was the result of prayer for divine inspiration by a ninety-year-old *kyai* (scholar), Bisri Syamsuri, and could not be rejected. The government side reluctantly gave way, allowing use of this immensely powerful religious emblem. As the PPP prepared for the 1977 election campaign a series of violent incidents, apparently based on religious bigotry, pointed up the dangers of Islamic fervour. A time bomb was found in the Baptist Hospital in Bukittinggi, West Sumatra. Then an explosion damaged the principal mosque nearby in Padang, as if in retaliation. On Christmas Day 1976, grenades went off in Medan (North Sumatra) nightspots, without causing injury. Early in 1977, the Muslim party began complaining of harassment in the provinces. As the campaign began in march 1977, the Jakarta press reported violent attacks on PPP activists in West Java and in the Muslim Horseshoe area around Surabaya in East Java. Two deaths were reported, one of a PPP supporter in Subang, West Java, and the other of a security guard in Madura at the hands of an anti-Golkar mob. Early in April, one month before the elections, Kopkamtib announced that some 700 people had been arrested for involvement in a Komando Jihad (Holy War Command), claimed to be a resurgence of the old Darul Islam movement for an Islamic republic.

The PPP campaign drew enormous and fervent crowds, despite official obstruction which became blatant in areas remote from independent observation. The party showed several faces. One was a communal appeal to the devout: it offered to the faithful the brotherhood of the Muslim *ummat* under the guidance of venerable scholars who sat on official platforms at most meetings. Another was the face of the *pribumi*, the indigenous Indonesian deprived of his rights by the triad of Chinese, foreigners and corrupt officialdom. Another showed the simplicity, homeliness and honesty of the Muslim in his daily round: Islam as a force that could lead a corrupt Indonesia to better ways. All these faces frowned in the same direction. While the influence of what the military, borrowing the language of Western social science, condemned as 'primordial' loyalties (religion and race) should not be underestimated, the 1977 election saw the emergence of leaders with secular appeal. Younger figures from the old Muslim Scholars' League, such as Chalik Ali and Chalid Mawardi, articulated a critique of development similar to that of the socialists. Often they were advised by even younger men, recent graduates and former campus activists who belonged to the influential Muslim student associations, the HMI (*Himpunan Mahasiswa Islam* which had survived the demise of its parent Masyumi party), and the PMII (formerly the Muslim Scholars' League student group). Thus in an election speech before a crowd of 40 000 in Bekasi, West Java, the East Javanese Chalik Ali raised the Marriage Law experience, compared the government's political and religious management tactics to those of the Dutch, and claimed that 20 per cent of development funds were 'leaking' because of corruption.

Events also ran against Golkar. In January 1977 the entire board of the largest government trading bank, Bank Bumi Daya, resigned after revelations of massive irregularities. What later proved to be $984 million in defaulted loans from the bank had been exposed by the financial difficulties of the Astra business empire backed by Ibnu Sutowo. The *New York Times* printed allegations of a $40 million payoff in connection with the most prestigious scheme of the New Order, the Palapa domestic satellite system. In February 1977 US authorities announced possible legal proceedings over the funding of a restaurant owned by Pertamina in New York. In March, Ibnu Sutowo was placed under loose arrest following an indiscreet and unrepentant press interview, and two of his closest lieutenants were arrested. In April 1977 a provincial chief of the food agency, Bulog, was put on trial for embezzling $4.5 million. At the same time a scandal enveloped the Indonesian soccer team in the preliminary World Cup regional tournament in Singapore, with newspapers printing details of bribes paid by Indonesian team managers to opposing players. In a comic parallel to the national political situation, the team manager who had been hand-picked by Suharto was also a practising mystic. Brigadier-General Bardosono, a former comrade of Suharto's in his old Jogjakarta Brigade, returned from Singapore flourishing a Buddha statuette which he claimed had been placed by the Thai team behind the Indonesian goal to exert a powerful attractive force on the ball. Replying to criticism, Bardosono said it was 'unconstitutional' for others to call for his resignation before his term expired in 1978.

In the 1977 election Golkar was hard pressed to stay close to its 'minimal' target of 62.8 per cent. Its share of the national vote dropped slightly from 62.8 per cent to 62.1 per cent; the Muslim Party gained 29.3 per cent as against the 27.1 per cent total of its constituent parties in 1971; the Indonesian Democratic Party's vote of 8.6 per cent was a distinct drop on the 10.1 per cent total of its predecessors. But in the Jakarta region, the only place where the government conceded that the election should be 'clean' because of the numerous foreign spectators, the PPP drew the largest proportion of votes, although not an absolute majority. Golkar was also under strong competition from the Muslims throughout Java. But with the exception of two strongly Islamic provinces, Aceh and South Kalimantan, Golkar's vote was healthier in proportion to distance from Jakarta and its foreign witnesses. The PPP immediately protested over alleged irregularities in East and Central Java. It charged that many known PPP supporters had not been issued with the voter registration certificates necessary to vote, that counting had often taken place secretly in government offices, and that some 1 million votes were 'missing' in East Java alone. The protest was eventually dropped when Suharto issued a pointed call for everyone to forget their grievances, warning that nobody should attempt to discredit the election results.

The election was merely the beginning of a more intense political struggle. For Suharto the next hurdle was the approaching convocation of the highest legislative body, the MPR, which would both debate the basic questions of development and endorse a president for the following five years. Some lessons had been drawn from the election, particularly that the level of corruption was causing unrest at home and unease among Indonesia's foreign friends. Soon after the election a new drive on corruption was announced: Opstib (from Operasi Tertib or Operation Order). It was spurred by the confession of Major-General Slamet Danusudirdjo that after six years on the job at the head of a specially empowered team he had failed to make any appreciable progress against corruption at Indonesian ports.

The Chief of Staff of Kopkamtib, Admiral Sudomo, soon became a national talking-point as he swooped on immigration offices, truck weighing stations, and markets to expose petty bribery. Within a few months the security agency listed several hundred officials up to regency head level who had been disciplined or charged. Results were mixed, however. Where truck owners were unable to bribe road inspectors to allow overloaded vehicles to pass, for example, transport charges rose and were passed on to consumers. The solution was to exempt certain key commodities from loading regulations, but it can be assumed all sorts of goods, at a price, soon came to be included on the list. More often, business simply slipped back into its old pattern once Kopkamtib moved on. The public reaction was amused, pleased, and highly cynical. All the trails of corruption pointed towards the top. It became plain that Opstib had its upper limits. The glaring inconsistency of General Ibnu Sutowo escaping prosecution after signing affidavits confessing gross irregularities in oil-tanker deals was widely noted but officially ignored.

Students and younger political activists opposed to the Golkar army ideology had stirred in 1976. Since the early 1970s a cross-fertilization of ideas had taken place among major non-campus youth organizations, encouraged by the threat of the Golkar-linked Indonesian National Youth Committee (KNPI) introduced as an umbrella organization and forum, 'with the sole right to speak for the youth of Indonesia'. Five important student groups (the Muslim HMI and PMII, the nationalist GMNI, the Protestant GMKI and the Catholic PMKRI) met for the third time in March 1976 at Cipayung, West Java, to discuss a campaign for 'social justice'. This 'Cipayung Group' visited parliamentary leaders shortly before the 1977 election to talk about the corruption cases of Pertamina, Bulog and the domestic satellite. Parallel with these activities, in January 1977 the students of Bandung had formed the 'Anti-Ignorance Movement' which pointed out Indonesia's uneven educational opportunities. It came under such heavy pressure from the government that it soon collapsed.

Private surveys of student opinion showed a heavy preference for the non-Golkar parties. Unlike in 1971, figures popular with students, such as Adnan Buyung Nasution and Rachman Tolleng, were not supporting Golkar, and indeed had just emerged from prison. At the University of Indonesia, the head of the student council, Dipo Alam, urged students to vote for one of the non-Golkar parties to restore a political 'balance'. Despite the high weighting of children of civil servants and servicemen at prestigious universities (put at 70 per cent by some estimates) the idea appeared to have wide favour. The appeal of the PPP's younger spokesmen, and the visible sympathy of General A. H. Nasution (who spoke frequently on campuses) to the Muslim Party, were probably influential in making the choice more positive in many cases. In two major tertiary networks, the IAIN (State Islamic Education Institutes) and IKIP (teacher training colleges) the Muslim connections were much stronger. The former were important Islamic strongholds; the latter were also said to have held a high proportion of students from *santri* families (which, in their position as the larger landowners, had tended to prosper more than others from the 'Green Revolution').[1] In one of the most telling incidents of the 1977 election campaign, students from the Jogjakarta IAIN had stoned a passing busload of army officers' wives, the army wives' association having become one of the most disliked representations of the Golkar corporatist mentality.

Tension built up and then relaxed over the 1977 election period. This relaxation of controls, the official anti-corruption campaign, and the abolition of highly restrictive regulations on student political activity imposed since January 1974, encouraged protest. A group of highly articulate young Muslims, who named themselves the 'Exponents of the Indonesian Young Generation', published a series of hard-hitting statements on current political developments. Various youth groups urged that Suharto not be unopposed as presidential candidate in the forthcoming MPR session. Dipo Alam and a group of fellow students from the University of Indonesia proposed the out-going Governor of Jakarta, Marine Lieutenant-General Ali Sadikin, for president, and Buyung Nasution as vice-president. Sadikin, a Sundanese whose blunt style and unwillingness to identify himself too closely with Golkar had made him unpopular with Suharto, responded with provocative statements. He claimed that Dipo Alam had as much right to nominate him as Golkar chairman, Amir Murtono, had to propose Suharto; that feudalism was far the worst threat to Indonesia; that most government contracts were won by giving 20 to 30 per cent kick-backs, and so on.

The opposition was all talk, until a large increase in the Jakarta public bus-fare was announced. Students seized upon the issue. One group occupied city bus depots, and some fifty students were briefly detained. The atmosphere was further charged by a wave of satire against bureaucratic attitudes. Early in 1977 one of Indonesia's most popular contemporary films, *Inem, the Sexy Servant*, was released. It had a similar theme to Richardson's *Pamela* and the same sort of impact on the society on which it was commenting. In mid-1977, the Jogjakarta poet and playwright W. S. Rendra staged his *Sedka* ('District Secretary'), a biting and cruelly witty portrayal of a provincial governor's clique plundering a famine relief programme. A Bandung rock group, Bimbo, produced a song called *Tante Sun* (Aunty Sun) about an elite businesswoman who was immediately identifiable as the president's wife. The popular singer, Titiek Puspa, satirized the consumption patterns of the Jakarta elite in an end-of-*Lebaran* (fasting month) operetta on the state television network. Newspaper reporting became increasingly direct.

During August and September 1977 the Suharto Government attempted to reason with its critics. Suharto ordered Dr Sumitro Djojohadikusumo and other ministers to meet students on campus, but this initiative failed. The minister's arguments about economic strategy were ignored, as the students raised questions about particular corruption allegations. Eventually the ministers withdrew in the face of rowdiness and walk outs by the students. Suharto himself came under some Muslim and student pressure to render his account to the outgoing MPR rather than the new, but firmly rejected this idea. Eight students were interrogated for operating a 'Provisional Parliament' during the DPR change-over recess in September 1977.

When the new MPR and DPR were sworn in on 1 October 1977 controversies broke out immediately over the government's legislative programme. The 'Broad Outlines of State Policy' that had been drafted by a military committee perpetuated the 'religion versus belief' arguments. An accompanying guideline on the Pancasila ideology added to the dismay of the Muslims, whose agreement to Pancasila was predicated on it remaining vague in interpretation. The Cipayung Group and student councils were equally alarmed by a provision to mention the National Youth Committee (KNPI) in the Broad Outlines for the first time.

While much of the lobbying around the MPR committees concentrated on these three issues, dissent had gained another forum. On 6 October 1977 the trial of Sawito Kartowibowo opened in Jakarta. The mystic launched a vigorous defence, with the aid of a team of lawyers provided free by the Jakarta Legal Aid Institute and the Indonesian Lawyers' Association. The accused man tackled head on the question of corruption involving Suharto. It became apparent that the chief of the defence team, the redoubtable human rights crusader, Yap Thian Hiem, was also going to make truth and public interest part of his plea. The timing of the Sawito trial remains intriguing. Convening at weekly and two-weekly intervals, it coincided with the entire span of MPR activity from October 1977 to March 1978. One line of speculation was that the military lawyers who managed the trial were using it to place pressure on Suharto as and when needed. Although some saw it as a lightening rod to draw off tension, the trial became a forum where the elsewhere unmentionable charges against Suharto were openly raised. (In mid-1978 Sawito was sentenced to eight years imprisonment.)

Over this period a sequence of historical anniversaries marked the progression of active student protest in the streets. Principally in Jakarta, Bandung, Jogjakarta and Surabaya (but with some participation in Bogor, Semarang and the Sumatran cities of Medan and Palembang), students held massive commemoration marches and assemblies, first on the anniversary of the 1928 nationalist Youth Pledge on 28 October, then Heroes' Day marking the Battle of Surabaya on 10 November, United Nations Human Rights Day on 10 December; and finally the anniversary of the 1966 'Three Demands' against Sukarno on 10 January. The slogans read: 'Return the Armed Forces to the People'; and in a reference to the Suharto family mausoleum: 'While the people starve, the boss builds his grave'. (The Suharto business associate, Sukamdani, ineptly admitted in reply that the mausoleum did not cost the rumoured $10 million, but 'only' about $1 million.) A new line of attack came from the exposure by newspapers of the starvation near Jakarta caused by crop failure late in 1977 and which was covered up by local officials.

Security officials watched uneasily but allowed the protest to continue to the point where speculation began that the student demands had some military support. In November 1977 the former Suharto aide, Lieutenant-General Alamsyah, as Vice-Chairman of the Supreme Advisory Council, addressed a social science convention, and in effect legitimized the complaints. Alamsyah pointed out that with the high incidence of corruption, the impact of the Pertamina affair, Indonesia's increasing reliance on imported rice and other foodstuffs, and development of the negara pejabat (bureaucratic state), it was not surprising that the public felt disturbed. At the end of November 1977, a widely read column in the armed forces newspaper, *Angkatan Bersenjata*, seemed to be suggesting that Suharto stand down while his reputation was still sound.

Midway in December 1977, the armed forces reacted. The Defence Minister, General Panggabean, assembled the entire senior leadership of all four services, pointedly including the most prominent officers (such as Alamsyah) in civilian secondment. After three days of private discussion, Panggabean and the service chief issued a statement warning against actions that would disturb the 'national leadership'. On 10 January 1978 the students gained a degree of support from two of the original Siliwangi Division 'New Order Radicals', Generals Dharsono and Kemal Idris. Kemal Idris told students of the University of Indonesia (UI) in Jakarta that 'the original ideals of the New Order are now receding.

These ideals now are clearly not upheld by several members of my generation.' In Bandung, Dharsono, then ASEAN Secretary-General, spoke in similar vein. On 14 January the student council of the Bandung Institute of Technology (ITB) published a manifesto, the *White Book*, which stated that because Indonesia's condition needed drastic change 'the target of our struggle is twofold: to replace Suharto via the general session of the MPR in March 1978, and to change the national development strategy'. The manifesto was endorsed by a mass meeting of Bandung's students on 16 January 1978. Two days later student council leaders from UI, ITB, and the principal universities in Bogor and Surabaya visited the presidential palace in Jakarta in an attempt to urge Suharto to step down. However, Suharto was not in. The next day Jakarta newspaper editors were warned by the government to tone down their reporting of the student movement. But they were given no chance to respond. On the evening of 20 January the press spokesman for the Jakarta army command telephoned the offices of *Kompas, Sinar Harapan, Merdeka, Pelita* and two other newspapers to inform them that they were closed. The same night security officials raided campuses and student lodgings in several cities, arresting over 140 students. Defence Minister Panggabean and Kopkamtib leaders stated that the action was pre-emptive, taken on information that massive demonstrations were planned for the next day in Jakarta. After their editors signed a letter of apology to Suharto (drafted by his State Secretary, General Sudharmono) the newspapers resumed publication within a fortnight.

The students, however, defied the 'freezing' of their councils. Over the following weeks universities in the major Java cities were disrupted by illegal student gatherings, sometimes violently dispersed by troops. At the ITB students declared a boycott of studies which was taken up by the UI student body on 5 March. Generals Kemal Idris and Dharsono received reprimands from Panggabean. Dharsono refused to withdraw his criticism

'Regeneration' 247

and at Indonesia's insistence was stood down from his position as Secretary-General by ASEAN. He was still defiant. While the Siliwangi Division may have shown some reluctance to use force against students in Bandung, no overt expression of support came from within the serving armed forces. But the unhappiness of several senior retired military personnel emerged in two forthright protests. Lieutenant-General Djatikusumo, an official in the retired officers' association, Pepabri, was one of six respected figures who signed a letter to the Supreme Advisory Council questioning the military crack-down. General Nasution gave similar views in a press interview. The public, he said, was 'shocked by this radical action which has no precedent in the past, and this shock will have its social and political consequences which will be felt for a long time'.[2] Nasution went on to state that the question of the armed forces link with Golkar 'is now being much discussed among fellow officers'.

Several universities and high schools were closed down, and military forces skirmished in several cities with demonstrators. However, the student protest was effectively stalled in Jakarta by the time the MPR assembled in March 1978 for its queen-bee-like moment of activity: two weeks in a five-year lifetime. The 920 members included 165 generals, admirals and air marshals. The 61 per cent of its members who were appointed or indirectly elected worked together with the Golkar fraction, and became known as the Trifaksi of Golkar, armed forces and provincial representatives. It was the Muslim Party which proved once again, through its Nahdatul Ulama component, that it alone could survive in this system and still retain some measure of independence. Out of all the speeches in reply to Suharto's account for his past five-year term, it was only that of Chalid Mawardi as chief spokesman for the PPP which took issue with him.

Chalid[3] spoke against the students' 'peaceful action being countered with force', of the suspicion engendered by the National Youth Committee 'orientating itself upwards' and acting as a loudspeaker for a particular election participant, i.e. Golkar. The PPP could not agree with Suharto that the 1977 election had been completely 'general, direct, free and secret', especially in the districts far from Jakarta and outside Java. Nor could state institutions function as intended given the existing dominance of presidential power. In foreign affairs Chalid saw the peak of Indonesian diplomatic success in the non-alignment of the 1955 Bandung Afro-Asia conference. Indonesia could not get international support over East Timor; it had not succeeded like other Islamic countries in Asia in gaining Arab finance; and it was overly dependent on the IGGI powers. Chalid went on to attack the growing imbalance of the economy and decreasing self-sufficiency which he attributed in part to 'perpetuation of the colonial economic structure'. Although spending had exceeded its estimates, physical targets had not been reached in rural and social infrastructure: government revenue growth was largely due to oil earnings and foreign borrowings; modern sector investment had created jobs for only a small fraction of the new entries to the workforce, and had displaced existing small-scale industry. The Muslim Party, he said, favoured a change towards a more autonomous economic structure, and more attention to basic needs, employment and equitable distribution of wealth.

The Muslim Party spokesman also outlined with remarkable frankness the PPP's view of Suharto's religious strategy. Chalid said the Muslim majority in Indonesia felt an 'Islamophobic' tendency among Suharto's advisers, whether or not this was known to the president. The traditional religious propagation, the *dakwah,* had been encumbered by bureaucratic procedures, partly through government-approved organizations such as the Majelis Ulama and the GUPPI. Promises given by Kopkamtib were ignored in the provinces. Islamic preachers of any spirit were haunted by accusations of sympathy for the Komando Jihad, which Chalid described as a 'hair-raising issue' (implying fabrication). Finally the question of 'belief' being separated from 'religion' could 'sharpen and strengthen the *santri–abangan* dichotomy developed by the Dutch colonial government... in the interest of prolonging power'. The institutionalization of mystic beliefs could bring a fracture in the nation, Chalid Mawardi said.

Enlivened by discovery of yet another alleged Muslim extremist organization, with the arrest of thirty-nine youths after a minor bomb explosion in the MPR building and the burning of a city taxi, it was this religious issue which brought the sharpest conflict in the MPR. The Muslim Party had attempted to have its 'reservations' about Suharto's speech of account inserted in the resolutions of the MPR. On a number of particular points of policy it proposed changes to government drafts, as with one amendment that would have questioned the continuance of press licensing. But having seen these rejected the PPP gracefully joined the concerted majority of the Trifraksi and its docile partner, the PDI. But on the *kepercayaan* (beliefs) clauses of the 'Broad Outlines of State Policy' and the Pancasila Guideline in toto, the PPP forced the MPR to a vote on amendments. This was the first time under the New Order that divisions had been taken. When the unamended portions were put to the MPR most of the PPP component walked out (those remaining, but abstaining from voting, were almost entirely from the non-Nahdatul Ulama section of the party).

Suharto was elected for another five-year term on 22 March 1978. The former Foreign Minister, Adam Malik, who had chaired the MPR and DPR since October 1977, replaced Sultan Hamengkubuwono as vice-president. The MPR went into recess.

Towards 21 June 1978 busloads of Javanese converged on the town of Blitar in East Java. On the eve of that day thousands jammed the garden and street outside the house owned by Mrs Wardoyo, the surviving sister of the late President Sukarno. In the front room family members and local Muslim elders sat in a circle to partake of a special meal of rice heaped in mountain-shape and side-dishes. It was a *slametan*, the Javanese religious ceremony marking great occasions, significant dates and new ventures. It was exactly eight years, in the Javanese reckoning of time, one *windu*, since Sukarno's lonely death.

For eight years Sukarno's body lay in an unmarked grave beside that of his Balinese mother in Blitar's tiny graveyard for local war veterans, a site selected by Suharto because it was so out of the way. Military authorities discouraged visits, for which special permits were required. Yet the 1978 remembrance was neither surreptitious nor defiant. For the first time since Sukarno's fall poster portraits of the old president were being sold openly in the streets. As the night wore on in Blitar, a screen was unrolled and a grainy, scratched film shone from an old projector. There was the familiar black cap, the beribboned uniform, the swagger-stick, as Sukarno faced a microphone at the Senayan stadium in Jakarta. '*Saudara-saudara* (Brothers) . . .' the faint voice began. The effect was electric.

The next morning soldiers marshalled the crowds around the graveyard. Army officers and senior officials had come from Surabaya. The former Nationalist Party (PNI) politician, Mohammad Isnaeni, now in the Indonesian Democratic Party (PDI) and Vice-Chairman of the Parliament, sat as guest of honour. There were comings and goings, delays, then speeches, and a ceremony marking the start of a government project to build a marble monument for Sukarno's remains, inscribed: 'Sukarno, Mouthpiece of the Indonesian People'. Tears were shed, and flower-petals scattered on the unmarked grave.

But among Sukarno's family in Jakarta there was not gratitude that the Suharto Government was at last giving Indonesia's founding president his due. Rather there was some bitterness. Sukarno's third wife, Hartini, held her own remembrance ceremony at her suburban Jakarta home, in a deliberate boycott of the Blitar celebration, and was joined by Sukarno's children. The newly appointed

Minister for Information, Ali Murtopo, chose to attend this Jakarta celebration even though he was identified as the moving force behind the government initiative. In effect he was hedging Suharto's political investment in Sukarnoism.

After ten years of pushing Sukarno's memory to the back of the Indonesian consciousness, Suharto was now engaged in a fight over Sukarno's body. After two Golkar victories in general elections and his own re-election more or less according to plan, Suharto and his advisers sought for new political directions to take. Golkar had reached a plateau and maintaining its level of popular support needed increasing amounts of official reinforcement. Far from becoming a galvanizer, it had become a casing to insulate the government apparatus. Moreover, Golkar was not achieving the secularization of Indonesian politics. A few of Golkar's more independent leaders, such as General 'Mas' Isman, openly spoke of a loss of credibility among young intellectuals. The strongest outside force had become the Muslims.

Sukarnoism offered one potentially effective counter-strategy, and it was taken. Official support became quite blatant for the Isnaeni faction in the PDI. At the party's congress in February 1978, Ali Murtopo made the first announcement of the Sukarno grave project, and lent funds throughout the year. Senior Opsus officials hovered at the 20 June ceremony. It appeared that in future the PDI, whose proportion of the vote had dwindled almost to insignificance, was now to become the semi-official partner of Golkar, with Sukarnoism as its ideology. The PDI would become more like the old Nationalist Party, reawakening the allegiances of *abangan* Java. Sukarnoism, as much a mood as a set of ideas, would perhaps revive lost enthusiasm and even bring some concern for the small man into the authority-oreinted Golkar–military–bureaucracy camp. With careful manipulation it need not present any great threat to the power-holders.

Immediately after his re-election in 1978 Suharto occasionally talked in a vein that suggested some rethinking of the 'floating mass' concept, once in a proposition that the political parties become more involved in rural enterprises and co-operatives. The Opstib (anti-corruption) campaign was stepped up to the point where it brought to court the deputy head of the Indonesian Police and caused the resignation in disgrace of the Chief of Police himself. A reorganization of Cabinet promoted General A. M. Yusuf, one of the three 'king-making' generàls behind the 1966 Supersemar decree, from Industries Minister to Defence Minister. Apart from his immediate military success in the Timor campaign, Jusuf brought distinctly new attributes to the second most powerful position in Indonesia. Seven years younger than Suharto, Jusuf is the son of a *raja* in the old Buginese principality of Bone in South Sulawesi. A devout Muslim, an efficient, partly American-trained soldier, Jusuf was something of a recluse and was not generally associated with the more controversial policies of his Industries Department. Immediately after his appointment, Jusuf began a round of unannounced visits to military installations, inspecting equipment and housing and made trips at three-week intervals to see troops in the field in Timor. Jusuf's expressed concern for the welfare of the rank-and-file soldiers, and his stern words for soft-living officers drew invidious comparisons upon the previous Defence Minister, Panggabean, who was stung to reply in a letter to the Jakarta newspaper *Kompas*. This was an unprecedented event.

In social and economic policy, too, Suharto appeared to have co-opted some ideas from his critics. The third five-year plan which started in April 1979 placed more emphasis in its rhetoric on spreading wealth more evenly. The long-debated devaluation took place on 15 November 1978, lowering the rate of rupiah 415 to the US dollar, maintained since August 1971, down to a new floating rate at 625 to the dollar. However, in the wake of attempted profiteering and subsequent price controls, it was not immediately clear that the main goal of encouraging exports and labour-intensive local industry had been greatly aided. New cabinet appointments indicated greater attention would be paid to food production, co-operatives and transmigration. The promotion of the Family Planning Board's head, Dr Suwardjono Suryaningrat, to Minister of Health likewise raised hopes that the successful, non-bureaucratic approach of the birth control project might be transferred to basic mass welfare programme, a kind of Indonesian 'barefoot doctor' scheme.

It was more easy to see a continuity of policy, however. The team of Technocrat ministers managing the economy remained virtually unchanged. The new five-year plan followed the same basic strategy, inasmuch as it went into detail, and was still highly reliant on large amounts of foreign aid, borrowing and investment. On the political side, encouragement of debate was ambiguous at best. The Jakarta press edged its way back to a degree of outspokenness. Most of those arrested in 1977–8 were released within a few months. But the government persisted with trials of key student leaders, including Heri Akmadi who as head of the Bandung Institute of Technology students council had signed the *White Book* in January 1978. And the case, in May 1979, of six peasants arrested for reporting to parliamentarians malpractice in village administration symbolized the unchanged state of official accountability at the local level. It said something that the case could be exposed in the press and rectified. So, too, did the fact that the original complaint needed a national *cause célèbre* to be heeded.

General Yusuf's appointment reflected a shift of emphasis in the application of the Dual Function Doctrine of the armed forces. At all levels, uniforms were to become less conspicuous. In his 1977 Armed Forces' Day speech Suharto had announced that civilian secondments were henceforth to be made on a more discriminating basis. But it would be a mistake to see this as a retreat from Dwi-Fungsi, a move back to the barracks. It was more a refinement, made in order to perpetuate the political role of the military.

Suharto gave every sign, too, that the successors to his '1945 Generation' of leaders would also come from the armed forces. A decision had been taken not to relinquish power until the first of the new 'Magelang Generation' of officers flowed into senior ranks. The first products of the Indonesian Armed Forces' Academy at Magelang had graduated in 1960. By the late 1970s the outstanding officers among them had reached the rank of colonel, and certain changes in the military structure were being made to move them more quickly into positions of responsibility. The Magelang graduates were expected to be more professional and more widely educated than the 1945 generation. But the very reason for nominating them as the successor generation was their thorough indoctrination in the Indonesian armed forces' own schools. In other words, they were drilled to uphold the Dual Function tradition. Another great hope was that they would be more 'clean' than the current leadership. The deciding factor in this would appear to be the budgetary limitations of the government. Should the armed forces need to keep relying on their own semi-official sources of income, as it would appear they must, the temptations for corruption will remain. Half-way through their 25-year programme of modernization and development the Indonesian Armed Forces appeared faced with declining public respect, reflected, among other things, by an inability to fill cadet intakes at the Magelang academy. With a slackening of the rate of economic advance, continuing population pressure, problems of inequality and rising expectations of political participation among the better educated civilians, the prospect of 'regeneration' planned for the mid-1980s appeared less than auspicious for the Magelang generation.

One evening in 1977 a crowd of Indonesians gathered at Jakarta's art centre, the Taman Ismail Marzuki, to hear an address by the author and journalist, Mochtar Lubis. His subject: the Indonesian character. The Indonesian, said

Lubis, was hypocritical, hence the corruption rampant throughout his country. He was irresponsible, as shown in the oil tanker deals between General Ibnu Sutowo and foreign shipbrokers. He was still feudal-minded, treating the new directors-general and managing directors like the rajahs and sultans of old. He was superstitious and believed in magic, hence the constant use of slogans and the trust that once the decision was taken the job was done. He was artistic, but weak-willed. His ideal was instant wealth, without having to work for it. He sought jobs with high status, with no corresponding dedication to the public good.[4]

Later that year, in a vastly different setting, another Indonesian writer took a different approach to the same theme. In a tiny, wooden cubicle with a bare light bulb hanging over an ancient typewriter, Pramoedya Ananta Toer summed up his thoughts on the Indonesian personality, worked out over twelve years of harsh confinement during which he had had ample opportunity to see the best and the worst in his fellow countrymen. History had made the people of the archipelago conservative, looking to their past, their arts decorative rather than functional. They had not worked out their own philosophy, but absorbed ideas from abroad. They had gone straight from feudalism to colonialism. No class had developed that worked on its own initiative, for itself, taking responsibility upon itself. The Indonesian's life was to work for other people. Thus arose the still pervasive ideal: *hidup senang, taupa kerja,* the contented life, without having to work.[5]

These are two explanations by once bitter ideological opponents that give grounds for some pessimism about any radical change in Indonesia's political system. Pramoedya was speaking from a prison camp on Buru Island, some 1500 kilometres from the centres of Indonesian political life on Java. Mochtar Lubis was addressing a well-dressed crowd of city intellectuals, who shared his agonies over the direction of Indonesia. Pramoedya's ideas will remain unshared with his fellow Indonesians at least until his release, likely to be at the end of 1979. Mochtar Lubis' speech gained a wider audience through the pages of the newspaper *Kompas* and was later available as a booklet. Even so, the people most likely to see it and respond must be counted as a small and rather powerless minority.

Indonesia will continue to hover somewhere between freedom and repression, which is why forecasts of cataclysmic change should be viewed cautiously. The Suharto Government has operated almost to a cycle of openness, abrupt clampdown, and then gradual easing of pressure. Since the slaughter and mass arrests that destroyed the Indonesian Communist Party, the regime has dealt more gently with its critics than many outsiders would suppose. Generally it has tried to buy off its opponents rather than eliminate them, with some success. A surprising level of debate about the basic issues facing the country is somehow managed by the press, the professions and other institutions. All Suharto's instincts are to envelop and neutralize independent sources of power. However, some still survive and may even be growing stronger.

For neighbouring countries such as Australia, living with Indonesia will not become very much easier. By the early 1980s the problem of political prisoners will be far less acute but doubts will remain, especially if the government persists with its controversial resettlement proposals. Every period of intensified political activity will no doubt see further arrests of students and harassment of the press. The army's rule may be a little less conspicuous, and the new generation of military leaders better educated and more worldly, but it has no intention of relinquishing power. With the massive problems Indonesia faces in creating jobs, increasing food production, developing new energy sources and shifting the population burden from Java, the question of political freedoms will continue to take second place for Suharto's Government.

Australian concerns about Indonesian 'expansionism' or

'aggression' should be put to rest. Indonesia will be inward-looking for the economic reasons just given, and all the signs point to the West Irian and Timor seizures being isolated cases. Dutch New Guinea had a special, emotional significance as a former component of the East Indies. Timor was a unique territory in the Indonesian area. Taking it proved a costly venture for Jakarta in both Indonesian lives and international reputation. An uprising that began in the West Irian highlands in May 1977 and spread to other areas, before being put down with the loss of at least 200 Irianese lives over the next year, caused friction with neighbouring Papua New Guinea. But the events of that period show Indonesian diplomacy to be directed at securing the border and obtaining the co-operation of Papua New Guinea in denying the rebel Free Papua Movement (OPM) any areas of sanctuary. In 1978 Indonesia joined Malaysia in endorsing the emergence of the tiny, petroleum-rich Borneo state of Brunei towards full independence. A limited re-equipment of the Indonesian Armed Forces began in 1976, but two years later certain of the larger purchases were deferred by the new Defence Minister, General A. M. Yusuf. The new military capability was intended to improve control of the archipelago and its enclosed waters, and to establish a 'security belt' to the north, facing Indo-China. Indonesia's prime concern in external defence was with Malaysia and the South China Sea, rather than areas to the south or east. This preoccupation was deepened in 1979 by the outbreak of another Indo-China War and a vast increase in the numbers of refugees escaping by sea towards Indonesia and Malaysia.

Despite its relative military weakness, Indonesia does have some weapons at hand. Its strategic position between the Indian and Pacific Oceans and across the air routes between Australia and South-East Asia make it a natural 'choke point' should it wish to deny passage, and this power would be strengthened by incorporation of the Archipelagic Concept into a new Law of the Sea. It is an essential source of raw materials and a major investment location for Japan. Indonesia has also become an important, if still minor, source of energy for the USA which also recognizes Indonesia's crucial importance to Japan, the principal US ally in the Pacific. In the Association of South-East Asian Nations (ASEAN) Indonesia, which contains over half the population in the five-nation grouping, tends to set the pace in economic cooperation. It is an influential member of other forums, such as the Non-aligned Movement, and the 'Group of 77' which in lesser developed countries are seeking a New International Economic Order. It is prepared to use the leverage these natural endowments and international links give it.

Conversely, Suharto's Indonesia is vulnerable to pressure from Western nations, on whom it relies for funding, investment, markets and arms supplies. Only two nations, however, have much capacity to exert this power individually: Japan and the USA. This factor has always been underrated by those in the smaller Western nations who urge greater criticism and persuasion to be applied to Jakarta to win changes in such areas as political detention and human rights. This applies particularly to Australia and the Netherlands, which in one case by history and the other by proximity have special concerns with Indonesia. It would be wrong to say that Indonesia does not appreciate this attention: few other countries, if any, look beyond Indonesia's economic attributes and its political-strategic alignments to the Indonesians as a people. But it will not accept that this contact gives Canberra or The Hague a pulpit from which to preach to Jakarta.

NOTES

1 Burhan Magenda, 'Student Movements and Political Systems', *Prisma* (Jakarta), no. 12, December 1977.
2 Interview with Kyodo Press Agency, Jakarta, 31 January 1978.

3 'Pemandangan Umum Fraksi Persatuan dalam MPR-RI terhadap Pidato Pertanggung-Jawaban Presiden/Mandataris MPR', given by H. A. Chalid Mawardi, MPR General Session, 15 March 1978.
4 Mochtar Lubis, *Manusia Indonesia*, Idayu Press, Jakarta, 1977.
5 Interview with the author, Buru Island, December 1977.

Glossary

Note Many Indonesian contractions are not acronyms as such, but formed from the initial syllable or first few letters of the composite words, eg Golkar from Golongan Karya. These are in lower case.

abangan from the Javanese for 'red'. Name given by sociologist Clifford Geertz to syncretist, nominal Muslims of village Java. cf. *santri*.

ABRI (Angkatan Bersenjata Republik Indonesia) Armed Forces of the Republic of Indonesia.

ani-ani traditional hand-held blade used in rice harvest.

Apodeti (Associação Popular Democrática Timorense) Popular Democratic Association of East Timor, the original pro-Indonesian party of Portuguese Timor.

ASEAN (Association of South-East Asian Nations) regional grouping of Indonesia, Malaysia, Singapore, Thailand and the Philippines.

Aspri (Asisten Pribadi) personal assistant (to Suharto).

Bakin (Badan Ko-ordinasi Inteligens Negara) State Intelligence Co-ordinating Agency, Indonesia's main external and internal intelligence body.

banjar term for hamlet in Bali.

Bapak, 'Pak literally 'father', hence respectful reference, address.

Bappenas (Badan Perencanaan Pembangunan Nasional) National Development Planning Council.

Batak   ethnic group from North Sumatra.

batik   traditional dyeing of cloth using wax as colour-separator.

becak   pedicab.

Bimas   (Bimbingan Massal) literally 'Mass guidance', a government rice intensification programme.

BPI   (Badan Pusat Intelijens) Central Intelligence Body, Sukarno's main intelligence agency.

Brawijaya   ancient East Java kingdom. Now name of army's East Java Division.

Bulog   (Badan Urusan Logistik) State Logistic Board, responsible for market stabilization for staple foodstuffs.

bupati   regent, administrative head of sub-provincial region.

buruh   labourer, worker.

cukong   pejorative term for Chinese financier.

Dakwah   Islamic evangelism.

Darul Islam   House of Islam, Muslim insurgent movement of 1950s and 1960s seeking Islamic state.

Diponegoro   Jogjakarta prince who led anti-Dutch uprising in the Java War, 1825–30. Now title of Army's Central Java Division.

DPR   (Dewan Perwakilan Raykat) People's Representative Council, the national Parliament.

dukun   mystic, folk healer, soothsayer.

Dwi-Fungsi   Dual Function, the armed forces doctrine claiming a 'social' role as well as a military one.

Finek   (Finansiil Ekonomi) Financial and Economic staff, Indonesian Army.

Fretilin   (Frente Revolucionária do Timor-Leste Independente) Revolutionary Front of Independent East Timor, a nationalist socialist-inclined party and guerilla movement.

fraksi fraction, parliamentary grouping.

GMNI (Gerakan Mahasiswa Nasional Indonesia) Nationalist Students' Movement of Indonesia.

Golkar (Golongan Karya) Functional Groups, the military-backed political organization.

gotong royong traditional mutual assistance in villages.

GUPPI (Gabungan Usaha-Usaha Perbaikan Pendidikan Islam) Union of Endeavours to Improve Islamic Education, a Golkar affiliate.

guru teacher, spiritual adviser.

Haji Muslim who has completed pilgrimage to Mecca.

halus refined.

Hankam (Departmen Pertahanan Keamanan) Department of Defence and Security.

Hisbullah Japanese-raised Islamic force in the Second World War.

HMI (Himpunan Mahasiswa Islam) Islamic Students' Association.

IAIN (Institut Agama Islam Negara) State Institute of Islamic Religion.

IBRD International Bank for Reconstruction and Development, part of the World Bank.

IGGI Intergovernmental Group on Indonesia, the major aid consortium of Western nations, Japan and international banks.

IMF International Monetary Fund.

Inkopad (Induk Koperasi Angkatan Darat) Central Board of Army Co-operatives.

Inpres (Instruksi Presiden) 'Presidential Instruction', system of direct presidential grants for public works.

ITB (Institut Teknoloji Bandung) Bandung Institute of Technology.

Glossary

Jakarta Charter   a draft prologue, subsequently rejected, to the 1945 Constitution requiring professed Muslims to follow Islamic law.

jalan   street.

Jihad   Holy War (Muslim).

Ka'abah   inner shrine at Mecca.

kabupaten   regency, sub-provincial region.

kampung   densely settled urban neighbourhood.

karya   occupation, function.

karyawan   person carrying out designated role.

kebatinan   Javanese mysticism.

Kekaryaan   secondment of armed forces personnel to civilian jobs.

kepercayaan   belief, often mystic.

KNIL   Royal Netherlands Indies Army.

KNPI (Komiti Nasional Pemuda Indonesia)   Indonesian National Youth Committee.

Kodam (Komando Daerah Militer)   military region, territorial command (including at least one province).

Kodim (Komando Distrik Militer)   military district command, a sub-provincial military area.

Kopkamtib (Komando Pemulihan Keamanan dan Ketertiban)   Operational Command for the Restoration of Security and Order, the main internal security command of the armed forces.

Koramil (Komando Rayon Militer)   Military Sub-District Command.

Kosgoro (Koperasi Serba Guna Gotongroyong)   multi-purpose Co-operative of Mutual Assistance, a component of the Functional Groups movement.

Kostrad (Komando Strategis Angkatan Darat)   Army Strategic Command.

kraton palace, court.

kretek clove-flavoured tobacco cigarette.

kris traditional dagger, often with a wavy blade.

kyai Muslim religious teacher.

Lekra (Lembaga Kesenian Rakyat) People's Cultural Institute, a PKI-sponsored body banned since 1965.

liurai traditional ruler in East Timor.

lurah village headman.

Madiun affair uprising by Indonesian leftists against the Republican Government begun at Madiun, 1948.

Mahabharata Great Epic (Hindu).

Malari (Malapetaka Limabelas Januari) '15 January Calamity', the Jakarta riots beginning on 15 January 1974.

Mangkunegaran the second royal house of Solo.

Marhaenism Sukarno's philosophy based on the typical Indonesian small landholder (Marhaen, a West Java peasant name).

Masyumi (Majelis Syoro Muslimin Indonesia) Council of Indonesian Muslim Associations, a political party banned in 1960.

Mbah grandfather/grandmother (Javanese).

Menteng prosperous suburb of Jakarta.

merdeka independence, national freedom.

Minangkabau ethnic group in West Sumatra.

MPR (Majelis Permusyawaratan Rakyat) People's Consultative Assembly, the Indonesian Congress which meets every five years to select the president and decide basic policy.

MPRS (MPR Sementara) Provisional MPR.

mufakat consensus.

Murba coined word, meaning 'proletariat'. Name of Marxist Party suspended in 1965.

musyawarah   process of consultation, village democracy.

Nahdatul Ulama (NU)   Muslim Scholars' League.

Nasakom (Nasionalisme, Agama, Komunisme)   Sukarno's ideological 'synthesis' of nationalism, religion and communism.

Operasi Komodo   Operation Dragon. Code name for Indonesian covert political campaign in Portuguese Timor, 1974–5.

OPM (Organisasi Papua Merdeka)   Free Papua Organization, separatist movement in Irian Jaya.

Opstib (Operasi Tertib)   Operation Order, an anti-corruption campaign begun in 1977.

Opsus (Operasi Khusus)   Special Operations group.

Pak   see *Bapak*.

Pancasila   five-point state ideology: belief in God, the sovereignty of the people, national unity, social justice, humanity.

pandito   wise man, elder.

Parmusi (Partai Muslim Indonesia)   Indonesian Muslim Party.

PDI (Partai Demokratis Indonesia)   Indonesian Democratic Party.

Permesta (Piagam Perjuangan Semesta)   Charter of Command Struggle the 1958 rebellion in Sulawesi.

Permigan   a state oil company, formed 1961, dissolved 1966.

Permina   state-owned oil company formed 1957, merged into Pertamina 1968.

Pertamin   state oil company established in 1961, merged into Pertamina in 1968.

Pertamina (Pertambangan Minyak dan Gas Bumi Nasional)   National Oil and Natural Gas Mining, the state petroleum monopoly.

pesantren   Islamic boarding school in Java.

PETA (Pembela Tanah Air)   Defenders of the Fatherland, Japanese-established force during the Second World War.

PKI (Partai Komunis Indonesia)   Indonesian Communist Party.

PMII (Pergerakan Mahasiswa Islam Indonesia)   Indonesian Islamic Students Movement), a Nahdatul Ulama affiliate.

PMKRI (Persatuan Mahasiswa Kristen Republik Indonesia) Indonesian Union of Christian Students, a Catholic students' group.

PN (Perusahan Negara)   state enterprise.

PNI (Partial Nasional Indonesia)   Indonesian Nationalist Party, now merged into PDI.

PPP (Partial Persatuan Pembangunan)   Development Unity Party, the amalgamated Muslim parties.

pribumi   'sons of the soil', indigenous Indonesians.

priyayi   lesser nobility in Java, officials.

PRRI (Pemerintah Revolusioner Republik Indonesia) Revolutionary Government of the Republic of Indonesia, anti-Sukarno uprising centred in Sumatra 1958–61.

PSI (Partai Serikat Islam Indonesia)   Indonesian Islamic League Party.

PSII (Partai Serikat Islam Indonesia)   Indonesian Islamic League Party.

PT (Perseroan Terbatas)   limited liability company.

pusaka   heirloom, often with magic qualities.

PWI (Persatuan Wartawan Indonesia)   Indonesian Journalist's Association.

Raden   title of minor nobility in Java.

raja   traditional ruler.

Ramayana   Indian epic drama.

ratu adil   'just prince', messianic leader.

Glossary 267

Repelita (Rencana Pembangunan Lima Tahun) Five Year Development Plan.

RMS (Republik Maluka Selatan) Republic of the South Moluccas, separatist movement crushed in 1950.

RPKAD (Resimen Pasukan Komando Angkatan Darat) Army Commando Regiment, now known as 'Kopassandha', for Special Forces.

santri term used by Clifford Geertz for devout Muslims in Java, cf. 'abangan'.

saudara brother, comrade, a fraternal form of address.

Seskoad (Sekolah Staf dan Komando Angkatan Darat) Army Staff and Command School in Bandung.

Siliwangi an ancient king of Sunda (in West Java). Now name of the army's West Java Division.

SKK (Sekretariat Kerjasama Kepercayaan) Joint Secretariat of Mystic Faiths.

SOBSI (Sentral Organisasi Buruh Selura Indonesia) Central all-Indonesia Workers' Organization, the PKI (Communist Party) trade union movement.

SOKSI (Swadiri Organisasi Karya Sosialis Indonesia) Union of Indonesian Socialist Workers' Organizations, former Functional Groups trade union body.

Sriwijaya ancient maritime kingdom centred in Sumatra. Now name of South and Central Sumatra Army Division.

Supersemar (Surat Perintahan Sebelas Maret) 11 March Order, the transfer of executive power from Sukarno to Suharto, 11 March 1966.

tapol (tahanan politik) political prisoner.

tepo seliru mutual understanding.

Tetum largest language group in Timor.

UDT (União Democrática Timorense) Timorese Democratic Union, a conservative party in East Timor.

UI (Universitas Indonesia)   the University of Indonesia, Jakarta.

ummat   Islamic community.

wahyu (kedaton)   divine revelation (kedaton is optional).

wayang   shadow-play, using leather or wooden puppets.

yayasan   foundation.

Index

abangan, 7, 18, 52, 88, 93, 249, 251
Aceh, 63
Adjie, Ibrahim, 40, 59
Adjitorop, Jusuf, 61
administration, 5, 70, 77, 106, 114-19;
  see also *pamong praja, priyayi*, and corruption
agriculture, 69, 70, 84, 129, 174-5, 245
  new rice techniques, 168-71, 187n
  employment in, 172-4
  see also Bulog
aid, see economy
Aidit, D. N., 39, 41, 43, 44, 51
air force, 38, 39, 50, 59, 210
Alamsjah, 92, 119
Aleida, Martin, 67n
Ali Murtopo, see Murtopo
Ali Sadikin, 122, 127, 242
Ali Sastroamidjojo, 59-60, 103, 236
Ali Wardhana, 55, 76, 77
Allies, 16, 17
Almeida Santos, 196-200, 208-9
Alves, Vitor, 201
Amaral, Xavier do, 213-14
Amir Machmud, 57, 98, 106, 108, 195
Amnesty International, 218-19
Anderson, Benedict O., 4-6, 45-6, 49, 112
Angola, 211
Ansor Youth, 54
Antunes, Melo, 210-11
Apodeti, 193-4, 199, 201-3, 209

Arab world, 248
Arabian Nights, 113
Araújo, Arnaldo dos Reis, 194, 212
Archipelagic Concept, 257
Arief Budiman, 125
Arief Husnie, see Ong Seng Keng
Arief Rachman Hakim, 56
Arjuna, PT, 199
army and armed forces
  business links of, 26-7, 114-15, 118, 213
  doctrine, political role of, 32-4, 40, 76, 94, 106-7, 242, 245, 247, 253-4;
    see also Golkar
  factions in, 37-8, 59, 91-3, 105, 134-41, 245
  foundation of, 13-17, 24-5
  strength, equipment of, 71, 115
  and Timor War, 189, 203, 211-14
ASEAN (Association of South-East Asian Nations), 161, 258
Asian Development Bank (ADB), 72
Aspri, 137, 139-40
Ataúro, 206, 209
Atsabe, 194, 203
Australia, 1-2, 72, 158-9, 191, 193, 195, 197, 198, 204, 207-8, 210, 256-7, 258
Aveling, Harry, 67n
Aziz, Andi Abdul, 24-5

Bakin (Intelligence Co-ordinating Agency), 101, 106, 124, 139;
  see also Opsus, BPI

270 Suharto's Indonesia

Bali, 53, 184
Balibo, 210
Bandung, 17, 33
Bandung Institute of Technology, see ITB
Bank Bumi Daya scandal, 238
Banteng Raiders, 25
Bappenas, 77, 141, 166
Bardosono, 238
Bartlett, Anderson G., 47n, 165n
batik, 22
Batugade, 210
Bayu Air, P. T., 233-4
Beek, Father J., 101-2, 130
Berita Yudha, 104, 194, 199
Berkeley Mafia, see Technocrats
Bimas scheme, 170-72, 177;
 see also agriculture
Biro Khusus, see Syam
birth control, see family planning
Blitar revolt, 14, 20
Boaventura, Dom, 190
Bogor, 42, 49, 54
Borobudur, 9
Boven Digul, 216
BPI (Sukarno-era Central Intelligence body), 55
Bratanata, Slamet, 151-2
Brawijaya Division, 55, 105
Britain, 16, 36-8, 40, 72, 82, 167
Buddhism, 9
Bugis, 25
Bulletin of Indonesian Economic Studies, 86n, 142n
Bulog, 124, 129, 169, 174-5, 239
bureaucracy, see administration, corruption
Buru Island, 220-28, 255

Cabinets, 37, 50, 57-9, 71, 75, 252-3
Caetano, 192
Caldwell, Malcolm, 48n
Caltex, 27, 148, 150, 156, 164
Canada, 82
Carrascalão, João, 205, 209-10

Carter, President Jimmy, 121, 219
Cendana group, 241
Centre for Strategic and International Studies, 198
Chalid Mawardi, 238, 247-9
Chalik Ali, 238
China, 37, 50, 56, 71, 210
Chinese in Indonesia, 13, 30, 51, 63, 83, 114, 118, 120, 129, 134, 167, 190, 192, 220, 237-8
Christianity, 130, 237
CIA (Central Intelligence Agency), 27, 45-6
Cipayung Group, 241
cities, 181-2;
 see also Jakarta
clove trade, 120-21
Collier, William A., 187n
Commission of Four, 124-6, 135, 154
Commander's Call, 105
communists, see PKI
Confrontation, see Malaysia
Constitution 96;
 see also human rights, corporatism
Cornell Paper, 45-6
corporatism, 95-7;
 see also Golkar
corruption, 30-32, 92, 99, 113-19, 123-4, 139, 157-8, 171, 238, 240-41, 252
'Council of Generals', 40
coup d'état of 1 October 1965, 40-47, 49-53, 88-9, 216-18
Crouch, Harold, 47n, 48n, 57, 93-4
cukong, 118, 136

Dading Kalbuardi, 209-10
dakwah, 248
Daryatmo, General, 97, 105
Daryatmo, *Kyai*, 12
Davies, Derek, 86n

Dayaks, 64
democracy, debate on, 95-6, 229;
    see also corporatism, Golkar,
    army doctrine
Des Alwi, 38
Dewi Sukarno, 41, 107, 146-7
Dhani, Omar, 38-9, 41, 50, 56, 59
Dharsono, H. R., 59, 92, 99,
    245-7
Diah, B. M., 60, 104
Dieng plateau, 1-2
Dili, 190;
    see also Timor
Dinuth, Alex, 199-200
Diponegoro, Prince, 19
Diponegoro Division, 25-6,
    28-32, 35, 43-4, 51-2, 93,
    119-22, 148
Djatikusumo, 247
DPR (Parliament), 93, 97-8, 108,
    110
Dual Function, see army and
    armed forces, doctrine of
Duta Masyarakat, 47n, 222
Dutch, 4-5, 11, 13, 15-20, 24-5,
    27-8, 35-6, 64-5, 72, 114,
    190-91, 216, 258

East, Roger, 212
economy
  before 1965, 69
  borrowing and aid, 69, 70-73,
    80, 144, 159-61, 163-4
  budgets and five-year plans,
    79-80, 158, 252
  currency, 55, 70, 252
  employment, 172-4, 180-82
  growth, 85-6, 174
  incomes, 166-87
  inflation, 55, 70, 78-9, 129
  investment, 80-82
  tax, 70, 74-5, 79, 129
  under Suharto, 68-86
Ekspres, 138, 140-41
elections and parties, 26, 87-90,
    97-8, 104-9, 232-40;
    see also Golkar, PNI, PDI,

Nahdatul Ulama, Parmusi,
    Masyumi, Partindo, PPP,
    PKI
Emmerson, Donald K., 142n
environment, 179-80

Fabrikant, Robert, 152
Fahmi Basya, 236
family planning, 183-5;
    see also population
Far Eastern Economic Review,
    67m, 142n
Feith, Herbert, 47n
FINEK staff, 30;
    see also Humardani S.
firewood crisis, 178-9
Fitzgerald, Stephen, 210
'Floating Mass', 109, 252
food, see agriculture
Ford Foundation, 76
France, 71
Fraser, Malcolm 204
Freeport Minerals, 81-2
Fretilin, 192-3, 195, 200-203,
    205-206, 209, 211-12
Functional Groups, see Golkar

Gatot Subroto, 29, 32
Geertz, C., 7-8, 87-9, 187n
Gestapu, see coup d'état of
    1 October 1965
Ghazalie Shafie, 38
'Gilchrist Letter', 40
Glassburner, Bruce, 86n
Goa, 200
Golkar, 8, 87, 89, 90, 95-7, 99,
    104, 106, 108-10, 132-35,
    140, 233, 238-41, 247, 251
Golongan Putih, 126
Gomez, da Costa, 196-7, 208
Gonçalves, Guilherme Maria,
    194, 203
gotong royong, 95
Guided Democracy, 26-8, 32, 39,
    96
Guntur Sukarnoputra, 107
GUPPI, 133

272 Suharto's Indonesia

Hadisubeno S., 28-9, 60, 103, 107
haj, 119
Halim airfield, 41-2
Hamengkubuwono, 9, 14, 19, 55, 57-8, 71-2, 122, 249
Hamka, Buya, 235
Hankam, 105
Hanna, Willard A., 23n
Harian Rakyat, 43, 45
Hartini Sukarno, 54, 107-8, 250-51
Haryono, Piet, 161
Hashim Ning, 114
Hassan, Bob, 31, 121
Hastings, Peter, 215n
Hasyim Rachman, 223
Hatta, Mohammad, 7, 15, 18, 95, 191, 234-5
health, 178-9, 253
Heri Akmadi, 253
Higgins, Benjamin, 86n
Hinduism, 8, 53, 69
Hisbullah, 25
HMI, 128, 238, 241
Hong Kong, 82, 83
Hugeng, 126, 235
Hughes, John, 67n
Hull, T. H. and V. J., 188n
human rights, 229-30, 256, 258
Humardani, Sujono, 30, 100, 120, 130-31, 133, 135-6, 138, 140, 208

Ibnu Sutowo, 31-2, 69-70, 92, 115, 122-3, 140, 143-65, 232, 238, 240-41, 255
IBRD, *see* World Bank
IGGI, 72-3, 85, 140-41, 154-6, 248
IMF, 71-2, 74, 154-6
Inco, 82
Independence struggle, 14-16, 20
Indo-China, 257
Indonesia Raya, 104, 138
Inkopad, 114-15
Inpres scheme, 180

Intermaritime group, *see* Rappaport
Irian Barat, 20, 27, 35-6, 64-6, 81-2, 102, 189, 191, 201, 257
Ishak Djuarsa, 234-6
Islam 8, 13, 24, 26, 27, 30, 32, 40, 119, 129-30, 133-4, 232, 235-6
  and communists, 52-4, 88-9, 226
  parties, 89, 91, 98-9, 103, 108-10, 128, 133-4, 237, 241-2, 247-9
  revolts, 24, 82
Ismael Saleh, 48n
Isman, Mas, 251
Isnaeni, Mohammad, 128, 250
ITB, 33, 246

Jakarta, 83-4, 181-2, 188n
Jakarta Charter, 91, 99, 103
Japan, 4, 13-15, 17, 41, 71, 82, 137-8, 141, 146-8, 190-91, 258
Java, influence of tradition, 1-23, 27, 33, 40, 95-7, 122-3, 130-31, 227, 234-6, 248-9
Jellinek, Lea, 188n
Jenkins, David, 67n
Jogjakarta, 8, 14-15, 19-20, 93
Jolliffe, Jill, 215n
Jonatas, Costa, 200, 206
Jones, Howard Palfrey, 48n
Joyoboyo, 4

Ka'abah, 237
Kahar Muzzakar, 214
Kalimantan—communist insurgency, 63-4
KAMI, 56
karyawan, 96
kebatinan, see Java
Kedaulatan Rakyat, 47n, 142n
Kediri, 87-9
Kemal Idris, 63, 92, 245-6

Index

Kissinger, Henry, 211
KNIL, 13, 24-5, 32
KNPI, 241, 244
Koentjaraningrat, 95
Komando Jihad, 237, 248
Komodo, Operasi, 198-201, 203, 207
Kompas, 230, 246, 252, 256
Kopassandha, 26, 35, 42, 51, 55-7, 209
Kopkamtib, 134-7, 139, 217, 240
Kosgoro, 97
Kostrad, 34-5, 54, 60, 97, 101, 105, 120
KOTA, 209
Krakatau Steel, 157, 160
kretek industry, 180;
 see also clove trade
kris, 14
Kurawa, 3

Lance, Bert, 121
land reform, 39-40, 88
Law of the Sea, 257
Lee Khoon Choy, 23n
Legal Aid Institute, 230, 244
legal system, 122, 229-30;
 see also prisoners, human rights
Lekra, 39, 220
Lev, Daniel S., 47n
Liem Bian-kie, see Yusuf Wanandi
Liem Siu Liong, 120-21, 123, 136
Lipsky, Seth, 156
Lisbon meeting on Timor, 196-7
liurai, 190, 194, 203
Lobato, Nicolau, 206, 213-14
Lockheed scandal, 223
London meeting on Timor, 201-2
Lopes da Cruz, F. X., 202-24, 209, 212-13
Lubang Buaya, 41
Lubis, Mochtar, 104, 123, 154, 217, 254-6
lurah, 171-2

Macao talks on Timor, 203-4
McCawley, Peter, 85, 158, 181
Mackie, J. A. C., 142n, 201
McVey, Ruth, 45-6, 48n, 49
Madiun Uprising, 18-19, 39, 52
Magelang generation, 254
Magenda, Burhan, 258n
Mahabharata, 3
Majelis Ulama, 235, 248
Makassar, 25
Malari affair, 134-41, 195
Malaysia, 36-9, 58, 63, 189, 191, 195, 201, 205, 208
Malik, Adam, 39, 55, 57, 58, 65-6, 71, 97, 193-4, 195, 207, 210, 211, 249
Maluku (Moluccas), 24-5
Mangkunegaran, 12, 21-2, 122
Marhaen, 107, 111n
Marine Corps, 55
Marriage law, 129-30, 133-4, 135, 142n
Mashuri, 42, 104
Masri Singarimbun, 177, 188n
Masyumi, 26-7, 54, 91, 98, 107, 140-41, 238
Matello, Major, 196-7
Mbah Suro, 132
Merdeka, 104, 246
Mini-Indonesia, 126-7
mining, 70, 80-81
Missen, G. J., 187n
Mochtar Ryadi, 121
Monoloyalty, 106
Mota, Francisco, 200-203, 206, 211
Mozambique, 192, 203
MPR(S), 58, 93, 98, 128-9, 243-9
mufakat, 26, 95
Murba, 55
Murdani, Benny, 35, 59, 207
Murtopo, Ali, 7, 35, 38-9, 58, 66, 99-103, 135-6, 138, 140, 193-204, 210, 233, 251
Muslims, see Islam
Musso, 18
musyawarah, 26, 95
mysticism, see Java

274 Suharto's Indonesia

Nahdatul Ulama, 26-7, 54, 91, 97, 108-10, 128, 133-4, 222, 238; see also PPP
Naro, John, 103, 193
Nasakom, 27-8, 44, 96
Nasution, Adnan Buyung, 137, 139, 230, 241-2
Nasution, General A. H., 20, 25, 31-5, 37, 40, 46, 50, 96, 233, 241, 247
nationalists, see PNI, PDI
navy, 38-9, 55, 60, 118, 207
New Guinea, see Irian Barat
Nicol, Bill, 215n
Nishihara, Masashi, 165n
Non-aligned Movement, 258
Nugroho Notosusanto, 23n, 48n
Nusakambangan, 223

Oecusse, 190
oil, 27, 30-31, 69, 77, 80, 143-65
   Japanese links, 146-8, 150
   OPEC, 149
   origins of industry, 146
   output, earnings, 156, 163-4
   production-sharing, 147-9, 151-3
Oliveira, Domingos, 195, 202, 205
Ong Hok-ham, 6
Ong Seng Keng, 121
OPM, 65, 257
Opsus, 36, 66, 100-101, 128, 130, 140-41, 196, 198, 201-2, 251

Padang, 27
Palembang, 145
Palmer, Ingrid, 86n
pamong praja, 93-4; see also administration
Pancasila, 91, 243-4
Pandawa, 3
Panggabean, M., 135, 207, 245, 252
Parliament, see DPR, MPR
Parmusi, 98-9, 103, 107, 108-10; see also PPP
Parsudi Suparlan, 142n
parties, see elections, Golkar, PNI, PDI, PKI, Nahdatul Ulama, Parmusi, PPP, Murba, Partindo.
Partindo, 55
Pauker, Guy S., 48n
PDI, 109-10, 239, 251; see also PNI
Pedoman, 104, 138
Pelita, 246
Permesta rebellion, 192, 217
Permigan, 30, 148-9
Permina, 31, 146-8
Pertamina, 77, 118-19, 124, 143-65, 238
   debts of, 147-8, 154-60, 163
   tankers, 161-3
pesantren, 89
PETA, 14-15; see also army, foundation of; Japan
Philippines, 26-7, 82
Pires, Lemos, 200, 202, 206
PKI, 8, 18, 26-8, 32, 37, 39-45, 50-53, 88-9, 97-8, 102
   attempts at regrouping, 60-62, 132
   leadership in exile, 61
PNI, 26, 28, 59, 91-4, 97, 99, 102-3, 107-10, 250; see also PDI
Polomka, Peter, 48n, 111n, 142n
'Pop' Affair, 9, 141, 198, 23n
population, 167-8, 180-86
poverty, 166-87
PPP, 128, 237, 239-40, 247-9; see also Nahdatul Ulama, Parmusi
Pramoedya Ananta Toer, 220-24, 225, 255-6
press, 104, 138-9, 246
pribumi, 114-15, 118, 139, 141, 237-8
prisoners, 37, 138, 216-31
priyayi, 8, 28, 93
Probosutedjo, 10, 120, 236

Protestants, 235, 241
PRRI, 27-8, 217
PSI, 27, 53-4, 91, 140-41
pusaka, 3, 5
PWI (Indonesian Journalists' Association), 104, 194

Rachman Tolleng, 104, 128, 138, 139, 241
Rachmat Saleh, 76, 159
Radius Prawiro, 55, 76-7, 162
Raffles, Stamford, 167
Ramayana, 3
Ramos Horta, Jose, 192-3
Rappaport, Bruce, 162-3
ratu adil, 4
Razak, Tun Abdul, 195
Reeve, David, 95, 106, 109, 231n
Reid, Anthony J. S., 165n
religion, 129-34;
    see also Islam, Java, Christianity, Hinduism, Buddhism, Protestants, Roman Catholics
Rendra, W. S., 125, 243
Renville Agreement, 17
rice, *see* agriculture
RMS, 25
Robison, R. A., 47n, 142n
Roeder, O. G., 23n, 47n
Rohde, Jon E., 178
Roman Catholics, 29, 53, 56, 101-2, 124, 130, 191, 194, 234, 241
Rosihan Anwan, 104
RPKAD, *see* Kopassandha
Ruslan Abdulgani, 58
Rusmin Nuryadin, 59

Sadli, Mohammad, 81, 161
Salazar, 190
Salim, Emil, 55, 76
Sandi Yudha, *see* Kopassandha
santri, 8, 18, 88, 240;
    see also Islam
Sarbini, 75, 139

Sarwo, Eddy Wibowo, 51, 55, 92
satellite, 158, 238
Sawito Kartowibowo, 6-7, 234-6, 244
Sayogyo, 175-7
Scott, Peter Dale, 48n
Seda, Frans, 56, 76-8, 196
Selosoemardjan, 55
Semar, 1-2
Semarang, 28, 30, 43, 45, 51
September 30th Movement, *see* coup d'état of 1 October 1965
Seroja, Operasi, 212
Seskoad, 32, 37, 53, 76, 93
Silalahi, Harry Tjan, 101, 128, 199
Siliwangi Division, 18, 20, 25, 33, 40, 53-4, 59, 92-3, 118, 234, 245-7
Simatupang, T. B., 235
Sinar Harapan, 125, 127, 230, 246
Sjahrir, Sutan, 16-17, 37, 191
SKK (Joint Secretariat of Mystic Faiths), 132, 234
smuggling, 26, 31-2, 38-9, 126, 145, 234-5
Soáres, Mario, 196-7
SOBSI, 96
soccer, 239
socialists, *see* PSI
Soemarwoto, Otto, 179
SOKSI, 96
Solo, 11-13, 21-2, 51-3, 93
South Blitar affair, 61-2
South China Sea, 257
Spinola, Antonio de, 192, 196
Sriwijaya Division, 92, 145
Staff and Command School, Army, *see* Seskoad
Stanvac, 27, 148, 150
Students, 54-6, 60, 70-71, 91, 98-9, 135-6, 229, 236, 241-6
Suara Karya, 104

Subandrio, 40, 55-7, 59, 191
Subroto, 55, 76
Subud, 132

276 Suharto's Indonesia

Sudarpo, 114
Sudharmono, 1
Sudirman, 17, 20
Sudisman, 39, 61, 217
Sudjatmoko, 139
Sudomo 35, 76, 78, 120, 179, 185
Sudono Salim, see Liem Siu Liong
Sudwikatmono, 121, 124
Sugianto, Aloysius, 198-9, 202-3, 205, 209, 211
Suharto,
  and army, 19-20, 25, 28
  assumption of power, 53-60, 97-8
  business links, 30-32, 119-23, 233, 236
  and Confrontation, 37-8
  and *coup*, 42-7, 49ff
  and critics, 97, 112-13, 122, 123, 125-7, 136-9, 171, 232, 235-7, 243, 252
  early life, 8-23
  and Ibnu Sutowo, 150-51
  Irian campaign, 35
  and Japanese, 14-16
  and Javanism, 1-23, 28, 97, 112-13, 130-31, 132, 208
  mausoleum, 234-5, 245
  re-election, 249
  and Timor, 1-2, 189, 195-6, 204, 207-8, 213, 233
  at Seskoad, 33
Suharto, Sigit, 233
Suharto, Tien, 21-2, 121-2, 126-7, 136-7, 235
Suhud, A. R., 78
Sukarno, 8, 15, 17-18, 26, 36-7, 40-41, 46, 50-55, 58, 60, 69, 107, 191, 216
Sukarnoism, revival of, 249-51
Sularto, 233
Sulawesi, 24-5
Sumarlin, J. B., 76, 160, 162
Sumatra, 27, 32, 63, 130
Sumitro Djojohadikusumo, 38, 76, 78, 120, 179, 185

Sumitro, General, 59, 105, 134-40
Sundhausen, Ulf, 47n, 48n
Supersemar, 2, 57-8, 235, 252
Surono, 139, 206, 235
Suryo, General, 120, 122, 124, 126, 140
Sutopo Yuwono, 106, 124, 134-40
Suwarma, 115
Suwarto, 33-4
Syam, 44-5

Tanjung Priok scandal, 31
Tanaka, Kakuei, 137-8
Taolin, Louis, 199, 202
Technocrats, 34, 75-8, 86, 98, 119, 140-41, 158-9, 253
Tempo, 23n, 48n, 67n, 116, 230
tepo seliru, 150, 195
territorial warfare, commands, 33, 94;
  see also army doctrine
30 September Movement, see *coup d'état*
Timah, PN, 233
timber, 82
Timor, 1-2, 24, 189-215, 252, 257;
  see also army, Suharto, Opsus, Ali Murtopo, Benny Murdani, Fretilin, UDT, Apodeti, Operasi Komodo, Australia, London meeting, Lisbon meeting, Macao meeting
Tjokropranolo, 38, 140
transmigration, 185-6
Tritura, 55, 244

UDT, 192-3, 195, 200-209
United Nations, 36, 66, 72, 212, 232
United States of America (USA), 17, 20, 34, 36, 56, 76, 80-82, 144, 149, 154-6, 199, 204, 211, 219, 233, 258

University of Indonesia, 34, 75, 241-2, 245-6
unrest, 129, 133-7, 236-49
Untung, 41-6, 48n
Union of Soviet Socialist Republics (USSR), 37, 71, 210

van der Kroef, J., 67n
Verchère, Ian, 142n
villages, 95, 171-2
Viqueque uprising, 192

wahyu, 6
wayang, 1-5
Ward, Ken, 111n
Westerling, Turk, 24
West Germany, 71, 157, 160
West Java, 24, 26;
see also Bandung, Siliwangi Division

White Book, 246, 253
Whitlam, Gough, 1-2, 195, 207
Widjojo Nitisastro, 55, 75-7, 160
Widodo, 43, 109
Wongsonegoro, 131-2
Wonogiri, 11
World Bank, 72-4, 140-41

Yamin, Mohammad, 191, 193
Yani, Ahmad, 25, 37-8, 40, 46
yayasan, 31, 122
Yoga Sugama, 139, 204, 207
Yusuf, Andi Mohammad, 57, 75, 214, 252, 257
Yusuf Muda Dalam, 58
Yusuf Wanandi, 101, 136, 199

Zulkifli Lubis Affair, 26

Fontana Politics

The English Constitution Walter Bagehot
edited by R. H. S. Crossman

Problems of Knowledge and Freedom Noam Chomsky

Understanding American Politics R. V. Denenberg

Marx and Engels: Basic Writings
edited by Lewis S. Feuer

Governing Britain A. H. Hanson and Malcolm Walles

Edmund Burke on Government, Politics and Society
edited by Brian Hill

Machiavelli: Selections
edited by John Plamenatz

Mao Ninian Smart

Lenin and the Bolsheviks Adam B. Ulam

The National Front Martin Walker

The Commons in the Seventies
edited by S. A. Walkland and Michael Ryle

John Stuart Mill on Politics and Society
Geraint Williams

To the Finland Station Edmund Wilson

The Anarchist Reader
Edited by George Woodcock

Understanding American Politics
R. V. Denenberg

In this concise guide to American politics, R. V. Denenberg offers an up-to-the-minute account of the workings, functions and relations of American institutions, from the Constitution and the Presidency, through Congress and the Supreme Court, to the bureaucracy and the mass media.

'Three cheers . . . for this brief, lucid, accurate and exceedingly informative study of a difficult and important subject.'

Hugh Brogan, *New Society*

'. . . a splendid introduction which avoids the patronizing tone that experts often assume when describing an unfamiliar political system, and also suceeds in being humorous without cynicism—not always an easy task.'

Sunday Telegraph

'. . . a quick, illuminating and often edgy account of some of the things in danger of falling apart.'

Martin Hillman, *Tribune*

Fontana Books

Fontana is a leading paperback publisher of fiction and non-fiction, with authors ranging from Alistair MacLean, Agatha Christie and Desmond Bagley to Solzhenitsyn and Pasternak, from Gerald Durrell and Joy Adamson to the famous Modern Masters series.

In addition to a wide-ranging collection of internationally popular writers of fiction, Fontana also has an outstanding reputation for history, natural history, military history, psychology, psychiatry, politics, economics, religion and the social sciences.

All Fontana books are available at your bookshop or newsagent; or can be ordered direct.